Creating Sketching for Embroidery

Creating Sketching for Embroidery

Darshan Chaturvedi

RANDOM PUBLICATIONS

NEW DELHI - 110 002 (INDIA)

Creating Sketching for Embroidery

ISBN 978-93-51112-58-7

Published in 2014 in India by

RANDOM PUBLICATIONS

4376-A/4B, Gali Murari Lal, Ansari Road
New Delhi-110 002
Phone: +9111-43580356, 23289044
E-mail: randomexports@gmail.com; sales@randompublications.com;
info@randompublications.com

Reprinted 2023

Type Setting by: Friends Media, Delhi-110089
Digitally Printed at: Replika Press Pvt. Ltd.

Preface

Art is the product of man's natural admiration for beauty awakened by what he sees, feels, and experiences. There are various forms of art that involve utilization of imagination and creativity. These forms require certain skills to create a so-called work of art. Music, literature, sculpture, architecture, and painting are just a few of the forms of art that serve as an outlet for man to freely express his thoughts and emotions. Art can be seen in everything that man does, ranging from his everyday duties and tasks to complex art forms and fields. The clothing that man uses to protect himself from the effects of his environment can also be transformed into a work of art. Embroidery is the fascinating cloth art that involves the use of needles and thread. The earliest forms of embroidery that survived the tests of time were found in ancient Egypt, probably because of the kind of climate there preserved these works. Embroidery was originally done manually, or by hand. It is basically done for decorative purposes by sewing various types of materials into a layer of cloth or fabric to create patterns and designs that are usually a reflection of the beauty of nature. It is a laborious threadwork, especially for starters since it requires not only the use of fingers but creativity and imagination as well. There is a need to critically choose the type of fabric or cloth, needles and threads to come up with a successfully embroidered product.

Embroidery is the handicraft of decorating fabric or other materials with needle and thread or yarn. Embroidery may also incorporate other materials such as metal strips, pearls, beads, quills, and sequins. Embroidery is most often used on caps, hats, coats, blankets, dress shirts, denim, stockings, and golf shirts. Embroidery is available with a wide variety of thread or yarn colour. An interesting characteristic of embroidery is that the basic techniques or stitches on surviving examples of the earliest embroidery—chain stitch, buttonhole or blanket stitch, running stitch, satin stitch, cross stitch—remain the fundamental techniques of hand embroidery today. Machine embroidery, which arose in the early stages of the Industrial Revolution, mimics hand embroidery, especially in the use of chain stitches, but the “satin stitch” and hemming stitches of machine work rely on the use of multiple threads and resemble hand work in their appearance but not their construction.

With just a few bold, quick, and spontaneous strokes, a sketch can capture the spirit of any subject. Using simple step by step instructions, this title helps aspiring fashion designers sketch trendy, fashion forward looks.

It’s comprehensive and unique book, filled with detail ideas for creating a variety of looks, highlights, and ornamental elements. This book contains all the basic information needed to begin stitching, from how to choose materials to how to develop new techniques that reflect contemporary style. A very useful book for the students and professionals of textile design industry.

I thank all members of my team who have helped in the preparation of the book. My special thanks go to “Random Publications” who have published the book.

—Darshan Chaturvedi

Contents

1

Introduction

A sketch is a rapidly executed freehand drawing that is not usually intended as a finished work. A sketch may serve a number of purposes: it might record something that the artist sees, it might record or develop an idea for later use or it might be used as a quick way of graphically demonstrating an image, idea or principle.

Sketches can be made in any drawing medium. The term is most often applied to graphic work executed in a dry media such as silverpoint, graphite, pencil, charcoal or pastel. But it may also apply to drawings executed in pen and ink, ballpoint pen, water colour and oil paint. The latter two are generally referred to as "water colour sketches" and "oil sketches". A sculptor might model three-dimensional sketches in clay, plasticine or wax.

Applications of Sketching

Sketching is generally a prescribed part of the studies of art students. This generally includes making sketches (croquis) from a live model whose pose changes every few minutes. A "sketch" usually implies a quick and loosely drawn work, while related terms such as study, modello and "preparatory drawing" usually refer to more finished and careful works to be used as a basis for a final work, often in a different medium, but the distinction is imprecise. Underdrawing is drawing underneath the final work, which may sometimes still be visible, or can be viewed by modern scientific methods such as x rays.

Most visual artists use, to a greater or lesser degree, the sketch as a method of recording or working out ideas. The sketchbooks of some individual artists have become very well known, including those of Leonardo da Vinci and Edgar Degas which have become art objects in their own right, with many pages showing finished studies as well as sketches.

The term "sketchbook" refers to a book of blank paper on which an artist can, (or has already) drawn sketches. The book might be purchased bound or might comprise loose leaves of sketches assembled or bound together.

The ability to quickly record impressions through sketching has found varied purposes in today's culture. Courtroom sketches record scenes and individuals in law courts. Sketches drawn to help authorities find or identify wanted people are called composite sketches. Street artists in popular tourist areas sketch portraits within minutes.

Art of Decorating Fabric

Textile Arts

Textile arts are those arts and crafts that use plant, animal, or synthetic fibres to construct practical or decorative objects.

Textiles have been a fundamental part of human life since the beginning of civilization, and the methods and materials used to make them have expanded enormously, while the functions of textiles have remained the same.

The history of textile arts is also the history of international trade. Tyrian purple dye was an important trade good in the ancient Mediterranean. The Silk Road brought Chinese silk to India, Africa, and Europe. Tastes for imported luxury fabrics led to sumptuary laws during the Middle Ages and Renaissance. The Industrial Revolution was a revolution of textiles technology: the cotton gin, the spinning jenny, and the power loom mechanized production and led to the Luddite rebellion.

The word *textile* is from Latin *texere* which means "to weave", "to braid" or "to construct". The simplest textile art is felting, in which animal fibres are matted together using heat and moisture. Most textile arts begin with twisting or spinning and plying fibres to make yarn (called *thread* when it is very fine and *rope* when it is very heavy). The yarn is then knotted, looped, braided, or woven to make flexible *fabric* or *cloth*, and cloth can be used to make clothing and soft furnishings. All of these items – felt, yarn, fabric, and finished objects – are collectively referred to as *textiles*.

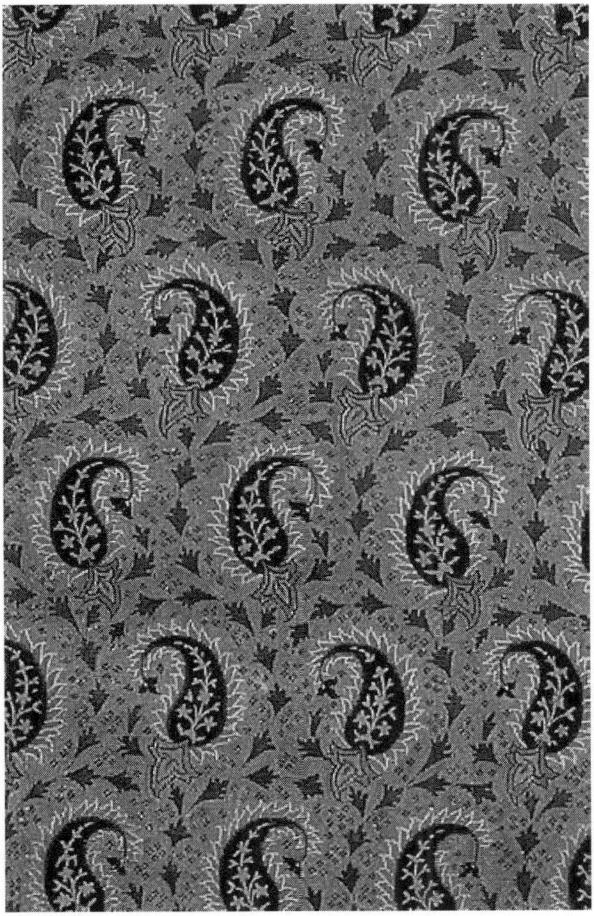

Figure: *Persian Silk Brocade. Persian Textile (The Golden Yarns of Zari - Brocade). Silk Brocade with Golden Thread (Golabetoon). Pattern and Design: Paisley Left and Right (Bote Jeghe), With Main Repeating Motif (Persian Paisley).*

The textile arts also include those techniques which are used to embellish or decorate textiles – dyeing and printing to add colour and pattern; embroidery and other types of needlework; tablet weaving; and lace-making.

Construction methods such as sewing, knitting, crochet, and tailoring, as well as the tools employed (looms and sewing needles), techniques employed (quilting and pleating) and the objects made (carpets, hooked rugs, and coverlets) all fall under the category of textile arts.

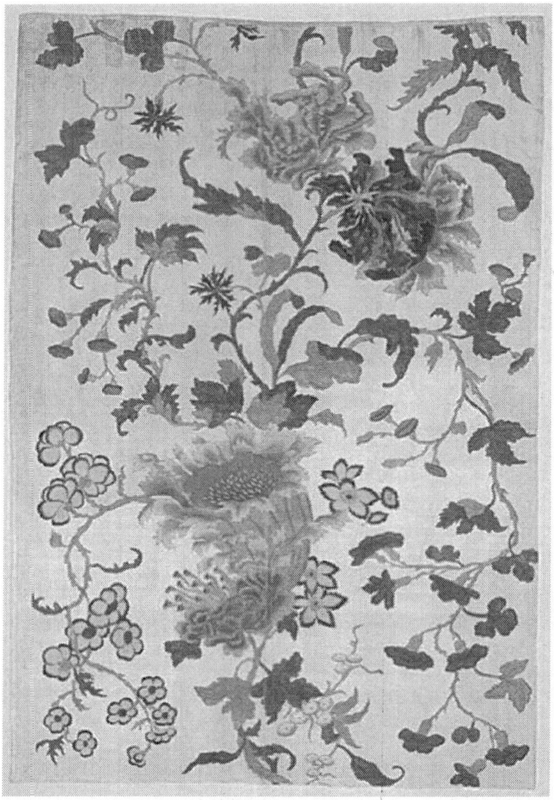

Figure: *Textile, painted silk, 45 × 29¹D ₂ in. (114.3 × 74.93 cm), Qing Dynasty, China, mid-18th century, LACMA textile collection*

Functions

From early times, textiles have been used to cover the human body and protect it from the elements; to send social cues to other people; to store, secure, and protect possessions; and to soften, insulate, and decorate living spaces and surfaces.

The persistence of ancient textile arts and functions, and their elaboration for decorative effect, can be seen in a Jacobean era portrait of Henry Frederick, Prince of Wales by Robert Peake the Elder (above). The prince's capotain hat is made of felt using the most basic of textile techniques. His clothing is made of woven cloth, richly embroidered in silk, and his stockings are knitted. He stands on an oriental rug of wool which softens and warms the floor, and heavy curtains both decorate the room and block cold drafts from the window. Goldwork embroidery on the tablecloth and curtains proclaim the status of the home's owner, in the same way that the felted fur hat, sheer linen shirt trimmed with reticella lace, and opulent embroidery on the prince's clothes proclaim his social position.

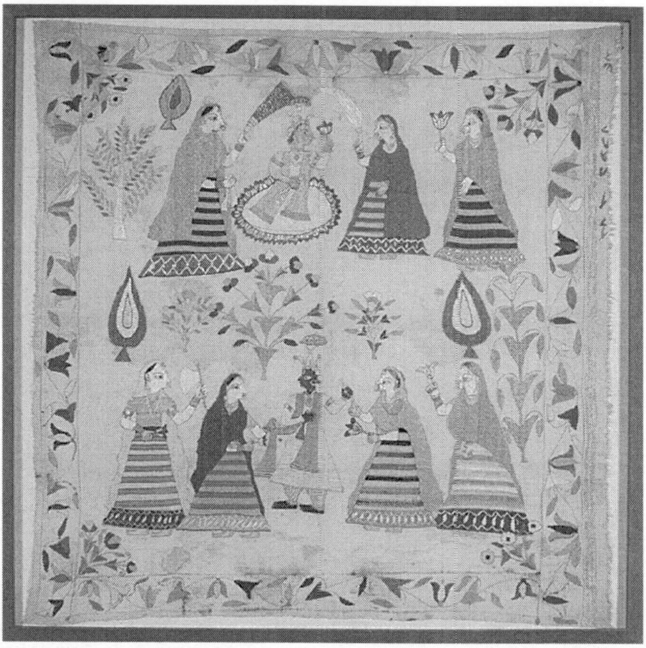

Figure: *Chamba* Rumâl *with scenes of* gopis *worshiping Krishna. Late 18th to early 19th century, Himachal Pradesh, India. Ceremonial/ritual furnishing, silk embroidery on cotton. LACMA textile collection*

Textiles as Art

Traditionally the term *art* was used to refer to any skill or mastery, a concept which altered during the Romantic period of the nineteenth century, when art came to be seen as "a special faculty of the human mind to be classified with religion and science".

This distinction between *craft* and fine art is applied to the textile arts as well, where the term *fibre art* or *textile art* is now used to describe textile-based decorative objects which are not intended for practical use.

Fundamentals

Applique

In its broadest tense, an *applique* is a smaller ornament or device applied to another surface. An appliqué is usually one piece. In the context of ceramics, for example, an appliqué is a separate piece of clay added to the primary work of clay, generally for the purpose of decoration. The term is borrowed from the French and, in this context, means "applied" or "thing that has been applied."

In the context of sewing, an appliqué refers to a needlework technique in which patterns or representational scenes are created by the attachment of smaller pieces of fabric to a larger piece of contrasting colour or texture. It is particularly suitable for work which is to be seen from a distance, such as in banner-making. A famous example of appliqué is the Hastings Embroidery.

Appliqued cloth is an important art form in Benin, West Africa, particularly in the area around Abomey, where it has been a tradition since the 18th century and the kingdom of Danhomè.

Appliqué is used extensively in quilting. "Dresden Plate" and "Sunbonnet Sue" are two examples of traditional American quilt blocks that are constructed with both patchwork and appliqué. Baltimore album quilts, Broderie perse, Hawaiian quilts, Amish quilts, Egyptian Khayamiya and the ralli quilts of India and Pakistan also use appliqué.

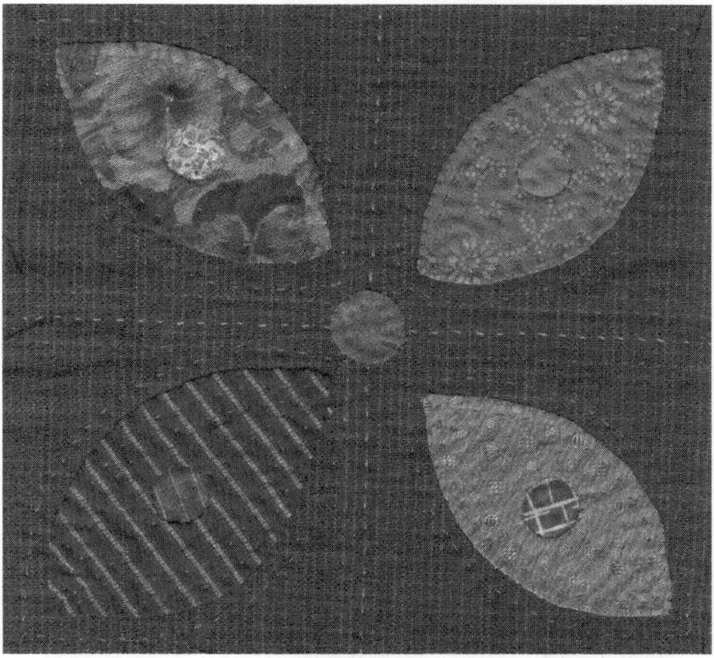

Figure: *Quilt block in appliqué and reverse applique*

Types

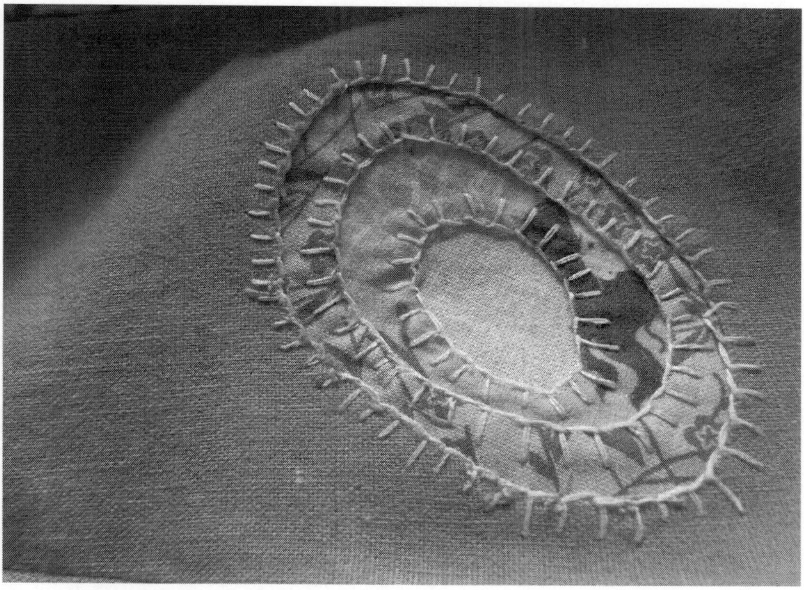

Figure: *A reverse appliqué decorating a linen dress.*

Applied pieces usually have their edges folded under, and are then attached by any of the following:

- Straight stitch, typically 20-30mm in from the edge.
- Satin stitch, all around, overlapping the edge. The patch may be glued or straight stitched on first to ensure positional stability and a neat edge.
- Reverse appliqué:several layers of material are stitched together, parts of the upper layers are cut áway, and the edges are stitched down. The largest cuts are made in the topmost layer.

Appliqué is also used for school badges.

Appliqué and Electronic Sewing Machines

Modern consumer embroidery machines quickly stitch appliqué designs by following a programme. The programmes have a minimum complexity of two thread colours, meaning the machine stops during stitching to allow the user to switch threads. First, the fabric that will be the background and the appliqué fabric are affixed into the machine's embroidery hoop. The programme is run and the machine makes a loose basting stitch over both layers of fabric. Next, the machine stops for a thread change, or other pre-programmed break. The user then cuts away the excess appliqué fabric from around the basting stitch. Following this, the machine continues on programme, automatically sewing the satin stitches and any decorative stitching over the appliqué for best results

Modern Fashion

In this sense,appliqué refers to using fabric shapes/designs usually on the trim of a garment. This can either be sewn or glued. Many appliques are more often imported from China and used here to keep costs down. Since many designers use appliques that are mass-produced, you can easily find matching accessories and such from competitive stores. Each store may carry various items with the same applique.

Beadwork

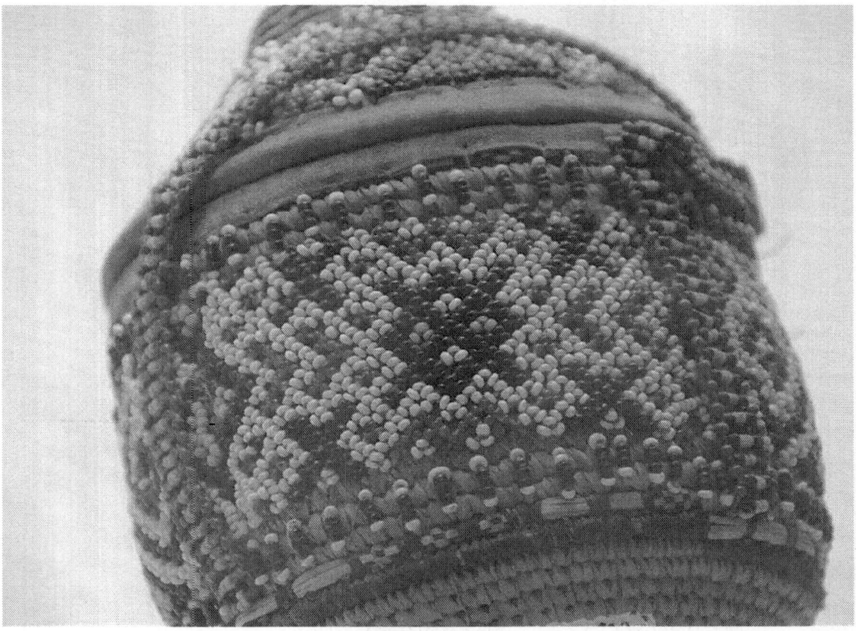

Figure: *Ethiopian beadwork on basket, from the ethnographic collection of the National Museum, Addis Ababa*

Beadwork is the art or craft of attaching beads to one another or to cloth, usually by the use of a needle and thread or soft, flexible wire. Most beadworking takes the form of jewellery or other personal adornment, but beads are also used in wall hangings and sculpture.

Beadwork techniques are broadly divided into loom and off-loom weaving, stringing, bead embroidery, bead crochet, and bead knitting.

Most cultures have employed beads for personal adornment. Archaeological records show that people made and used beads as long as 5,000 years ago. Beads have also been used for religious purposes, as good luck talismans, and as curative agents.

Modern Beading

Modern beadwork is often used as a creative hobby to create jewellery, purses, coasters, and dozens of other crafts. Beads are available in many different designs, sizes, colours, and materials, allowing much variation among bead artisans and projects. Simple projects can be created in less than an hour by novice beaders, while complex beadwork may take weeks of meticulous work with specialized tools and equipment.

3D Beading

3D, or three-dimensional, beading is less common than 2D, or two-dimensional, beading largely because free 3D beading patterns are not widely available on the internet. Resources are scarce and difficult to find. It is mainly an East Asian art form, and most 3D beading resources are written in East Asian languages such as Japanese and Chinese, further impeding access for those in English-speaking countries. 3D beading is widely considered too complex for most beaders to manage although this sentiment is largely due to the apparent complexity of many Asian beading diagrams. It is a challenge for pattern designers to create 2D beading patterns that portray 3D beaded objects. However, there are resources available that facilitate this design process by offering free instructions on how to draw a 3D beading diagram using free software available from inkscape.org in the hope that clearer beading diagrams will allow greater understanding of 3D beading patterns.

3D beading generally uses the techniques of bead weaving, which can be further divided into right angle weave and peyote stitch. Most 3D beading patterns are done in right angle weave, but sometimes both techniques are combined in the same piece. Both stitches are done using either fishing line (most popular brand: fireline) or nylon thread (most popular brand: nymo). Fishing line lends itself better to right angle weave because it is stiffer than nylon thread, so it holds the beads in a tighter arrangement and does not easily break when tugged upon. On the other hand, nylon thread is more suited to peyote stitch because it is softer and more pliable than fishing line, which permits the beads of the stitch to sit straight without undue tension bending the arrangement out of place.

Right angle weave is done using both ends of the fishing line, in which beads are strung in repeated circular arrangements, and the fishing line is pulled tight after each bead circle is made. Peyote stitch is stitched using only one end of the nylon thread.

The other end of the string is left dangling at the beginning of the piece, while the first end of the thread progresses through the stitch. In peyote stitch, beads are woven into the piece in a very similar fashion to knitting or cross stitching.

In fact, it is not uncommon for cross stitch patterns to be beaded in peyote stitch technique. Peyote stitch patterns are very easy to depict diagrammatically because they are typically stitched flat and then later incorporated into the piece or simply left as a flat tapestry. Right angle weave lends itself better to 3D beading, but peyote stitch offers the advantage of allowing the beads to be more tightly knit, which is sometimes necessary to portray an object properly in three dimensions.

Jewellery and patterns such as animals, hearts, and flowers can be stitched using 3D beading. Although it may take a little searching, there are resources available on the internet which provide 3D patterns in English for animals, hearts, flowers, and jewellery.

European Beadwork

Beadwork in Europe has a history dating back millennia to a time when shells and animal bones were used as beads in necklaces.

Glass beads were being made in Murano by the end of the 14th century. French beaded flowers were being made as early as the 16th century, and lampwork glass was invented in the 18th century. Seed beads began to be used for embroidery, crochet, and numerous off-loom techniques.

Native American Beadwork

Beadwork is a quintessentially Native American art form but, ironically, uses beads imported from Europe and Asia. Glass beads have been in use for almost five centuries in the Americas. Today a wide range of beading styles flourish.

In the Great Lakes, Ursuline nuns introduced floral patterns to tribes who quickly applied them to beadwork. Great Lakes tribes are known for their bandolier bags that might take an entire year to complete. During the 20th century the Plateau tribes, such as the Nez Perce, perfected contour-style beadwork in which the lines of beads are stitched to emphasize the pictorial imagery. Plains tribes are master beaders, and today dance regalia for men and women feature a variety of beadwork styles.

While Plains and Plateau tribes are renowned for their beaded horse trappings, Subarctic tribes such as the Dene create lavish beaded floral dog blankets. Eastern tribes have a completely different beadwork aesthetic: Innu, Mi'kmaq, Penobscot, and Haudenosaunee tribes are known for symmetrical scroll motifs in white beads, called the "double curve." Iroquois are also known for "embossed" beading in which strings pulled taut force beads to pop up from the surface, creating a bas-relief. Tammy Rahr (Cayuga) is a contemporary practitioner of this style. Zuni artists have developed a tradition of three-dimensional beaded sculptures.

Huichol Indians of Jalisco and Nayarit, Mexico have a completely unique approach to beadwork. They adhere beads one by one to a surface such as wood or a gourd with a mixture of resin and beeswax.

Most Native beadwork is created for tribal use, but beadworkers also create conceptual work for the art world. Richard Aitson (Kiowa-Apache), enjoying both an Indian and non-Indian audience, is known for his fully beaded cradleboards. Another Kiowa beadworker, Teri Greeves, has won top honours for her beadwork which consciously integrates both traditional and contemporary motifs such as beaded dancers on Converse high-tops. Greeves also beads on buckskin and explores such issues as warfare or Native American voting rights.

Marcus Amerman, Choctaw, one of today's most celebrated bead artists, pioneered a movement of highly realistic beaded portraits. His imagery ranges from 19th century Native leaders to pop icons including Janet Jackson and Brooke Shields.

Roger Amerman, Marcus' brother, and Martha Berry, Cherokee, have effectively revived Southeastern beadwork, a style that had been lost because of the forced removal of their tribes to Indian Territory. Their beadwork commonly features white bead outlines, an echo of the shell beads or pearls Southeastern tribes used before contact.

Jamie Okuma (Luiseño-Shoshone-Bannock) has won top awards with her beaded dolls, which can include entire families or horses and riders, all with fully beaded regalia. The antique Venetian beads she uses can be as small as size 22°, about the size of a grain of salt. Juanita Growing Thunder Fogarty, Rhonda Holy Bear, and Charlene Holy Bear are also prominent beaded doll makers.

The widespread popularity of glass beads does not mean aboriginal bead making is dead. Perhaps the most famous Native bead is wampum, a cylindrical tube of quahog or whelk shell. Both shells produce white beads, but only parts of the quahog produce purple. These are ceremonially and politically important to a range of Eastern tribes.

Beetlewing

Beetlewing, or beetlewing art, is an ancient craft technique using iridescent beetle wings practiced traditionally in Thailand, Myanmar, India, China and Japan.

Tradition

It was common in some of the ancient refined cultures of Asia to attach beetlewing pieces as an adornment to paintings, textiles and jewellery. Different species of metallic wood-boring beetle wings were used depending on the region, but traditionally the most valued were those from beetles belonging to genus *Sternocera*. Their wings were valued for their beautiful and hardy metallic emerald iridescence. The shiny appearance of beetlewings is long-lasting. They are surprisingly durable if subject to normal non-abusive use.

In Thailand beetlewings of wood–boring beetles *Sternocera spp.*, like *Sternocera aequisignata*, were preferred to decorate clothing (shawls and Sabai cloth) and jewellery in former court circles. The beetles have a short life span of 3 to 4 weeks in their adult stage. To avoid killing the beetles, only those that die of natural causes are collected.

In 19th-century India exquisite masterpieces of embroidered textiles were produced using beetlewing pieces. These cloth items have survived the passage of time without losing their splendor.

In some instances, the beetle wings will retain their natural sparkle, even though the cloth surrounding them may have decayed.

The species of beetle traditionally used in decorative work in Japan is *Chrysochroa fulgidissima*, known also as *Tamamushi*.

Survival

In Thailand this ancient tradition has mostly died out. In Bangkok, rare pieces of crafts and jewellery made with beetlewing are displayed at the Dusit Palace complex of King Chulalongkorn (Rama V), now a museum.

Thanks to the encouragement and support of HRH Queen Sirikit, efforts are being made to preserve this traditional art at the Chitralada Centre by supporting artisans who have kept the skill alive.

Modern beetlewing work is usually applied on simple items, like earrings and collage work. These are marketed mostly through tourist-oriented shops.

Crochet

Crochet is a process of creating fabric from yarn, thread, or other material strands using a crochet hook. The word is derived from the French word "crochet", meaning *hook*. Hooks can be made of materials such as metals, woods or plastic and are commercially manufactured as well as produced by artisans. Crocheting, like knitting, consists of pulling loops through other loops, but additionally incorporates wrapping the working material around the hook one or more times. Crochet differs from knitting in that only one stitch is active at one time (exceptions being Tunisian crochet and broomstick lace), stitches made with the same diameter of yarn are comparably taller, and a single crochet hook is used instead of two knitting needles. Additionally, crochet has its own system of symbols to represent stitch types.

The word crochet comes from Old French crochet, *hook*, diminutive of croche, feminine of croc, *of Germanic origin.*

History

Origins: Lis Paludan theorizes that crochet evolved from traditional practices in Iran, South America, or China, but there is no decisive evidence of the craft being performed before its popularity in Europe during the 19th century. The earliest written reference to crochet refers to *slip stitch crochet | shepherd's knitting* from *The Memoirs of a Highland Lady* by Elizabeth Grant (1797–1830) in the 19th century. Some claim that the first published crochet patterns appeared in the Dutch magazine *Pénélopé* in 1824. Crochet patterns have recently been found in the Swedish magazine "Konst och nyhetsmagasin för medborgare av alla klasser" from 1819, discarding this earlier notion. There might exist even earlier examples in publications not previously scrutinised. Other indicators that crochet was new in the 19th century include the 1847 publication *A Winter's Gift*, which provides detailed instructions for performing crochet stitches, although it presumes that readers understand the basics of other needlecrafts.

Early references to the craft in *Godey's Lady's Book* in 1846 and 1847 refer to *crotchet* before the spelling standardized in 1848.

Kooler proposes that early industrialization is key to the development of crochet. Machine spun cotton thread became widely available and inexpensive in Europe and North America after the invention of the cotton gin and the spinning jenny, displacing hand spun linen for many uses. Crochet technique consumes more thread than comparable textile production methods and cotton is well suited to crochet.

Knit and knotted textiles survive from very early periods, but there are no surviving samples of crocheted fabric in any ethnological collection, or archeological source prior to 1800. These writers point to the tambour hooks used in tambour lace | tambour embroidery in France in the 18th century, and contend that the hooking of loops through fine fabric in tambour work evolved into "crochet in the air." Most samples of early work claimed to be crochet turn out to actually be samples of nålebinding.

Donna Kooler identifies a possible problem with the tambour hypothesis: period tambour hooks that survive in modern collections cannot produce crochet because the integral wing nut necessary for tambour work interferes with attempts at crochet.

However, Mrs. Gaugain, in her 1840 *The Lady's Assistant for Executing Useful and Fancy Designs in Knitting, Netting, and Crotchet Work*, refers to "Tambour, or Crotchet," then proceeds to call it "tambour" in all the instructions, indicating a strong connection believed in at the time of crochet's beginning, and that it was, perhaps, the older name.

That those hooks that survive cannot be used is the constant problem in archaeology: what was commonly used may have been usually worn out and didn't survive. Tambour lace on fine net is commonly taught with the crochet hook, these hooks with "integral wing nuts" being an expensive item.

Early crochet hooks ranged from primitive bent needles in a cork handle, used by poor Irish lace workers, to expensively crafted silver, brass, steel, ivory and bone hooks set into a variety of handles, some of which were better designed to show off a lady's hands than they were to work with thread. By the early 1840s, instructions for crochet were being published in England, particularly by Eleanor Riego de la Blanchardiere and Frances Lambert. These early patterns called for cotton and linen thread for lace, and wool yarn for clothing, often in vivid colour combinations.

Early History

In the 19th century, as Ireland was facing the Great Irish Famine (1845-1849), crochet lace work was introduced as a form of famine relief (the production of crocheted lace being an alternative way of making money for impoverished Irish workers). Mademoiselle Riego de la Blanchardiere is generally credited with the invention of Irish Crochet, publishing the first book of patterns in 1846. Irish lace became popular in Europe and America, and was made in quantity until the first World War.

Modern Practice and Culture

Fashions in crochet changed with the end of the Victorian era in the 1890s. Crocheted laces in the new Edwardian era, peaking between 1910 and 1920, became even more elaborate in texture and complicated stitching.

The strong Victorian colours disappeared, though, and new publications called for white or pale threads, except for fancy purses, which were often crocheted of brightly coloured silk and elaborately beaded. After World War I, far fewer crochet patterns were published, and most of them were simplified versions of the early 20th century patterns. After World War II, from the late 40s until the early 60s, there was a resurgence in interest in home crafts, particularly in the United States, with many new and imaginative crochet designs published for colourful doilies, potholders, and other home items, along with updates of earlier publications. These patterns called for thicker threads and yarns than in earlier patterns and included wonderful variegated colours. The craft remained primarily a homemaker's art until the late 1960s and early 1970s, when the new generation picked up on crochet and popularized granny squares, a motif worked in the round and incorporating bright colours.

Although crochet underwent a subsequent decline in popularity, the early 21st century has seen a revival of interest in handcrafts and DIY, as well as great strides in improvement of the quality and varieties of yarn. There are many more new pattern books with modern patterns being printed, and most yarn stores now offer crochet lessons in addition to the traditional knitting lessons. There are many books you can purchase from local book stores to teach yourself how to crochet whether it be as a beginner or more intermediate, there are also many books for children and teenagers who are hoping to take up the hobby. Filet crochet, Tunisian crochet, tapestry crochet, broomstick lace, hairpin lace, cro-hooking, and Irish crochet are all variants of the basic crochet method.

Crochet has experienced a revival on the catwalk. Christopher Kane's Fall 2011 Ready-to-Wear collection makes intensive use of the granny square, one of the most basic of crochet motifs. Crochet has been utilized many a time by designers on the popular reality show *Project Runway*. Additionally, websites such as Etsy and Ravelry have made it easier for individual hobbyists to sell and distribute their patterns or projects across the internet.

Laneya Wiles released a music video titled "Straight Hookin'" which makes a play on the word "hookers," which has a double meaning for both "one who crochets" and "a prostitute."

Materials

Basic materials required for crochet are a hook and some type of material that will be crocheted, most commonly yarn or thread. Additional tools are convenient for keeping stitches counted, measuring crocheted fabric, or making related accessories. Examples include cardboard cutouts, which can be used to make tassels, fringe, and many other items; a pom-pom circle, used to make pom-poms; a tape measure and a gauge measure, both used for measuring crocheted work and counting stitches; a row counter; and occasionally plastic rings, which are used for special projects. In recent years, yarn selections have moved beyond synthetic and plant and animal-based fibres to include bamboo, qiviut, hemp, and banana stalks, to name a few.

Hook

The crochet hook comes in many sizes and materials, such as bone, bamboo, aluminium, plastic and steel. Sizing is categorized by the diameter of the hook's shaft, and a crafter aims to create stitches of a certain size in order to reach a particular gauge specified in a given pattern. If gauge is not reached with one hook, another is used until the stitches made are the needed size. Crafters may have a preference for one type of hook material over another due to aesthetic appeal, yarn glide, or hand disorders such as arthritis, where bamboo or wood hooks are favored over metal for the perceived warmth and flexibility during use. Hook grips and ergonomic hook handles are also available to assist crafters.

Steel crochet hooks range in size from 0.4 to 3.5 millimeters, or from 00 to 16 in American sizing. These hooks are used for fine crochet work such as doilies and lace.

Aluminium, bamboo, and plastic crochet hooks are available from 2.5 to 19 millimeters in size, or from B to S in American sizing.

Artisan-made hooks are often made of hand-turned woods, sometimes decorated with semi-precious stones or beads.

Crochet hooks used for Tunisian crochet are elongated and have a stopper at the end of the handle, while double-ended crochet hooks have a hook on both ends of the handle. There is also a double hooked apparatus called a Cro-hook that has become popular.

A hairpin loom is often used to create lacey and long stitches, known as hairpin lace. While this is not in itself a hook, it is a device used in conjunction with a crochet hook to produce stitches.

Yarn

Yarn for crochet is usually sold as balls or skeins (hanks), although it may also be wound on spools or cones. Skeins and balls are generally sold with a *yarn band,* a label that describes the yarn's weight, length, dye lot, fibre content, washing instructions, suggested needle size, likely gauge, etc. It is a common practice to save the yarn band for future reference, especially if additional skeins must be purchased. Crocheters generally ensure that the yarn for a project comes from a single dye lot. The dye lot specifies a group of skeins that were dyed together and thus have precisely the same colour; skeins from different dye lots, even if very similar in colour, are usually slightly different and may produce a visible stripe when added onto existing work. If insufficient yarn of a single dye lot is bought to complete a project, additional skeins of the same dye lot can sometimes be obtained from other yarn stores or online.

The thickness or weight of the yarn is a significant factor in determining the gauge, i.e., how many stitches and rows are required to cover a given area for a given stitch pattern. Thicker yarns generally require large-diameter crochet hooks, whereas thinner yarns may be crocheted with thick or thin hooks. Hence, thicker yarns generally require fewer stitches, and therefore less time, to work up a given project. Patterns and motifs are coarser with thicker yarns and produce bold visual effects, whereas thinner yarns are best for refined or delicate patternwork. Yarns are standardly grouped by thickness into six categories: superfine, fine, light, medium, bulky and superbulky. Quantitatively, thickness is measured by the number of wraps per inch (WPI). The related *weight per unit length* is usually measured in tex or denier.

Before use, hanks are wound into balls in which the yarn emerges from the centre, making crocheting easier by preventing the yarn from becoming easily tangled. The winding process may be done by hand, or with a ballwinder and swift.

A yarn's usefulness is judged by several factors, such as its *loft* (its ability to trap air), its *resilience* (elasticity under tension), its washability and colourfastness, its *hand* (its feel, particularly softness vs. scratchiness), its durability against abrasion, its resistance to pilling, its *hairiness* (fuzziness), its tendency to twist or untwist, its overall weight and drape, its blocking and felting qualities, its comfort (breathability, moisture absorption, wicking properties) and its appearance, which includes its colour, sheen, smoothness and ornamental features. Other factors include allergenicity, speed of drying, resistance to chemicals, moths, and mildew, melting point and flammability, retention of static electricity, and the propensity to accept dyes. Desirable properties may vary for different projects, so there is no one "best" yarn.

Although crochet may be done with ribbons, metal wire or more exotic filaments, most yarns are made by spinning fibres. In spinning, the fibres are twisted so that the yarn resists breaking under tension; the twisting may be done in either direction, resulting in an Z-twist or S-twist yarn. If the fibres are first aligned by combing them and then the spinner uses a worsted type drafting method such as the short forward draw, the yarn is smoother and called a *worsted*; by contrast, if the fibres are carded but not combed and the spinner uses a woolen drafting method such as the long backward draw, the yarn is fuzzier and called *woolen-spun*. The fibres making up a yarn may be continuous *filament* fibres such as silk and many synthetics, or they may be *staples* (fibres of an average length, typically a few inches); naturally filament fibres are sometimes cut up into staples before spinning. The strength of the spun yarn against breaking is determined by the amount of twist, the length of the fibres and the thickness of the yarn. In general, yarns become stronger with more twist (also called *worst*), longer fibres and thicker yarns (more fibres); for example, thinner yarns require more twist than do thicker yarns to resist breaking under tension. The thickness of the yarn may vary along its length; a *slub* is a much thicker section in which a mass of fibres is incorporated into the yarn.

The spun fibres are generally divided into animal fibres, plant and synthetic fibres. These fibre types are chemically different, corresponding to proteins, carbohydrates and synthetic polymers, respectively. Animal fibres include silk, but generally are long hairs of animals such as sheep (wool), goat (angora, or cashmere goat), rabbit (angora), llama, alpaca, dog, cat, camel, yak, and muskox (qiviut). Plants used for fibres include cotton, flax (for linen), bamboo, ramie, hemp, jute, nettle, raffia, yucca, coconut husk, banana trees, soy and corn. Rayon and acetate fibres are also produced from cellulose mainly derived from trees.

Common synthetic fibres include acrylics, polyesters such as dacron and ingeo, nylon and other polyamides, and olefins such as polypropylene. Of these types, wool is generally favored for crochet, chiefly owing to its superior elasticity, warmth and (sometimes) felting; however, wool is generally less convenient to clean and some people are allergic to it. It is also common to blend different fibres in the yarn, e.g., 85% alpaca and 15% silk. Even within a type of fibre, there can be great variety in the length and thickness of the fibres; for example, Merino wool and Egyptian cotton are favored because they produce exceptionally long, thin (fine) fibres for their type.

A single spun yarn may be crochet as is, or braided or plied with another. In plying, two or more yarns are spun together, almost always in the opposite sense from which they were spun individually; for example, two Z-twist yarns are usually plied with an S-twist. The opposing twist relieves some of the yarns' tendency to curl up and produces a thicker, *balanced* yarn. Plied yarns may themselves be plied together, producing *cabled yarns* or *multi-stranded yarns*.

Sometimes, the yarns being plied are fed at different rates, so that one yarn loops around the other, as in bouclé. The single yarns may be dyed separately before plying, or afterwords to give the yarn a uniform look.

The dyeing of yarns is a complex art. Yarns need not be dyed; or they may be dyed one colour, or a great variety of colours. Dyeing may be done industrially, by hand or even hand-painted onto the yarn. A great variety of synthetic dyes have been developed since the synthesis of indigo dye in the mid-19th century; however, natural dyes are also possible, although they are generally less brilliant. The colour-scheme of a yarn is sometimes called its colourway. Variegated yarns can produce interesting visual effects, such as diagonal stripes.

Process

Crocheted fabric is begun by placing a slip-knot loop on the hook (though other methods, such as a magic ring or simple folding over of the yarn may be used), pulling another loop through the first loop, and repeating this process to create a chain of a suitable length. The chain is either turned and worked in rows, or joined to the beginning of the row with a slip stitch and worked in rounds. Rounds can also be created by working many stitches into a single loop. Stitches are made by pulling one or more loops through each loop of the chain. At any one time at the end of a stitch, there is only one loop left on the hook. Tunisian crochet, however, draws all of the loops for an entire row onto a long hook before working them off one at a time. Like knitting, crochet can be worked either flat or in the round.

International Crochet Terms and Notations

In the English-speaking crochet world, basic stitches have different names that vary by country. The differences are usually referred to as UK/US or British/American. To help counter confusion when reading patterns, a diagramming system using a standard international notation has come into use.

Another terminological difference is known as *tension* (UK) and *gauge* (US). Individual crocheters work yarn with a loose or a tight hold and, if unmeasured, these differences can lead to significant size changes in finished garments that have the same number of stitches. In order to control for this inconsistency, printed crochet instructions include a standard for the number of stitches across a standard swatch of fabric. An individual crocheter begins work by producing a test swatch and compensating for any discrepancy by changing to a smaller or larger hook. North Americans call this *gauge*, referring to the end result of these adjustments; British crocheters speak of *tension*, which refers to the crafter's grip on the yarn while producing stitches.

Differences from and Similarities to Knitting

One of the more obvious differences is that crochet uses one hook while much knitting uses two needles. In most crochet, the artisan usually has only one live stitch on the hook (with the exception being Tunisian crochet), while a knitter keeps an entire row of stitches active simultaneously.

Dropped stitches, which can unravel a fabric, rarely interfere with crochet work, due to a second structural difference between knitting and crochet.

In knitting, each stitch is supported by the corresponding stitch in the row above and it supports the corresponding stitch in the row below, whereas crochet stitches are only supported by and support the stitches on either side of it. If a stitch in a finished crocheted item breaks, the stitches above and below remain intact, and because of the complex looping of each stitch, the stitches on either side are unlikely to come loose unless heavily stressed.

Round or cylindrical patterns are simple to produce with a regular crochet hook, but cylindrical knitting requires either a set of circular needles or three to five special double-ended needles. Many crocheted items are composed of individual motifs which are then joined together, are by sewing or crocheting, whereas knitting is usually composed of one fabric, such as entrelac.

Freeform crochet is a technique that can create interesting shapes in three dimensions because new stitches can be made independently of previous stitches almost anywhere in the crocheted piece. It is generally accomplished by building shapes or structural elements onto existing crocheted fabric at any place the crafter desires.

Knitting can be accomplished by machine, while many crochet stitches can only be crafted by hand. The height of knitted and crocheted stitches is also different: a single crochet stitch is twice the height of a knit stitch in the same yarn size and comparable diameter tools, and a double crochet stitch is about four times the height of a knit stitch.

While most crochet is made with a hook, there is also a method of crocheting with a knitting loom. This is called loomchet. Slip stitch crochet is very similar to knitting. Each stitch in slip stitch crochet is formed the same way as a knit or purl stitch which is then bound off. A person working in slip stitch crochet can follow a knitted pattern with knits, purls, and cables, and get a similar result.

It is a common perception that crochet produces a thicker fabric than knitting, tends to have less "give" than knitted fabric, and uses approximately a third more yarn for a comparable project than knitted items. Though this is true when comparing a single crochet swatch with a stockinette swatch, both made with the same size yarn and needle/hook, it is not necessarily true for crochet in general.

Most crochet uses far less than 1/3 more yarn than knitting for comparable pieces, and a crocheter can get similar feel and drape to knitting by using a larger hook or thinner yarn. Tunisian crochet and slip stitch crochet can in some cases use less yarn than knitting for comparable pieces.

According to sources claiming to have tested the 1/3 more yarn assertion, a single crochet stitch (sc) uses approximately the same amount of yarn as knit garter stitch, but more yarn than stockinette stitch. Any stitch using yarnovers uses less yarn than sc to produce the same amount of fabric. Cluster stitches, which are in fact multiple stitches worked together, will use the most length.

Standard crochet stitches like sc and dc also produce a thicker fabric, more like knit garter stitch. This is part of why they use more yarn. Slip stitch can produce a fabric much like stockinette that is thinner and therefore uses less yarn.

Charity

It has been very common for people and groups to crochet clothing and other garments and then donate them to soldiers during war. People have also crocheted clothing and then donated it to hospitals, for sick patients and also for newborn babies. Sometimes groups will crochet for a specific charity purpose, such as crocheting for homeless shelters, nursing homes, etc. It is also becoming increasingly popular to crochet hats (commonly referred to as "chemo caps") and donate them to cancer treatment centres, for those undergoing chemotherapy. During the month of October pink hats and scarves are made and proceeds are donated to breast cancer funds.

Mathematics and Hyperbolic Crochet

Crochet patterns have an underlying mathematical structure—the pattern created by the regular presence or omission of stitches is the very essence of this artform. The similarities to Base2 math, with its series of 0s and 1s, are obvious. That is to say, a present stitch is like a "1", and a missing stitch is like a "0". The craft has been used to illustrate shapes in hyperbolic space that are difficult to reproduce using other media or are difficult to understand when viewed two-dimensionally. A hyperbolic model of a coral reef has also been constructed for environmental purposes

A paper model based on the pseudosphere was created by William Thurston, however, it was quite delicate. Crochet has been used by mathematician Daina Taimina in order to create a version of the hyperbolic plane. Daina Taimina used the art of crochet to create a strong, durable model, which received an exhibition by the Institute For Figuring.

Architecture

In "Style in the technical arts", Gottfried Semper looks at the textile with great promise and historical precedent. In Section 53, he writes of the "loop stitch, or Noeud Coulant: a knot that, if untied, causes the whole system to unravel." In the same section, Semper confesses his ignorance of the subject of crochet but believes strongly that it is a technique of great value as a textile technique and possibly something more.

There are a small number of architects currently interested in the subject of crochet as it relates to architecture. The following publications, explorations and thesis projects can be used as a resource to see how crochet is being used within the capacity of architecture.

- Emergent Explorations: Analog and Digital Scripting - Alexander Worden
- Research and Design: The Architecture of variation - Lars Spuybroek
- YurtAlert - Kate Pokorny

Graffiti

In the past few years, a practice called yarn bombing, or the use of knitted or crocheted cloth to modify and beautify one's (usually outdoor) surroundings, emerged in the US and spread worldwide.

Yarn bombers sometimes target existing pieces of graffiti for beautification.

Felting

Felt is a non-woven textile that is produced by matting, condensing and pressing fibres together. Felt can be made of natural fibres such as wool or synthetic fibres such as acrylic. There are many different types of felts for industrial, technical, designer and craft applications. While some types of felt are very soft, some are tough enough to form construction materials. Felt can vary in terms of fibre content, colour, size, thickness, density and more factors depending on the use of the felt.

Many cultures have legends as to the origins of feltmaking. Sumerian legend claims that the secret of feltmaking was discovered by Urnamman of Lagash. The story of Saint Clement and Saint Christopher relates that while fleeing from persecution, the men packed their sandals with wool to prevent blisters. At the end of their journey, the movement and sweat had turned the wool into felt socks.

Feltmaking is still practised by nomadic peoples (Altaic people:Mongols;Turkic people) in Central Asia, where rugs, tents and clothing are regularly made. Some of these are traditional items, such as the classic yurt (Gers), while others are designed for the tourist market, such as decorated slippers. In the Western world, felt is widely used as a medium for expression in textile art as well as design, where it has significance as an ecological textile.

Construction

Wet Felting: Felt is made by a process called *wet felting* where the natural wool fibres, stimulated by friction and lubricated by moisture (usually soapy water), move at a 90 degree angle towards the friction source and then away again, in effect making little "tacking" stitches. While at any given moment only 5% of the fibres are active, the process is continual, so different 'sets' of fibres become activated and then deactivated, thereby building up the cloth.

This "wet" process takes advantage of the inherent nature of wool and other animal hairs. The hairs are made up of unidirectional scales, and they are also naturally kinked. It is this combination which reacts to the friction of the felting process, forcing the scales on the hairs to lock together and thus causing the phenomenon of felting. It tends to work well with wool fibres because their scales, when aggravated, readily bond together.

It is also possible to produce artificial felts. If made using the wet method, an artificial felt will contain a minimum of 30% wool fibres with the rest being artificial fibres. This is the minimum composition necessary to hold a fabric together with the fibres alone; it would be difficult to form a stable fabric by hand below this ratio. Wholly artificial felts are actually needle-felts.

An alternative felting process involves a steam roller rolling over the unwoven fibres in a shallow pool of water with the cloth rotating as the steam roller passes over it. This method is widely used in small towns in India where mass manufacturing of clothing is performed.

Needle Felt

Needle felting is a popular fibre arts craft that creates felt without the use of water. Special needles that are used in industrial felting machines are used by the artist as a sculpting tool. While erroneously referred to as "barbed" needles, they in fact have notches along the shaft of the needle that grab the top layer of fibres and tangle them with the inner layers of fibres as the needle enters the wool. Since these notches face down towards the tip of the needle, they do not pull the fibres out as the needle exits the wool.

Once tangled and compressed using the needle, the felt can be strong and used for creating jewellery or sculpture. Using a single needle or a small group of needles (2-5) in a hand-held tool, fine details can be achieved using this technique, and it is popular for 2D and 3D felted work.

Carroting

From the mid-17th to the mid-20th centuries, a process called "carroting" was used in the manufacture of good quality felt for making men's hats. Beaver, rabbit or hare skins were treated with a dilute solution of the mercury compound mercuric nitrate.

The skins were dried in an oven where the thin fur at the sides turned orange — the colour of carrots. Pelts were stretched over a bar in a cutting machine and the skin sliced off in thin shreds, the fleece coming away entirely.

The fur was blown onto a cone-shaped colander, treated with hot water to consolidate it, the cone peeled off and passed through wet rollers to cause the fur to felt. These 'hoods' were then dyed and blocked to make hats. This toxic solution and the vapours it produced resulted in widespread cases of mercury poisoning among hatters, possibly giving rise to the expression "mad as a hatter".

Uses

Felt is used everywhere from the automotive industry, to musical instruments and home construction. It is often used as a damper. In the automotive industry, for example, it damps the vibrations between interior panels and also stops dirt entering into some ball/cup joints. Felt is used on the underside of a car bra to protect the body.

Many musical instruments use felt. On drum cymbal stands, it protects the cymbal from cracking and ensures a clean sound. It is used to wrap bass drum and timpani mallets. Felt is used extensively in pianos; for example, piano hammers are made of wool felt around a wooden core.

The density and springiness of the felt is a major part of what creates a piano's tone. As the felt becomes grooved and "packed" with use and age, the tone suffers. Felt is placed under the piano keys on accordions to control touch and key noise; it is also used on the *pallets* to silence notes not sounded by preventing air flow.

Felt is used for framing paintings. It is laid between the slip mount and picture as a protective measure to avoid damage from rubbing to the edge of the painting. This is commonly found as a preventive measure on paintings which have already been restored or professionally framed. It is widely used to protect paintings executed on various surfaces including canvas, wood panel and copper plate.

A felt-covered board can be used in storytelling to small children. Small felt cutouts or figures of animals, people, or other objects will adhere to a felt board, and in the process of telling the story, the storyteller also acts it out on the board with the animals or people. Puppets can also be made with felt.

German artist Josef Beuys used felt in a number of works.

In the early part of the 20th century, felt hats, such as fedoras, trilbies and homburgs, were worn by many men in the western world.

Knitting

Knitting is a method by which thread or yarn is used to create a cloth.

Knitted fabric consists of a number of consecutive rows of loops, called stitches.

As each row progresses, a new loop is pulled through an existing loop. The active stitches are held on a needle until another loop can be passed through them. This process eventually results in a fabric, often used for garments.

Knitting may be done by hand or by machine. There exist numerous styles and methods of hand knitting.

Different types of yarns and needles may be used to achieve a plethora of knitted materials; these tools give the final piece a different colour, texture, weight, and/or integrity.

Other factors that affect the end result include the needle's shape, thickness and malleability, as well as the yarn's fibre type, texture and twist.

Structure

Courses and wales:

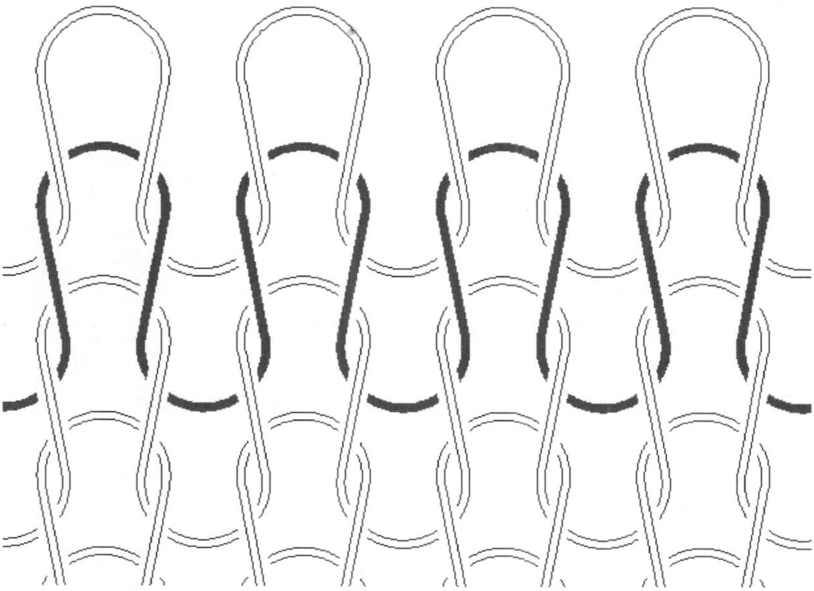

Figure: *Structure of stockinette, a common knitted fabric. The meandering red path defines one* course, *the path of the yarn through the fabric. The uppermost white loops are unsecured and "active", but they secure the red loops suspended from them. In turn, the red loops secure the white loops just below them, which in turn secure the loops below them, and so on.*

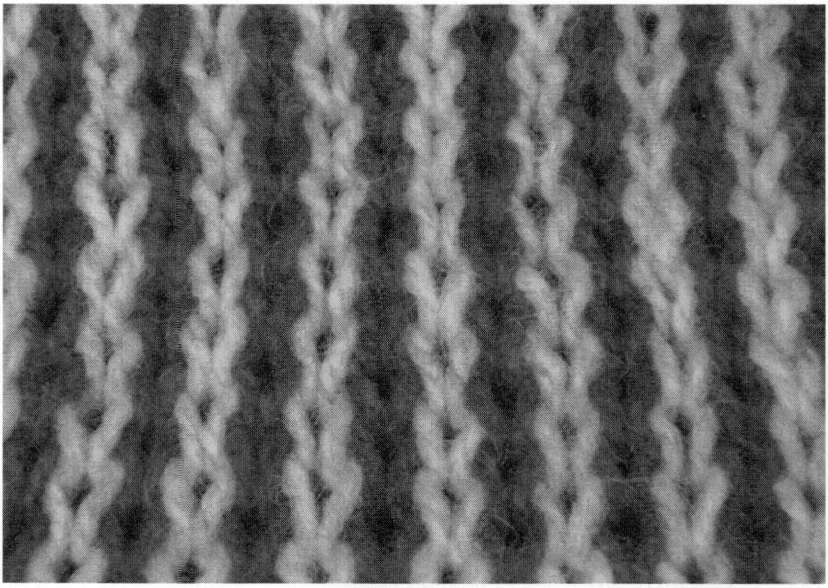

Figure: *Alternating wales of red and white knit stitches. Each stitch in a wale is suspended from the one above it.*

Like weaving, knitting is a technique for producing a two-dimensional fabric made from a one-dimensional yarn or thread. In weaving, threads are always straight, running parallel either lengthwise (warp threads) or crosswise (weft threads). By contrast, the yarn in knitted fabrics follows a meandering path (a *course*), forming symmetric loops (also called bights) symmetrically above and below the mean path of the yarn.

These meandering loops can be stretched easily in different directions, which gives knitting much more elasticity than woven fabrics; depending on the yarn and knitting pattern, knitted garments can stretch as much as 500%. For this reason, knitting was initially developed for garments that must be elastic or stretch in response to the wearer's motions, such as socks and hosiery.

For comparison, woven garments stretch mainly along one direction (the *bias*) and are not very elastic, unless they are woven from stretchable material such as spandex. Knitted garments are often more form-fitting than woven garments, since their elasticity allows them to contour to the body's outline more closely; by contrast, curvature is introduced into most woven garments only with sewn darts, flares, gussets and gores, the seams of which lower the elasticity of the woven fabric still further. Extra curvature can be introduced into knitted garments without seams, as in the heel of a sock; the effect of darts, flares, etc. can be obtained with short rows or by increasing or decreasing the number of stitches. Thread used in weaving is usually much finer than the yarn used in knitting, which can give the knitted fabric more bulk and less drape than a woven fabric.

If they are not secured, the loops of a knitted course will come undone when their yarn is pulled; this is known as *ripping out*, *unravelling* knitting, or humorously, *frogging* (because you 'rip it', this sounds like a frog croaking: 'rib-bit'). To secure a stitch, at least one new loop is passed through it.

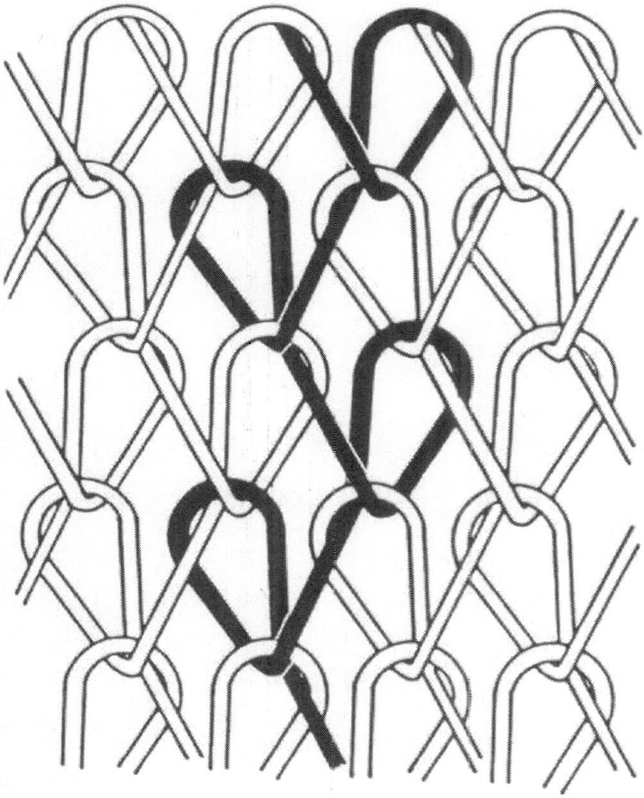

Figure: *Basic pattern of warp knitting. Parallel yarns zigzag lengthwise along the fabric, each loop securing a loop of an adjacent strand from the previous row.*

Although the new stitch is itself unsecured ("active" or "live"), it secures the stitch(es) suspended from it. A sequence of stitches in which each stitch is suspended from the next is called a *wale*. To secure the initial stitches of a knitted fabric, a method for casting on is used; to secure the final stitches in a wale, one uses a method of binding off. During knitting, the active stitches are secured mechanically, either from individual hooks (in knitting machines) or from a knitting needle or frame in hand-knitting.

Weft and Warp Knitting

There are two major varieties of knitting: weft knitting and warp knitting. In the more common *weft knitting*, the wales are perpendicular to the course of the yarn. In warp knitting, the wales and courses run roughly parallel. In weft knitting, the entire fabric may be produced from a single yarn, by adding stitches to each wale in turn, moving across the fabric as in a raster scan.

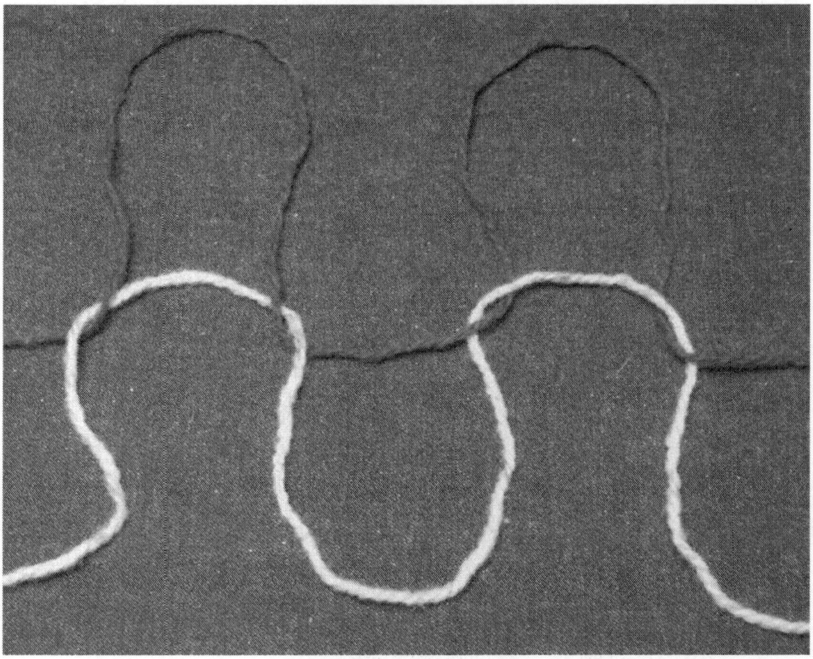

Figure: *In the knit stitch on the left, the next (red) loop passes through the previous (white) loop from* below, *whereas in the purl stitch (right), the next stitch enters from above. Thus, a knit stitch on one side of the fabric appears as a purl stitch on the other, and vice versa.*

By contrast, in warp knitting, one yarn is required for every wale. Since a typical piece of knitted fabric may have hundreds of wales, warp knitting is typically done by machine, whereas weft knitting is done by both hand and machine. Warp-knitted fabrics such as tricot and milanese are resistant to runs, and are commonly used in lingerie.

Weft-knit fabrics may also be knit with multiple yarns, usually to produce interesting colour patterns. The two most common approaches are intarsia and stranded colourwork. In intarsia, the yarns are used in well-segregated regions, e.g., a red apple on a field of green; in that case, the yarns are kept on separate spools and only one is knitted at any time. In the more complex stranded approach, two or more yarns alternate repeatedly within one row and all the yarns must be carried along the row, as seen in Fair Isle sweaters. Double knitting can produce two separate knitted fabrics simultaneously, e.g., two socks; however, the two fabrics are usually integrated into one, giving it great warmth and excellent drape.

Knit and Purl Stitches

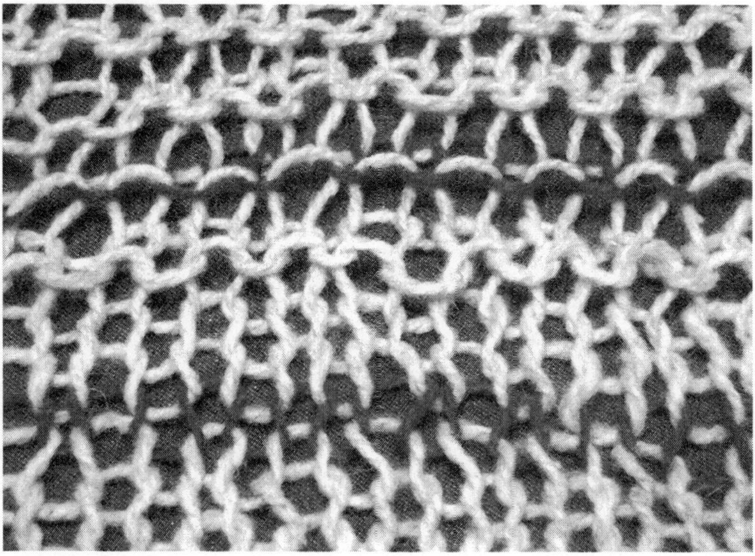

Figure: *Two courses of red yarn illustrating two basic fabric types. The lower red course is knit into the white row below it and is itself knit on the next row; this produces* stockinette *stitch. The upper red course is purled into the row below and then is knit, consistent with* garter *stitch.*

In securing the previous stitch in a wale, the next stitch can pass through the previous loop from either below or above. If the former, the stitch is denoted as a *knit stitch* or a *plain stitch*; if the latter, as a *purl stitch*. The two stitches are related in that a knit stitch seen from one side of the fabric appears as a purl stitch on the other side.

The two types of stitches have a different visual effect; the knit stitches look like "V"'s stacked vertically, whereas the purl stitches look like a wavy horizontal line across the fabric. Patterns and pictures can be created in knitted fabrics by using knit and purl stitches as "pixels"; however, such pixels are usually rectangular, rather than square, depending on the gauge of the knitting.

Individual stitches, or rows of stitches, may be made taller by drawing more yarn into the new loop (an elongated stitch), which is the basis for uneven knitting: a row of tall stitches may alternate with one or more rows of short stitches for an interesting visual effect. Short and tall stitches may also alternate within a row, forming a fish-like oval pattern.

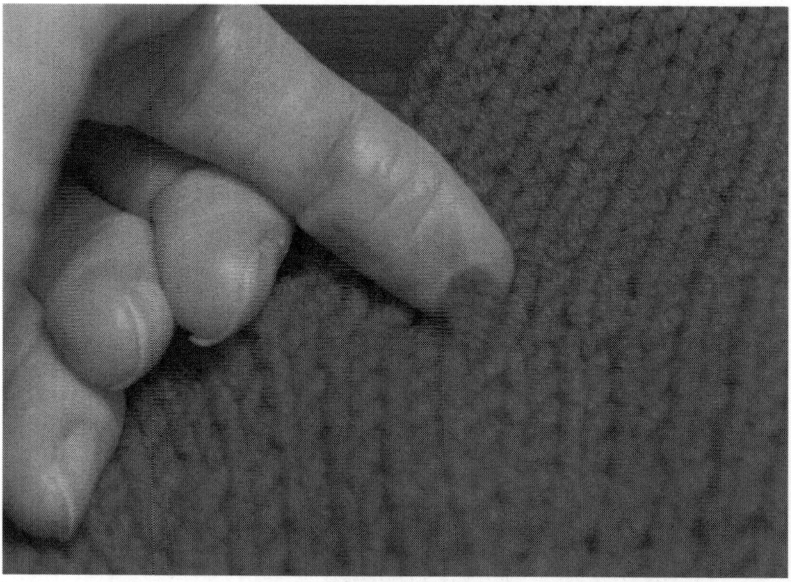

Figure: *A dropped stitch, or missed stitch, is a common error that creates an extra loop to be fixed.*

In the simplest knitted fabrics, all of the stitches are knit or purl; this is known as a garter stitch. Alternating rows of knit stitches and purl stitches produce what is known as a stockinette pattern. Vertical stripes (ribbing) are possible by having alternating wales of knit and purl stitches; for example, a common choice is 2x2 ribbing, in which two wales of knit stitches are followed by two wales of purl stitches, etc. Horizontal striping (welting) is also possible, by alternating *rows* of knit and purl stitches. Checkerboard patterns (basketweave) are also possible, the smallest of which is known as *seed stitch*: the stitches alternate between knit and purl in every wale and along every row.

Fabrics in which the number of knit and purl stitches are not the same, such as stockinette, have a tendency to curl; by contrast, those in which knit and purl stitches are arranged symmetrically (such as ribbing, garter stitch or seed stitch) tend to lie flat and drape well. Wales of purl stitches have a tendency to recede, whereas those of knit stitches tend to come forward.

Thus, the purl wales in ribbing tend to be invisible, since the neighbouring knit wales come forward. Conversely, rows of purl stitches tend to form an embossed ridge relative to a row of knit stitches. This is the basis of shadow knitting, in which the appearance of a knitted fabric changes when viewed from different directions.

Typically, a new stitch is passed through a single unsecured ("active") loop, thus lengthening that wale by one stitch. However, this need not be so; the new loop may be passed through an already secured stitch lower down on the fabric, or even between secured stitches (a dip stitch). Depending on the distance between where the loop is drawn through the fabric and where it is knitted, dip stitches can produce a subtle stippling or long lines across the surface of the fabric, e.g., the lower leaves of a flower.

The new loop may also be passed between two stitches in the *present* row, thus clustering the intervening stitches; this approach is often used to produce a smocking effect in the fabric. The new loop may also be passed through *two or more* previous stitches, producing a decrease and merging wales together. The merged stitches need not be from the same row; for example, a tuck can be formed by knitting stitches together from two different rows, producing a raised horizontal welt on the fabric.

Not every stitch in a row need be knitted; some may be left as is and knitted on a subsequent row. This is known as slip-stitch knitting. The slipped stitches are naturally longer than the knitted ones. For example, a stitch slipped for one row before knitting would be roughly twice as tall as its knitted counterparts. This can produce interesting visual effects, although the resulting fabric is more rigid, because the slipped stitch "pulls" on its neighbours and is less deformable. Slip-stitch knitting plays an important role in *mosaic knitting*, an important technique in hand-knitting patterned fabrics; mosaic-knit fabrics tend to be stiffer than patterned fabrics produced by other methods such as Fair-Isle knitting.

In some cases, a stitch may be deliberately left unsecured by a new stitch and its wale allowed to disassemble. This is known as drop-stitch knitting, and produces a vertical ladder of see-through holes in the fabric, corresponding to where the wale had been.

Right- and Left-plaited Stitches

Both knit and purl stitches may be twisted: usually once if at all, but sometimes twice and (very rarely) thrice. When seen from above, the twist can be clockwise (right yarn over left) or counterclockwise (left yarn over right); these are denoted as right- and left-plaited stitches, respectively.

Hand-knitters generally produce right-plaited stitches by knitting or purling through the back loops, i.e., passing the needle through the initial stitch in an unusual way, but wrapping the yarn as usual.

By contrast, the left-plaited stitch is generally formed by hand-knitters by wrapping the yarn in the opposite way, rather than by any change in the needle. Although they are mirror images in form, right- and left-plaited stitches are functionally equivalent. Both types of plaited stitches give a subtle but interesting visual texture, and tend to draw the fabric inwards, making it stiffer. Plaited stitches are a common method for knitting jewellery from fine metal wire.

Edges and Joins Between Fabrics

The initial and final edges of a knitted fabric are known as the *cast-on* and *bound-off* edges. The side edges are known as the *selvages*; the word derives from "self-edges", meaning that the stitches do not need to be secured by anything else. Many types of selvages have been developed, with different elastic and ornamental properties.

Vertical and horizontal edges can be introduced within a knitted fabric, e.g., for button holes, by binding off and re-casting on again (horizontal) or by knitting the fabrics on either side of a vertical edge separately.

Two knitted fabrics can be joined by embroidery-based grafting methods, most commonly the Kitchener stitch. New wales can be begun from any of the edges of a knitted fabric; this is known as picking up stitches and is the basis for entrelac, in which the wales run perpendicular to one another in a checkerboard pattern.

Cables, Increases, and Lace

Ordinarily, stitches are knitted in the same order in every row, and the wales of the fabric run parallel and vertically along the fabric. However, this need not be so, since the order in which stitches are knitted may be permuted so that wales cross over one another, forming a cable pattern. Cables patterns tend to draw the fabric together, making it denser and less elastic; Aran sweaters are a common form of knitted cabling.

Arbitrarily complex braid patterns can be done in cable knitting, with the proviso that the wales must move ever upwards; it is generally impossible for a wale to move up and then down the fabric. Knitters have developed methods for giving the illusion of a circular wale, such as appear in Celtic knots, but these are inexact approximations. However, such circular wales are possible using Swiss darning, a form of embroidery, or by knitting a tube separately and attaching it to the knitted fabric.

A wale can split into two or more wales using increases, most commonly involving a yarn over. Depending on how the increase is done, there is often a hole in the fabric at the point of the increase. This is used to great effect in lace knitting, which consists of making patterns and pictures using such holes, rather than with the stitches themselves. The large and many holes in lacy knitting makes it extremely elastic; for example, some Shetland "wedding-ring" shawls are so fine that they may be drawn through a wedding ring.

By combining increases and decreases, it is possible to make the direction of a wale slant away from vertical, even in weft knitting. This is the basis for bias knitting, and can be used for visual effect, similar to the direction of a brush-stroke in oil painting.

Ornamentations and Additions

Various point-like ornaments may be added to knitting for their look or to improve the wear of the fabric. Examples include various types of bobbles, sequins and beads. Long loops can also be drawn out and secured, forming a "shaggy" texture to the fabric; this is known as loop knitting. Additional patterns can be made on the surface of the knitted fabric using embroidery; if the embroidery resembles knitting, it is often called Swiss darning. Various closures for the garments, such as frogs and buttons can be added; usually buttonholes are knitted into the garment, rather than cut.

Ornamental pieces may also be knitted separately and then attached using applique. For example, differently coloured leaves and petals of a flower could be knit separately and attached to form the final picture. Separately knitted tubes can be applied to a knitted fabric to form complex Celtic knots and other patterns that would be difficult to knit.

Unknitted yarns may be worked into knitted fabrics for warmth, as is done in tufting and "weaving" (also known as "couching").

Types

Flat Knitting Versus Circular Knitting

Circular knitting (also called "knitting in the round") is a form of knitting that can be used to create a seamless tube. Knitting is worked in rounds (the equivalent of rows in flat knitting) in a helix. Originally, circular knitting was done using a set of four or five double-pointed knitting needles.

Later, circular needles were invented. A circular needle resembles two short knitting needles connected by a cable between them. Flat knitting, on the other hand, is used, in its most basic form, to make flat, rectangular pieces of cloth. It is done with two straight knitting needles and is worked in rows, horizontal lines of stitches. A circular knitting needle can also be used to create flat-knitted pieces that are too large for ordinary straight knitting needles, such as afghans and blankets.

Circular knitting is employed to create pieces that are circular or tube-shaped, such as hats, socks, mittens, and sleeves. Flat knitting is usually used to knit flat pieces like scarves, blankets, afghans, and the backs and fronts of sweaters.

There is also such a thing as finger knitting. Instead of needles, fingers are used to produce a tube of knitted fabric.

Felting

Felting is the hand-knitters' term for fulling, a technique for joining knitted or woven wool fibres (only animal yarn fibres can be felted. Acrylic or any fibre that can be machine washed cannot be felted). The finished product is put in a hot wash and the yarn fibres become agitated until it starts to shrink. While the knitted project is in the washing machine, it is important to check the progress. Depending on the size of the project, some may felt faster than others. The end result typically has reduced dimensions. Bags, mittens, vests, socks, slippers and hats are just a few items that can be felted.

Needle Felting

Needle felting is a technique used to add decoration to a knitted or felted piece, where raw roving is applied using a very sharp barbed felting needle by repeatedly piercing the roving and background together. Once washed in hot water, the appliqued decoration is fused with the background. Felted knitting can be cut with scissors without concern about fraying. This is also a good method to use when attempting to give structure to what can be frail knitted fabrics.

History and Culture

The word is derived from *knot* and ultimately from the Old English *cnyttan,* to knot. One of the earliest known examples of knitting was cotton socks with stranded knit colour patterns, found in Egypt from the end of the first millennium AD. Originally a male-only occupation, the first knitting trade guild was started in Paris in 1527. With the invention of the knitting machine, however, knitting "by hand" became a useful but non-essential craft. Similar to quilting, spinning, and needlepoint, knitting became a leisure activity.

Hand-knitting has gone into and out of fashion many times in the last two centuries, and at the turn of the 21st century it is enjoying a revival. According to the industry group Craft Yarn Council of America, the number of women knitters in the United States age 25–35 increased 150% in the two years between 2002 and 2004. The latest incarnation is less about the "make-do and mend" attitude of the 1940s and early 50s and more about making a statement about individuality as well as developing an innate sense of community.

During the 1940s, English knitting rose in popularity while Continental knitting fell. This is due to the fact that continental knitting originated within Germany and was spread by immigrants. During World War II, continental knitting fell out of style due to its relationship with Germany. It wasn't until Elizabeth Zimmermann publicized continental knitting in the 1980s that it again was popularized.

Additionally, many contemporary knitters have an interest in blogging about their knitting, patterns, and techniques, or joining a virtual community focused on knitting, such as the extremely popular Ravelry. There are also a number of popular knitting podcasts, and various other knitting websites. Contemporary knitting groups may be referred to in the U.S. as a "Stitch 'N Bitch" where a group of knitters get together to work on projects, discuss patterns, troubleshoot their work and just socialize. In the UK, the term has been "knitting circle" since the early 20th century.

Properties of Fabrics

The topology of a knitted fabric is relatively complex. Unlike woven fabrics, where strands usually run straight horizontally and vertically, yarn that has been knitted follows a loopy path along its row, as with the red strand in the diagram at left, in which the loops of one row have all been pulled through the loops of the row below it.

Because there is no single straight line of yarn anywhere in the pattern, a knitted piece can stretch in all directions. This elasticity is unavailable from woven fabrics, which only stretch along the bias. Many modern stretchy garments, even as they rely on elastic synthetic materials for some stretch, also achieve at least some of their stretch through knitted patterns.

The basic knitted fabric (as in the diagram, and usually called a *stocking* or *stockinette* pattern) has a definite "right side" and "wrong side". On the right side, the visible portions of the loops are the verticals connecting two rows, arranged in a grid of *V* shapes. On the wrong side, the ends of the loops are visible, both the tops and bottoms, creating a much more bumpy texture sometimes called *reverse stockinette.* (Despite being the "wrong side," reverse stockinette is frequently used as a pattern in its own right.) Because the yarn holding rows together is all on the front, and the yarn holding side-by-side stitches together is all on the back, stockinette fabric has a strong tendency to curl toward the front on the top and bottom, and toward the back on the left and right side.

Stitches can be worked from either side, and various patterns are created by mixing regular knit stitches with the "wrong side" stitches, known as purl stitches, either in columns (ribbing), rows (garter, welting), or more complex patterns. Each such fabric has different properties: a garter stitch has much more vertical stretch, while ribbing stretches much more horizontally. Because of their front-back symmetry, these two fabrics have little curl, making them popular as edging, even when their stretch properties are not desired.

Different combinations of knit and purl stitches, along with more advanced techniques, generate fabrics of considerably variable consistency, from gauzy to very dense, from highly stretchy to relatively stiff, from flat to tightly curled, and so on.

Texture

The most common texture for a knitted garment is that generated by the flat stockinette stitch, though very small, in machine-made stockings and T-shirts—which is worked in the round as nothing but knit stitches, and worked flat as alternating rows of knit and purl. Other simple textures can be made with nothing but knit and purl stitches, including garter stitch, ribbing, and moss and seed stitches. Adding a "slip stitch" (where a loop is passed from one needle to the other) allows for a wide range of textures, including heel and linen stitches, and a number of more complicated patterns.

Some more advanced knitting techniques create a surprising variety of complex textures. Combining certain increases, which can create small eyelet holes in the resulting fabric, with assorted decreases is key to creating knitted lace, a very open fabric resembling lace. Changing the order of stitches from one row to the next, usually with the help of a cable needle or stitch holder, is key to cable knitting, producing an endless variety of cables, honeycombs, ropes, and Aran sweater patterning. Entrelac forms a rich checkerboard texture by knitting small squares, picking up their side edges, and knitting more squares to continue the piece.

The appearance of a garment is also affected by the *weight* of the yarn, which describes the thickness of the spun fibre. The thicker the yarn, the more visible and apparent stitches will be; the thinner the yarn, the finer the texture.

Colour

Plenty of finished knitting projects never use more than a single colour of yarn, but there are many ways to work in multiple colours. Some yarns are dyed to be either *variegated* (changing colour every few stitches in a random fashion) or *self-striping* (changing every few rows). More complicated techniques permit large fields of colour (intarsia, for example), busy small-scale patterns of colour (such as Fair Isle), or both (double knitting and slip-stitch colour, for example).

Yarn with multiple shades of the same hue are called *ombre*, while a yarn with multiple hues may be known as a given *colourway* — a green, red and yellow yarn might be dubbed the "Parrot Colourway" by its manufacturer, for example. *Heathered* yarns contain small amounts of fibre of different colours, while *tweed* yarns may have greater amounts of different coloured fibres.

Process

There are many hundreds of different knitting stitches used by knitters. A piece of knitting begins with the process of *casting on* (also known as "binding on"), which involves the initial creation of the stitches on the needle. Different methods of casting on are used for different effects: one may be stretchy enough for lace, while another provides a decorative edging — *Provisional* cast-ons are used when the knitting will continue in both directions from the cast-on. There are various method employed to "cast on," such as the "thumb method" (also known as "slingshot" or "long-tail" cast-ons), where the stitches are created by a series of loops that will, when knitted, give a very loose edge ideal for "picking up stitches" and knitting a border; the "double needle method" (also known as "knit-on" or "cable cast-on"), whereby each loop placed on the needle is then "knitted on," which produces a firmer edge ideal on its own as a border; and many more. The number of active stitches remains the same as when cast on unless stitches are added (an increase) or removed (a decrease).

Most Western-style knitters follow either the English style (in which the yarn is held in the right hand) or the Continental style (in which the yarn is held in the left hand).

There are also different ways to insert the needle into the stitch. Knitting through the front of a stitch is called Western knitting. Going through the back of a stitch is called Eastern knitting. A third method, called combination knitting, goes through the front of a knit stitch and the back of a purl stitch.

Once the knitted piece is finished, the remaining live stitches are "cast off". Casting (or "binding") off loops the stitches across each other so they can be removed from the needle without unravelling the item. Although the mechanics are different from casting on, there is a similar variety of methods.

In knitting certain articles of clothing, especially larger ones like sweaters, the final knitted garment will be made of several knitted pieces, with individual sections of the garment knit separately and then sewn together. Seamless knitting, where a whole garment is knit as a single piece, is also possible. Elizabeth Zimmermann is probably the best-known proponent of seamless or circular knitting techniques. Smaller items, such as socks and hats, are usually knit in one piece on double-pointed needles or circular needles.

Mega Knitting

Mega knitting is a term recently coined and relates to the use of knitting needles greater than or equal to half an inch in diameter. Mega knitting uses the same stitches and techniques as conventional knitting, except that hooks are carved into the ends of the needles. The hooked needles greatly enhance control of the work, catching the stitches and preventing them from slipping off.

It was the development of the knitting machine that introduced hooked needles and enabled faultless, automated knitting. Most knitters probably aren't even aware of the many processes that their fingers perform in the making of a single stitch. However, large gauge needles emphasise those actions and knitting becomes increasingly more awkward when the needle diameter is greater than the width of the knitters finger.

On a one inch diameter (size 50) needle for instance, the shaft begins to taper one and three quarter inches from the tip. This means that the stitches are spread much further apart on mega knitting needles, making them more difficult to control. The hook catches the loop of yarn as each stitch is knitted, meaning that wrists and fingers don't have to work so hard and there is less chance of stitches slipping off the needle. The position of the hook is most important. Turn the left (non-working) hook to face away at all times; turn the right (working) hook toward you up whilst knitting (plain stitch) and away whilst purling. Mega knitting produces a chunky, bulky fabric or an open lacy weave, depending on the weight and type of yarn used.

Materials

Yarn: Yarn for hand-knitting is usually sold as balls or skeins (hanks), although it may also be wound on spools or cones. Skeins and balls are generally sold with a *yarn-band*, a label that describes the yarn's weight, length, dye lot, fibre content, washing instructions, suggested needle size, likely gauge, etc. It is common practice to save the yarn band for future reference, especially if additional skeins must be purchased. Knitters generally ensure that the yarn for a project comes from a single dye lot. The dye lot specifies a group of skeins that were dyed together and thus have precisely the same colour; skeins from different dye-lots, even if very similar in colour, are usually slightly different and may produce a visible stripe when knitted together. If a knitter buys insufficient yarn of a single dye lot to complete a project, additional skeins of the same dye lot can sometimes be obtained from other yarn stores or online. Otherwise, knitters can alternate skeins every few rows to help the dye lots blend together easier.

The thickness or weight of the yarn is a significant factor in determining the gauge, i.e., how many stitches and rows are required to cover a given area for a given stitch pattern. Thicker yarns generally require thicker knitting needles, whereas thinner yarns may be knit with thick or thin needles. Hence, thicker yarns generally require fewer stitches, and therefore less time, to knit up a given garment. Patterns and motifs are coarser with thicker yarns; thicker yarns produce bold visual effects, whereas thinner yarns are best for refined patterns. Yarns are grouped by thickness into six categories: superfine, fine, light, medium, bulky and superbulky; quantitatively, thickness is measured by the number of wraps per inch (WPI). The related *weight per unit length* is usually measured in tex or dernier.

Before knitting, the knitter will typically transform a hank into a ball where the yarn emerges from the centre of the ball; this making the knitting easier by preventing the yarn from becoming easily tangled. This transformation may be done by hand, or with a device known as a ballwinder. When knitting, some knitters enclose their balls in jars to keep them clean and untangled with other yarns; the free yarn passes through a small hole in the jar-lid.

A yarn's usefulness for a knitting project is judged by several factors, such as its *loft* (its ability to trap air), its *resilience* (elasticity under tension), its washability and colourfastness, its *hand* (its feel, particularly softness vs. scratchiness), its durability against abrasion, its resistance to pilling, its *hairiness* (fuzziness), its tendency to twist or untwist, its overall weight and drape, its blocking and felting qualities, its comfort (breathability, moisture absorption, wicking properties) and of course its look, which includes its colour, sheen, smoothness and ornamental features. Other factors include allergenicity; speed of drying; resistance to chemicals, moths, and mildew; melting point and flammability; retention of static electricity; and the propensity to become stained and to accept dyes. Different factors may be more significant than others for different knitting projects, so there is no one "best" yarn.

The resilience and propensity to (un)twist are general properties that affect the ease of hand-knitting. More resilient yarns are more forgiving of irregularities in tension; highly twisted yarns are sometimes difficult to knit, whereas untwisting yarns can lead to split stitches, in which not all of the yarn is knitted into a stitch. A key factor in knitting is *stitch definition*, corresponding to how well complicated stitch patterns can be seen when made from a given yarn. Smooth, highly spun yarns are best for showing off stitch patterns; at the other extreme, very fuzzy yarns or eyelash yarns have poor stitch definition, and any complicated stitch pattern would be invisible.

Although knitting may be done with ribbons, metal wire or more exotic filaments, most yarns are made by spinning fibres. In spinning, the fibres are twisted so that the yarn resists breaking under tension; the twisting may be done in either direction, resulting in a Z-twist or S-twist yarn. If the fibres are first aligned by combing them, the yarn is smoother and called a *worsted*; by contrast, if the fibres are carded but not combed, the yarn is fuzzier and called *woolen-spun*. The fibres making up a yarn may be continuous *filament* fibres such as silk and many synthetics, or they may be *staples* (fibres of an average length, typically a few inches); naturally filament fibres are sometimes cut up into staples before spinning.

The strength of the spun yarn against breaking is determined by the amount of twist, the length of the fibres and the thickness of the yarn. In general, yarns become stronger with more twist (also called *worst*), longer fibres and thicker yarns (more fibres); for example, thinner yarns require more twist than do thicker yarns to resist breaking under tension. The thickness of the yarn may vary along its length; a *slub* is a much thicker section in which a mass of fibres is incorporated into the yarn.

The spun fibres are generally divided into animal fibres, plant and synthetic fibres. These fibre types are chemically different, corresponding to proteins, carbohydrates and synthetic polymers, respectively. Animal fibres include silk, but generally are long hairs of animals such as sheep (wool), goat (angora, or cashmere goat), rabbit (angora), llama, alpaca, dog, cat, camel, yak, and muskox (qiviut). Plants used for fibres include cotton, flax (for linen), bamboo, ramie, hemp, jute, nettle, raffia, yucca, coconut husk, banana trees, soy and corn. Rayon and acetate fibres are also produced from cellulose mainly derived from trees.

Common synthetic fibres include acrylics, polyesters such as dacron and ingeo, nylon and other polyamides, and olefins such as polypropylene. Of these types, wool is generally favored for knitting, chiefly owing to its superior elasticity, warmth and (sometimes) felting; however, wool is generally less convenient to clean and some people are allergic to it. It is also common to blend different fibres in the yarn, e.g., 85% alpaca and 15% silk.

Even within a type of fibre, there can be great variety in the length and thickness of the fibres; for example, Merino wool and Egyptian cotton are favored because they produce exceptionally long, thin (fine) fibres for their type.

A single spun yarn may be knitted as is, or braided or plied with another. In plying, two or more yarns are spun together, almost always in the opposite sense from which they were spun individually; for example, two Z-twist yarns are usually plied with an S-twist. The opposing twist relieves some of the yarns' tendency to curl up and produces a thicker, *balanced* yarn. Plied yarns may themselves be plied together, producing *cabled yarns* or *multi-stranded yarns*. Sometimes, the yarns being plied are fed at different rates, so that one yarn loops around the other, as in bouclé. The single yarns may be dyed separately before plying, or afterwards to give the yarn a uniform look.

The dyeing of yarns is a complex art that has a long history. However, yarns need not be dyed. They may be dyed just one colour, or a great variety of colours. Dyeing may be done industrially, by hand or even hand-painted onto the yarn. A great variety of synthetic dyes have been developed since the synthesis of indigo dye in the mid-19th century; however, natural dyes are also possible, although they are generally less brilliant. The colour-scheme of a yarn is sometimes called its colourway. Variegated yarns can produce interesting visual effects, such as diagonal stripes; conversely, a variegated yarn may frustrate an otherwise good knitting pattern by producing distasteful colour combination.

Glass/Wax

Knitted Glass combines knitting, lost-wax casting, mold-making, and kiln-casting. The process involves

1. *knitting* with wax strands,
2. surrounding the knitted wax piece with a heat-tolerant refractory material,
3. removing the wax by melting it out, thus creating a mold;
4. placing the mold in a kiln where lead crystal glass melts into the mold;
5. after the mold cools, the mold material is removed to reveal the knitted glass piece.

Tools

The process of knitting has three basic tasks:

1. the active (unsecured) stitches must be held so they don't drop
2. these stitches must be released sometime after they are secured
3. new bights of yarn must be passed through the fabric, usually through active stitches, thus securing them.

In very simple cases, knitting can be done without tools, using only the fingers to do these tasks; however, knitting is usually carried out using tools such as knitting needles, knitting machines or rigid frames. Depending on their size and shape, the rigid frames are called knitting boards, knitting rings (also called knitting looms) or knitting spools (also known as knitting knobbies, knitting nancies, or corkers). There is also a technique of knitting with a crochet hook that has a cord attached to the end, to hold the stitches while they're being worked. This technique is called knooking. Other tools are used to prepare yarn for knitting, to measure and design knitted garments, or to make knitting easier or more comfortable.

Needles

There are three basic types of knitting needles (also called "knitting pins"). The first and most common type consists of two slender, straight sticks tapered to a point at one end, and with a knob at the other end to prevent stitches from slipping off. Such needles are usually 10–16 inches (250–410 mm) long but, due to the compressibility of knitted fabrics, may be used to knit pieces significantly wider. The most important property of needles is their diameter, which ranges from below 2 to 25 mm (roughly 1 inch). The diameter affects the size of stitches, which affects the gauge of the knitting and the elasticity of the fabric. Thus, a simple way to change gauge is to use different needles, which is the basis of uneven knitting. Although the diameter of the knitting needle is often measured in millimeters, there are several different measurement systems, particularly those specific to the United States, the United Kingdom and Japan; a conversion table is given at knitting needle. Such knitting needles may be made out of any materials, but the most common materials are metals, wood, bamboo, and plastic. Different materials have different frictions and grip the yarn differently; slick needles such as metallic needles are useful for swift knitting, whereas rougher needles such as bamboo offer more friction and are therefore less prone to dropping stitches. The knitting of new stitches occurs only at the tapered ends. Needles with lighted tips have been sold to allow knitters to knit in the dark.

The second type of knitting needles are straight, double-pointed knitting needles (also called "DPNs"). Double-pointed needles are tapered at both ends, which allows them to be knit from either end. DPNs are typically used for circular knitting, especially smaller tube-shaped pieces such as sleeves, collars, and socks; usually one needle is active while the others hold the remaining active stitches. DPNs are somewhat shorter (typically 7 inches) and are usually sold in sets of four or five.

Cable needles are a special case of DPNs, although they usually are not straight, but dimpled in the middle. Often, they have the form of a hook. When cabling a knitted piece, a hook is easier to grab and hold the yarn. Cable needles are typically very short (a few inches), and are used to hold stitches temporarily while others are being knitted. Cable patterns are made by permuting the order of stitches; although one or two stitches may be held by hand or knit out of order, cables of three or more generally require a cable needle.

The third needle type consists of circular needles, which are long, flexible double-pointed needles. The two tapered ends (typically 5 inches (130 mm) long) are rigid and straight, allowing for easy knitting; however, the two ends are connected by a flexible strand (usually nylon) that allows the two ends to be brought together. Circular needles are typically 24-60 inches long, and are usually used singly or in pairs; again, the width of the knitted piece may be significantly longer than the length of the circular needle.

A developing trend in the knitting world is interchangeable needles. These kits consist of pairs of needles with usually nylon cables or cords. The cables/cords are screwed into the needles, allowing the knitter to have both flexible straight needles or circular needles. This also allows the knitter to change the diameter and length of the needles as needed.

The ability to work from either end of one needle is convenient in several types of knitting, such as slip-stitch versions of double knitting. Circular needles may be used for flat or circular knitting.

Cable needles are a specific design, and are used to create the twisting motif of a knitted cable. They are made in different sizes, which produces cables of different widths. When in use, the cable needle is used at the same time as two regular needles.

It functions by holding together the stitches creating the cable as the other needles create the rest of the stitches for the knitted piece. At specific points indicated by the pattern, the cable needle is moved, the stitches on it are worked by the other needles, then the cable needle is turned around to a different position to create the cable twist.

Mega Needles

Mega knitting needles are generally considered to be any knitting needles larger than size 17 (half inch diameter). Mega needles may or may not have hooks carved in the ends. Hooks on large diameter needles help enormously to control the stitches whilst knitting.

Largest Circular Knitting Needles

The largest aluminium circular knitting needles on record are size US 150 and are nearly 7 feet tall. They are owned by Paradise Fibres and are currently on display in the Paradise Fibres retail showroom.

Record

The current holder of the Guinness World Record for Knitting with the Largest Knitting Needles is Julia Hopson of Penzance in Cornwall.

Julia knitted a square of ten stitches and ten rows in stockinette stitch using knitting needles that were 6.5 centimeters in diameter and 3.5 metres long.

Ancillary Tools

Various tools have been developed to make hand-knitting easier. Tools for measuring needle diameter and yarn properties have been discussed above, as well as the yarn swift, ballwinder and "yarntainers". Crochet hooks and a darning needle are often useful in binding off or in joining two knitted pieces edge-to-edge. The darning needle is used in duplicate stitch (also known as Swiss darning), while the crochet hook is also essential for repairing dropped stitches and some speciality stitches such as tufting.

Other tools are used to prepare specific ornaments include the pompom tree for making pompoms conveniently. For large or complex patterns, it is sometimes difficult to keep track of which stitch should be knit in a particular way; therefore, several tools have been developed to identify the number of a particular row or stitch, including circular stitch markers, hanging markers, extra yarn and row counters. A second potential difficulty is that the knitted piece will slide off the tapered end of the needles when unattended; this is prevented by "point protectors" that cap the tapered ends. Another problem is that too much knitting may lead to hand and wrist troubles; for this, special stress-relieving gloves are available. Finally, there are sundry bags and containers for holding knitting, yarns and needles.

Commercial Applications

Industrially, metal wire is also knitted into a metal fabric for a wide range of uses including the filter material in cafetieres, catalytic converters for cars and many other uses. These fabrics are usually manufactured on circular knitting machines that would be recognised by conventional knitters as sock machines. Many fashion designers make heavy use of knitting in their fashion collections. Gordana Gelhausen, who appeared in season six of the television show *Project Runway*, is primarily a knit designer. Other designers and labels that make heavy use of knitting include Michael Kors, Fendi, and Marc Jacobs. For individual hobbyists, websites such as Etsy,Liz and Ravelry have made it easy to sell patterns on a small scale, in a way similar to eBay.

Graffiti

In the last decade, a practice called knitting graffiti, guerilla knitting, or yarn bombing— the use of knitted or crocheted cloth to modify and beautify one's (usually outdoor) surroundings—emerged in the U.S. and spread worldwide. Magda Sayeg is credited with starting the movement in the US and Knit the City are a prominent group of graffiti knitters in the United Kingdom. Yarn bombers sometimes target existing pieces of graffiti for beautification. For instance, Dave Cole is a contemporary sculpture artist who practiced knitting as graffiti for a large-scale public art installation in Melbourne, Australia for the Big West Arts Festival in 2009. The work was vandalized the night of its completion. A new movie, shot by a Tasmanian filmmaker on a set made almost entirely out of yarn, was partially inspired by "knitted graffiti".

Charity

Knitting garments for free distribution to others has become common practice among knitting groups. Girls and women knitted socks, sweaters, scarves, mittens, gloves, and hats for soldiers in Crimea, the American Civil War, and the Boer Wars; this practice continued in World War I, World War II and the Korean War, and continues for soldiers in Iraq and Afghanistan. In the historical projects, yarn companies provided patterns approved by the various branches of the armed services; often they were distributed by local chapters of the American Red Cross. Modern projects usually entail the knitting of hats or helmet liners; the liners provided for soldiers must be of 100% worsted weight wool and be crafted using specific colours.

Clothing and afghans are frequently made for children, the elderly, and the economically disadvantaged in various countries. Pine Ridge Indian Reservation accepts donations for the Lakota people in the United States.

Prayer shawls, or shawls in which the crafter meditates or says prayers of their faith while knitting with the intent on comforting the recipient, are donated to those experiencing loss or stress.

Many knitters today knit and donate "chemo caps," soft caps for cancer patients who lose their hair during chemotherapy. Yarn companies offer free patterns for these caps.

Penguin sweaters were knitted by volunteers for the rehabilitation of penguins contaminated by exposure to oil slicks. The project is now complete.

Chicken sweaters were also knitted to aid battery hens that had lost their feathers. The organization is not currently accepting donations, but maintains a list of volunteers.

Originally started after the 2004 Indonesian tsunami, Knitters Without Borders is a charity challenge issued by knitting personality Stephanie Pearl-McPhee that encourages knitters to donate to Médecins Sans Frontières (Doctors Without Borders). Instead of knitting for charity, knitters are encouraged to a week's worth of disposable income, including money that otherwise might have been spent on yarn. Knitted items are occasional offered as prizes to donors. As of September 2011, Knitters Without Borders donors have contributed CAD$1,062,217.

Security blankets can also be made through the Project Linus organization which helps needy children.

There are organizations that help reach other countries in need such as afghans for Afghans. This outreach is described as, "afghans for Afghans is a humanitarian and educational people-to-people project that sends hand-knit and crocheted blankets and sweaters, vests, hats, mittens, and socks to the beleaguered people of Afghanistan."

Health Benefits

Studies have shown that knitting, along with other forms of needlework, provide several significant health benefits. These studies have found the rhythmic and repetitive action of knitting can "help prevent and manage stress, pain and depression, which in turn strengthens the body's immune system", as well as create a relaxation response in the body which can decrease blood pressure, heart rate, help prevent illness, and have a calming effect. Pain specialists have also found that the brain chemistry is changed when one knits, resulting in an increase in "feel good" hormones (i.e. serotonin and dopamine), and a decrease in stress hormones.

Knitting, along with other leisure activities has been linked to reducing the risk of developing Alzheimer's disease and dementia. Much like physical activity strengthens the body, mental exercise makes our brains more resilient.

Lace

Lace is an openwork fabric, patterned with open holes in the work, made by machine or by hand. The holes can be formed via removal of threads or cloth from a previously woven fabric, but more often open spaces are created as part of the lace fabric. Lace-making is an ancient craft. True lace was not made until the late 15th and early

16th centuries. A true lace is created when a thread is looped, twisted or braided to other threads independently from a backing fabric.

Originally linen, silk, gold, or silver threads were used. Now lace is often made with cotton thread, although linen and silk threads are still available. Manufactured lace may be made of synthetic fibre. A few modern artists make lace with a fine copper or silver wire instead of thread.

Types

There are many types of lace, classified by how they are made. These include:

- Needle lace; such as Venetian Gros Point is made using a needle and thread. This is the most flexible of the lace-making arts. While some types can be made more quickly than the finest of bobbin laces, others are very time-consuming. Some purists regard needle lace as the height of lace-making. The finest antique needle laces were made from a very fine thread that is not manufactured today.
- Cutwork, or whitework; lace constructed by removing threads from a woven background, and the remaining threads wrapped or filled with embroidery.
- Bobbin lace; as the name suggests, made with bobbins and a pillow. The bobbins, turned from wood, bone or plastic, hold threads which are woven together and held in place with pins stuck in the pattern on the pillow. The pillow contains straw, preferably oat straw or other materials such as sawdust, insulation styrofoam or ethafoam. Also known as Bone-lace. Chantilly lace is a type of bobbin lace.
- Tape lace; makes the tape in the lace as it is worked, or uses a machine- or hand-made textile strip formed into a design, then joined and embellished with needle or bobbin lace.
- Knotted lace; including macramé and tatting. Tatted lace is made with a shuttle or a tatting needle.
- Crocheted lace; including Irish crochet, pineapple crochet, and filet crochet.
- Knitted lace; including Shetland lace, such as the “wedding ring shawl”, a lace shawl so fine that it can be pulled through a wedding ring.

- Machine-made; any style of lace created or replicated using mechanical means.
- Chemical lace; The stitching area is stitched with embroidery threads that form a continuous motif. Afterwards, the stitching areas are removed and only the embroidery remains. The stitching ground is made of water-soluble or non heat-resistant material.

Etymology

The word lace is from Middle English, from Old French las, *noose, string*, from Vulgar Latin **laceum*, from Latin *laqueus, noose*; probably akin to *lacere, to entice, ensnare.*

History

In the late 16th century there was a rapid development in the field of lace. There was an openwork fabric where combinations of open spaces and dense textures form designs. These forms of lace were dominant in both fashion as well as home décor during the late 1500s. For enhancing the beauty of collars and cuffs, needle lace was embroidered with loops and picots.

Objects resembling lace bobbins have been found in Roman remains, but there are no records of Roman lace-making. Lace was used by clergy of the early Catholic Church as part of vestments in religious ceremonies, but did not come into widespread use until the 16th century in northwestern part of the European continent.

The popularity of lace increased rapidly and the cottage industry of lace making spread throughout Europe. Countries like Italy, France, Belgium, Germany (then Holy Roman Empire), Czech Republic (town of Vamberk), Slovenia (town of Idrija), Finland (town of Rauma) England (town of Honiton), Hungary, Ireland, Malta, Russia, Spain, Turkey and others all have established heritage expressed through lace.

In North America in the 19th century, lace making was spread to the Native American tribes through missionaries.

St. John Francis Regis helped many country girls stay away from the cities by establishing them in the lacemaking and embroidery trade, which is why he became the Patron Saint of lace-making. In 1837, Samuel Ferguson first used jacquard looms with Heathcoat's bobbin net machine, resulting in endless possibilities for lace designs.

Traditionally, lace was used to make tablecloths and doilies and in both men's and women's clothing.

The English diarist Samuel Pepys often wrote about the lace used for his, his wife's, and his acquaintances' clothing, and on May 7, 1669 noted that he intended to remove the gold lace from the sleeves of his coat "as it is fit [he] should", possibly in order to avoid charges of ostentatious living.

Industrial Revolution

With the passage of time and an increasing demand in the market for lace, the way the world produced goods changed. This led to the production of machine lace. In 1768, John Heathcoat invented the bobbin net machine. This machine made the production of complex lace designs more quickly. This Industrial Revolution was the downfall for the handmade lace industry. The teaching of handmade lacemaking disappeared in schools as emphasis shifted from trades to academics, which paved the way for lacemaking to become a hobby instead of the business it once was.

Military Uniforms

The term 'lace' is used by the British to refer to the gold bands sewn onto the sleeves of naval officers' uniforms to indicate rank, and to name the similar decoration elsewhere on other uniforms (such as Italian caps and Polish collars) because of the procedure used to make it. In America, the term is not used for this purpose because the bands are metal compactly sewn, while 'lace' seems to imply cloth sewn into patterns with holes in them.

Macramé

Macramé or macrame is a form of textile-making using knotting rather than weaving or knitting. Its primary knots are the square knot and forms of "hitching": full hitch and double half hitches. It was long crafted by sailors, especially in elaborate or ornamental knotting forms, to decorate anything from knife handles to bottles to parts of ships.

Cavandoli macramé is a variety of macramé used to form geometric patterns and free-form patterns like weaving. The Cavandoli style is done mainly in a single knot, the double half-hitch knot. Reverse half hitches are sometimes used to maintain balance when working left and right halves of a balanced piece.

Leather or fabric belts are another accessory often created via macramé techniques. Most friendship bracelets exchanged among schoolchildren and teens are created using this method. Vendors at theme parks, malls, seasonal fairs and other public places may sell macramé jewellery or decoration as well.

Materials

Materials used in macramé include cords made of cotton twine, linen, hemp, jute, leather or yarn. Cords are identified by construction, such as a 3-ply cord, made of 3 lengths of fibre twisted together. Jewellery is often made in combination of both the knots and various beads (glass, wooden, and so on), pendants or shells. Sometimes 'found' focal points are used for necklaces, such as rings or gemstones, either wire-wrapped to allow for securing or captured in a net-like array of intertwining overhand knots. A knotting board is often used to mount the cords for macramé work. Cords may be held in place using a C-clamp, straight pins, T-pins, U-pins, or upholstery pins.

For larger decorative pieces, such as wall hangings or window coverings, a work of macramé might be started out on a wooden or metal dowel, allowing for a spread of dozens of cords that are easy to manipulate. For smaller projects, push-pin boards are available specifically for macramé, although a simple corkboard works adequately. Many craft stores offer beginners' kits, work boards, beads and materials ranging in price for the casual hobbyist or ambitious craftsperson.

History of Macramé

In the Western Hemisphere, macramé is believed to have originated with 13th-century Arab weavers. These artisans knotted the excess thread and yarn along the edges of hand-loomed fabrics into decorative fringes on bath towels, shawls, and veils. The Spanish word *macramé* is derived from the Arabic *migramah,* believed to mean "striped towel", "ornamental fringe" or "embroidered veil." After the Moorish conquest, the art was taken to Spain, then to Italy, especially in the region of Liguria, and then spread through Europe. It was introduced into England at the court of Mary II in the late 17th century. Queen Mary taught the art of macramé to her ladies-in-waiting.

Sailors made macramé objects in off hours while at sea, and sold or bartered them when they landed, thus spreading the art to places like China and the New World. Nineteenth-century British and American sailors made hammocks, bell fringes, and belts from macramé. They called the process "square knotting" after the knot they used most frequently. Sailors also called macramé "McNamara's Lace".

Macramé was most popular in the Victorian era. *Sylvia's Book of Macramé Lace* (1882), a favorite, showed readers how "to work rich trimmings for black and coloured costumes, both for home wear, garden parties, seaside ramblings, and balls—fairylike adornments for household and underlinens ..." Most Victorian homes were adorned by this craft. Macramé was used to make household items such as tablecloths, bedspreads and curtains.

Though the craze for macramé faded, it has regained popularity since the 1970s as a means to make wall hangings, articles of clothing, bedspreads, small jean shorts, tablecloths, draperies, plant hangers and other furnishings.

Macramé jewellery has become popular among the American neo-hippie and grunge crowd, starting in the early 1970s. Using mainly square knots and granny knots, this jewellery often features handmade glass beads and natural elements such as bone and shell. Necklaces, anklets and bracelets have become popular forms of macramé jewellery.

Nålebinding

Nålebinding (Danish: literally "binding with a needle" or "needle-binding", also naalbinding, nålbinding or naalebinding) is a fabric creation technique predating both knitting and crochet. Also known in English as "knotless netting," "knotless knitting," or "single needle knitting," the technique is distinct from crochet in that it involves passing the full length of the working thread through each loop, unlike crochet where the work is formed only of loops, never involving the free end. It also differs from knitting in that lengths must be pieced together during the process of nålebinding, rather than a continuous strand of yarn that can easily be pulled out. Archaeological specimens of fabric made by nålebinding can be difficult to distinguish from knitted fabric.

Nålebinding is still practiced by women of the Nanti tribe, an indigenous people of the Camisea region of Peru. They use it to make bracelets. Nålebinding also remains popular in the Scandinavian countries as well as in the Balkans.

History

Nålebinding works well with short pieces of yarn; based on this, scholars believe that the technique may be ancient, as long continuous lengths of yarn are not necessary. The term "nålebinding" was introduced in the 1970s.

The oldest known samples of single-needle knitting include the colour-patterned sandal socks of the Coptic Christians of Egypt (4th century CE), and hats and shawls from the Paracas and Nazca cultures in Peru, dated between 300 BCE and 300 CE.

Technique

The basic technique involves the use of a single flat needle. A loop is formed, and the needle passed through the loop. The thread is pulled through the loop, but the knot is not snugged up. Left loose, the yarn forms a new loop. The needle is passed through the new loop, forming a chain. At the end of a row, the work may be turned, and each stitch passed through both its partner loop and a loop in the previous row. The work may be performed in a single direction "in the round", forming circles and tubes for socks and mittens.

Characteristics

Due to the "pulling through", this technique is well adapted to short lengths of yarn which can be joined together to form a textile.

Although nålebinding is slower and more laborious than knitting, it is easier on the shoulders, back and hands, and the fabric it produces can be more dense and durable than knitted fabric. It is still used in Peru, in Iran to make socks, and in parts of Scandinavia to make hats, gloves and other items that are very warm.

Needlework

Needlework is a broad term for the handicrafts of decorative sewing and textile arts. Anything that uses a needle for construction can be called needlework. The definition may expand to include related textile crafts such as a crochet hook or tatting shuttles.

Similar abilities often transfer well between different varieties of needlework, such as fine motor skill and a knowledge of textile fibres. Some of the same tools may be used in several different varieties of needlework. For instance, a needle threader is useful in nearly all needlecrafts.

Types of Needlework

Needle Lace

Needle lace (also known as needlelace or needle-made lace or point lace) is a type of lace created using a needle and thread to stitch up hundreds of small stitches to form the lace itself.

In its purest form the only equipment and materials used are a needle, thread and scissors. This form of lace making originated in Armenia where there is evidence of an Armenian needle lace making tradition dating back to the pre-Christian era. Turkish needle lace is also very popular around the world. This form however arose separately from what is usually termed needle lace and is generally referred to as knotted lace. Such lace is very durable and will not unravel if one or more loops are broken.

Beginning in the 17th century in Italy, a variety of styles developed where the work is started by securing heavier guiding threads onto a stiff background (such as thick paper) with stitches that can later be removed. The work is then built up using a variety of stitches - the most basic being a variety of buttonhole or blanket stitch. When the entire area is covered with the stitching, the stay-stitches are released and the lace comes away from the paper.

Needle lace is also used to create the fillings or insertions in cutwork.

Cutwork

Cutwork or cut work is a needlework technique in which portions of a textile are cut away and the resulting "hole" is reinforced and filled with embroidery or needle lace.

Cutwork is related to drawn thread work. In drawn thread work, typically only the warp or weft threads are withdrawn (cut and removed), and the remaining threads in the resulting hole are bound in various ways. In other types of cutwork, both warp and weft threads may be drawn.

Needlework styles that incorporate cutwork include broderie anglaise, Carrickmacross lace, whitework, and early reticella.

Quilting

Quilting can refer either to the process of creating a quilt or to the sewing of two or more layers of material together to make a thicker padded material. "Quilting" as the process of creating a quilt uses "quilting" as the joining of layers as one of its steps, often along with designing, piecing, appliqué, binding and other steps. A quilter is the name given to someone who works at quilting. Quilting can be done by hand, by sewing machine, or by a specialist longarm quilting system.

The process of quilting uses a needle and thread to join two or more layers of material to make a quilt. Typical quilting is done with 3 layers: the top fabric or quilt top, batting or insulating material and backing material. The quilter's hand or sewing machine passes the needle and thread through all layers and then brings the needle back up. The process is repeated across the entire area where quilting is wanted.

A rocking, straight or running stitch is commonly used and these stitches can be purely functional or decorative and elaborate. Quilting is done to create bed spreads, art quilt wall hangings, clothing, and a variety of textile products. Quilting can make a project thick, or with dense quilting, can raise one area so that another stands out.

Quilt stores often sell fabric, thread, patterns and other goods that are used for quilting. They often have group sewing and quilting classes, where one can learn how to sew or quilt and work with others to exchange skills. Quilt stores often have quilting machines that can be rented out for use, or customers can drop off their quilts and have them professionally quilted.

Early Functional Quilting

The word "quilt" comes from the Latin *culcita* meaning a large stuffed sack, but it came into the English language from the French word *cuilte*. The origins of quilting remain unknown, but sewing techniques of piecing, applique, and quilting have been used for clothing and furnishings in diverse parts of the world for several millennia.

The earliest known quilted garment is depicted on the carved ivory figure of a Pharaoh of the Egyptian First Dynasty, about 3400 B.C.

In 1924 archaeologists discovered a quilted floor covering in Mongolia. They estimated its date as between 100 BC to 200 AD. There are numerous references to quilts in literature and inventories of estates. Crusaders brought quilted objects from the Middle East to Europe in the late 11th century. Quilted garments known as gambesons were popular in the European Middle Ages. Knights wore them under their armor for comfort and sometimes as an outer garment to protect the metal armor from the weather. The earliest known surviving European bed quilt is from late 14th century Sicily. It is made of linen and padded with wool. The blocks across the centre are scenes from the legend of Tristan. The quilt is 122" by 106" and is in the Victoria and Albert Museum in London.

Quilting has been part of the needlework tradition in Europe from about the 5th century CE. Early objects contain Egyptian cotton, which may indicate that Egyptian and Mediterranean trade provided a conduit for the technique. Quilted objects were relatively rare in Europe until approximately the 12th century, when quilted bedding and other items appeared after the return of the Crusaders from the Middle East. The medieval quilted gambeson, aketon and arming doublet were garments worn under, or instead of, armor of maille or plate armor. These developed into the later quilted doublet worn as part of fashionable European male clothing from the 14th to 17th century. Quilting clothing began to be generally used in the 14th century, with quilted doublets and armor worn in France, Germany, and England and quilted tunics in Italy.

American Quilts

In American Colonial times, most women were busy spinning, weaving, and making clothing. Meanwhile, women of the wealthier classes prided themselves on their fine quilting of wholecloth quilts with fine needlework. Quilts made during the early 19th century were not constructed of pieced blocks but were instead whole cloth quilts. Broderie perse quilts and medallion quilts were made. Some antique quilts made in North America have worn-out blankets or older quilts as the internal batting layer, quilted between new layers of fabric and thereby extending the usefulness of old material.

During American pioneer days, "paper" quilting became popular. Paper was used as a pattern and each individual piece of cut fabric was basted around the paper pattern. Paper was a scarce commodity in the early American west, and women would save letters from home, newspaper clippings, and catalogues to use as patterns. The paper not only served as a pattern but as an insulator. The paper found between the old quilts has become a primary source of information about pioneer life.

Quilts made without any insulation or batting were referred to as summer quilts. They were not made for warmth, only to keep the chill off during cooler summer evenings.

African-American Quilts

African-American women developed a distinctive style of quilting, notably different from the style most strongly associated with the Amish. Harriet Powers, a slave-born African American woman, made two famous story quilts. She was just one of the many African American quilters who contributed to the evolution of quilting.

The Gee's Bend quilting community was celebrated in an exhibition that travelled to museums including the Smithsonian. The contributions made by her and other quilters of Gee's Bend, Alabama has been recognized by the US Postal Service with a series of stamps. The *communal* nature of the quilting process (and how it can bring together women of varied races and backgrounds) was honoured in the series of stamps.

During the American Civil War, slaves used quilts as a means to share and transmit secret messages to escape slavery and travel the Underground Railroad. A lack of written record on the topic has created debate among historians and scholars. However, an oral history has been told and preserved.

Hawaiian Quilting

"Hawaiian quilting was well established by the beginning of the twentieth century. Hawaiian women learned to quilt from the wives of missionaries from New England in the 1820s. Though they learned both pieced work and applique; by the 1870s they had adapted applique techniques to create a uniquely Hawaiian mode of expression. The classic Hawaiian quilt design is a large, bold, curvilinear appliqué pattern that covers much of the surface of the quilt, and the symmetrical design is cut from only one piece of fabric."

Art Quilting

During the late 20th century, art quilts became popular for their aesthetic and artistic qualities rather than for functionality (they are displayed on a wall or table rather than spread on a bed). "It is believed that decorative quilting came to Europe and Asia during the Crusades (A.D. 1100-1300), a likely idea because textile arts were more developed in China and India than in the West."

Quilting in Fashion and Design

Unusual quilting designs have increasingly become popular as decorative textiles. Industrial sewing technology has become more precise and flexible, and quilting using exotic fabrics and embroidery began to appear in home furnishings in the early 21st century.

Types and Equipment

Many types of quilting exist today. The two most widely used are hand-quilting and machine quilting. Hand quilting is the process of using a needle and thread to sew a running stitch by hand across the entire area to be quilted. This binds the layers together. A quilting frame or hoop is often used to assist in holding the piece being quilted off the quilter's lap. A quilter can make one stitch at a time by first driving the needle through the fabric from the right side, then pushing it back up through the material from the wrong side to complete the stitch; this is called a stab stitch. Another option is called a rocking stitch, where the quilter has one hand, usually with a finger wearing a thimble, on top of the quilt, while the other hand is located beneath the piece to push the needle back up. A third option is called "loading the needle" and involves doing four or more stitches before pulling the needle through the cloth. Hand quilting is still practiced by the Amish and Mennonites within the United States and Canada, and is enjoying a resurgence worldwide.

Machine quilting is the process of using a home sewing machine or a longarm machine to sew the layers together. With the home sewing machine, the layers are tacked together before quilting. This involves laying the top, batting, and backing out on a flat surface and either pinning (using large safety pins) or tacking the layers together. Longarm Quilting involves placing the layers to be quilted on a special frame. The frame has bars on which the layers are rolled, keeping these together without the need for tacking or pinning. These frames are used with a professional sewing machine mounted on a platform. The platform rides along tracks so that the machine can be moved across the layers on the frame. A Longarm machine is moved across the fabric. In contrast, the fabric is moved through a home sewing machine.

Tying is another technique of fastening the three layers together (and is not a form of quilting at all). This is done primarily on quilts that are made to be used and are needed quickly. The process of tying the quilt is done with yarns or multiple strands of thread. Square knots are used to finish off the ties so that the quilt may be washed and used without fear of the knots coming undone. This technique is commonly called "tacking." In the Midwest, tacked bed covers are referred to as comforters.

Quilting is now taught in some American schools. It is also taught at senior centres around the U.S., but quilters of all ages attend classes. These forms of workshop or classes are also available in other countries in guilds and community colleges.

Contemporary quilters use a wide range of quilting designs and styles, from ancient and ethnic to post-modern futuristic patterns. There is no one single school or style that dominates the quilt-making world.

Processes and Definitions

Traditional: Traditional quilting is a six-step process that includes:

1) selecting a pattern, fabrics and batting;
2) measuring and cutting fabrics to the correct size to make blocks from the pattern;
3) piecing (sewing cut pieces of fabric together using a sewing machine or by hand to make blocks) blocks together to make a finished "top";
4) layering the quilt top with batting and backing, to make a "quilt sandwich";
5) quilting by hand or machine through all layers of the quilt sandwich; and
6) squaring up and trimming excess batting from the edges, machine sewing the binding to the front edges of the quilt and then hand-stitching the binding to the quilt backing.

   Note: If the quilt will be hung on the wall, there is an additional step: making and attaching the hanging sleeve.

In China

Throughout China, a simple method of producing quilts is employed. It involves setting up a temporary roadside site. A frame is assembled within which a lattice work of cotton thread is made. Cotton batting, either new or retrieved from discarded quilts, is prepared in a mobile carding machine. The mechanism of the carding machine is powered by a small, petrol motor. The batting is then added, layer by layer, to the area within the frame. Between each layer, a new lattice of thread is created with a wooden disk used to tamp down the layer.

About 4 of these can be produced by a two-person team each day. They are sold to local shops for 60 RMB or more depending on size and thickness.

Definitions

- Piecing: Sewing small pieces of cloth into patterns, called blocks, that are then sewn together to make a finished quilt top. These blocks may be sewn together, edge to edge, or separated by strips of cloth called sashing. Note: Whole cloth quilts typically are not pieced, but are made using a single piece of cloth for the quilt top.
- Borders: Typically strips of fabric of various widths added to the perimeter of the pieced blocks to complete the quilt top. Note: borders may also be made up of simple or patterned blocks that are stitched together into a row, before being added to the quilt top.
- Layering: Placing the quilt top over the batting and the backing.
- Quilting: Stitching through all three layers of the quilt (the quilt top, the batting, and the quilt back), typically in decorative patterns, which serves three purposes:
  1. To secure the layers to each other,
  2. To add to the beauty and design of the finished quilt, and
  3. To trap air within the quilted sections, making the quilt as a whole much warmer than its parts.
- Binding: Long fabric strips cut on the bias that are attached to the borders of the quilt. Binding is typically machine sewn to the front side of the edge of the quilt, folded over twice, and hand sewn to the back side of the quilt.

Quilting is usually completed by starting from the middle, and moving outward toward the edges of the quilt.

Quilting can be elaborately decorative, comprising stitching fashioned into complex designs and patterns, simple or complex geometric grids, “motifs” traced from published quilting patterns or traced pictures, freehand, or complex repeated designs called tessellations. The quilter may choose to emphasize these designs by using threads that are multicoloured or metallic, or that contrast highly to the fabric.

Conversely, the quilter may choose to make the quilting disappear, using "invisible" nylon or polyester thread,thread that matches the quilt top, or stitching within the patchwork seams themselves (commonly known as "stitch in the ditch"). Some quilters draw the quilting design on the quilt top before stitching, while others prefer to stitch "freehand."

Quilting is often combined with embroidery, patchwork, applique, and other forms of needlework.

Tatting

Tatting is a technique for handcrafting a particularly durable lace constructed by a series of knots and loops. Tatting can be used to make lace edging as well as doilies, collars, and other decorative pieces. The lace is formed by a pattern of rings and chains formed from a series of cow hitch, or half-hitch knots, called double stitches (ds), over a core thread. Gaps can be left between the stitches to form picots, which are used for practical construction as well as decorative effect.

Tatting dates to the early 19th century. The term for tatting in most European languages is derived from French *frivolité*, which refers to the purely decorative nature of the textiles produced by this technique. The technique was developed to imitate point lace

In German tatting is called *Schiffchenarbeit*, which means the work of the little boat, referring to the boat-shaped shuttle, and in Italian tatting is called *chiacchierino*, which means taking.

Technique and Materials

Shuttle Tatting: Tatting with a shuttle is the earliest method of creating tatted lace. A tatting *shuttle* facilitates tatting by holding a length of wound thread and guiding it through loops to make the requisite knots. It is normally a metal or ivory pointed oval shape less than 3 inches (76 mm) long, but shuttles come in a variety of shapes and materials. Shuttles often have a point or hook on one end to aid in the construction of the lace. Antique shuttles and unique shuttles have become highly sought after by collectors — even those who do not tat.

To make the lace, the tatter wraps the thread around one hand and manipulates the shuttle with the other hand. No tools other than the thread, the hands, and the shuttle are used, though a crochet hook may be necessary if the shuttle does not have a point or hook.

Needle Tatting

Traditional shuttle tatting may be simulated using a tatting needle or doll needle instead of a shuttle. There are two basic techniques for needle tatting. With the more widely disseminated technique a double thread passes through the stitches. The result is similar to shuttle tatting but is slightly thicker and looser. The second technique approximates shuttle tatting because a single thread passes through the stitches.

Needle tatting originated in the early twentieth century, but did not become popular until much later. A tatting needle is a long, blunt needle that does not change thickness at the eye of the needle. The needle used must match the thickness of the thread chosen for the project. Rather than winding the shuttle, the needle is threaded with a length of thread. To work with a second colour, a second needle is used. Although needle tatting looks similar to shuttle tatting, it differs in structure and is slightly thicker and looser because both the needle and the thread must pass through the stitches.

In the late twentieth century, tatting needles became commercially available in a variety of sizes, from fingering yarn down to size 80 tatting thread. Patterns are written specifically for needle tatting, although shuttle tatting patterns may be used without modification. There are currently two manufacturers of tatting needles.

Cro-tatting

Cro-tatting combines needle tatting with crochet. The cro-tatting tool is a tatting needle with a crochet hook at the end. One can also cro-tat with a bullion crochet hook or a very straight crochet hook. In the nineteenth century, "crochet tatting" patterns were published which simply called for a crochet hook. One of the earliest patterns is for a crocheted afghan with tatted rings forming a raised design. Patterns are available in English and are equally divided between yarn and thread. In its most basic form the rings are tatted with a length of plain thread between them, as in single shuttle tatting. In modern patterns, beginning in the early twentieth century, the rings are tatted and the arches or chains are crocheted. Many people consider cro-tatting more difficult than crochet or needle tatting. Some tatting instructors recommend using a tatting needle and a crochet hook to work cro-tatting patterns. Cro-tatting is most popular in Japan.

The stitches of cro-tatting (and needle tatting before you close a ring) unravel easily, unlike tatting that is made with a shuttle.

Materials

Older designs, especially through the early 1900s, tend to use fine white or ivory thread (50 to 100 widths to the inch) and intricate designs. This thread was either made of silk or a silk blend, to allow for improper stitches to be easily removed. Newer designs from the 1920s and onward often use thicker thread in one or more colours.

The best thread for tatting is a "hard" thread that does not untwist readily. DMC Cordonnet thread is a common tatting thread; Perl cotton is an example of a beautiful cord that is nonetheless a bit loose for tatting purposes. Some tatting designs incorporate ribbons and beads.

Patterns

Older patterns use a long hand notation to describe the stitches needed while newer patterns tend to make extensive use of abbreviations and an almost mathematical looking notation. The following examples describe the same small piece of tatting (the first Ring in the *Hen and Chicks* pattern)

Ring five ds, three picots separated by five ds, five ds, close, turn, space

R 5ds, 3 p sep by 5ds, 5ds, cl, turn, sp

R 5-5-5-5 cl rw sp

Some tatters prefer a visual pattern where the design is drawn schematically with annotations indicating the number of ds and order of construction. This can either be used on its own or alongside a written pattern.

History

Some believe that tatting may have developed from netting and decorative ropework as sailors and fishers would put together motifs for girlfriends and wives at home. Decorative ropework employed on ships includes techniques (esp. coxcombing) that show striking similarity with tatting. A good description of this can be found in *Knots, Splices and Fancywork.*

Some believe tatting originated over 200 years ago, often citing shuttles seen in eighteenth century paintings of women such as Charlotte of Mecklenburg-Strelitz, Madame Adelaide (daughter of Louis XV of France), and Anne, Countess of Albemarle. A close inspection of those paintings shows that the shuttles in question are too large to be tatting shuttles, and that they are actually knotting shuttles. There is no documentation, nor any examples of tatted lace, that date prior to 1800. All of the available evidence shows that tatting originated in the early 19th century.

As most fashion magazines and home economics magazines from the first half of the 20th century attest, tatting had a substantial following. When fashion included feminine touches such as lace collars and cuffs, and inexpensive yet nice baby shower gifts were needed, this creative art flourished. As the fashion moved to a more modern look and technology made lace an easy and inexpensive commodity to purchase, hand-made lace began to decline.

Lucet

A lucet is a tool used in cordmaking or braiding which is believed to date back to the Viking and Medieval periods, when it was used to create cords that were used on clothing, or to hang items from the belt. Lucet cord is square, strong, and slightly springy. It closely resembles knitted I-cord or the cord produced on a knitting spool. Lucet cord is formed by a series of loops, and will therefore unravel if cut. Unlike other braiding techniques such as kumihimo, finger-loop braiding or plaiting, where the threads are of a finite length, lucetted braids can be created without pre-measuring threads and so it is a technique suited for very long cords.

Archaeological finds and a literary description of lucets strongly suggest that its use declined after the 12th century, but was revived in the 17th century. Its use waned again in the early 19th century.

A modern lucet fork, like that pictured, is normally made of wood, with two prongs at one end and a handle on the other. It may also have a hole through which the cord can be pulled. Medieval lucets, in contrast, appear to be double-pronged, straight-sided implements, often made of bone. Some were shaped from hollowed bones, left tubular, presumably so that the cord could be drawn through the centre hole.

Creating Lucet Braids

The only materials necessary to lucet are a length of yarn and a lucet fork, also called a lucet or a chain fork. However, one can also use skewer-like sticks to pull the yarn over in addition to this. Lucets can be bought in shops as kits that are designed for children.

To cast on, the yarn is put through the hole in the lucet from the front, and the yarn in front of the lucet is wound around the prongs twice in a figure-of-eight. The two lower loops are then lifted over the two upper loops using either the fingers or a stick until they come over the horns, and the thread behind the lucet is pulled to tighten the knot. The process is then repeated, but this time only winding the yarn once around the prongs, as there is already a figure-of-eight on the fork. When the desired length is reached, the lucet can be cast off by carefully lifting the loops off the prongs, passing the remaining thread through them and pulling the knot tight. Any loose thread can be cut off with scissors or tied together to form a closed circle. The cord can be wrapped around the lucet handle as it grows.

Note that this is only one technique. There are many techniques used for making lucet, all of which produce slightly different cords. It is also possible to produce a two-coloured cord by using two strands of yarn.

Lucet cord can be used for decorative edging, draw-strings, lacing, and any other use where a strong cord is needed.

2

Braiding and Tassel Making

A braid (also called plait) is a complex structure or pattern formed by intertwining three or more strands of flexible material such as textile fibres, wire, or human hair. Compared to the process of weaving a wide sheet of cloth from two separate, perpendicular groups of strands (warp and weft), a braid is usually long and narrow, with each component strand functionally equivalent in zigzagging forward through the overlapping mass of the others.

The simplest possible braid is a flat, solid, three-strand structure in some countries/cases called a plait. More complex braids can be constructed from an arbitrary (but usually odd) number of strands to create a wider range of structures: wider ribbon-like bands, hollow or solid cylindrical cords, or broad mats which resemble a rudimentary perpendicular weave.

Braids are commonly used to make rope, decorative objects, and hairstyles. Complex braids have been used to create hanging fibre artworks. Braiding is also used to prepare horses' manes and tails for showing, polo and polocrosse.

History

Hair braiding has long been thought to have originated in East Africa. The oldest known image of hair braiding was traced back to a burial site called Saqqara located on the Nile river during the first dynasty of Pharaoh Menes. It was a means of communication so that at a glance one individual could distinguish a wealth of information about another, whether they were married, mourning, or of age for courtship, simply by observing their hairstyle. Certain hairstyles were distinctive to particular tribes or nations. Other styles spoke to an individual's status in society.

Braiding is traditionally a social art. Because of the time it takes to braid hair the women took time to socialize while braiding and having their hair done. It begins with the elders making simple knots and braids for younger children. Older children watch and learn from them, start practicing on younger girls and eventually learn the traditional designs. In the US, you see mothers and grandmothers braiding and putting colourful beads in little children's hair. This carries on a tradition of bonding between elders and the new generation.

Braiding hair down to the scalp has been traditional in many African ethnic groups such as the Tuareg, Bushmen, Copts, Amhara, Nubian, Akan, Beja, Himba, Somali, Ababda, Dogon, Fula, Bedouin, Pygmies, Tigraway, and the Yoruba. Asian ethnic groups such as the Sumerians, Akkadians, Babylonians, Phoenicians and Assyrians, the ethnic groups of North and South America such as the Cherokee, Sioux, Blackfoot Confederacy, Inca, Maya, Aztec and the Olmec, and European ethnic groups such as the Spanish, Dutch, French, Hellenes and Italians.

Ropes and Cables

Braiding creates a composite rope that is thicker and stronger than the non-interlaced strands of yarn. Braided ropes are preferred by arborists, rock climbers and in sport sailing because they do not twist under load, as does an ordinary twisted-strand rope. These ropes consist of one or more concentric tubular braided jackets surrounding either several small twisted fibre cords, or a single untwisted yarn of straight fibres, and are known as Kernmantle ropes.

In electrical and electronic cables, *braid* is a tubular sheath made of braided strands of metal placed around a central cable for shielding against electromagnetic interference. The braid is grounded while the central conductor(s) carry the signal. The braid may be used in addition to a foil jacket to increase shielding and durability.

Another use is for litz wire which uses braids of thin insulated wires to carry high frequency signals with much lower losses from skin effect or to minimise proximity effect in transformers.

Flat braids made of many copper wires are also sometimes used for flexible electrical connections between large components. The numerous smaller wires comprising the braid are much more resistant to breaking under repeated motion and vibration than is a cable of larger wires. A common example of this may be found connecting a car battery's negative terminal to the metal chassis.

Similar braiding is used on pressurized rubber hoses, such as in plumbing and hydraulic brake systems in automobiles. Braiding is also used for fibres for composite reinforcements.

A property of the basic braid is that removing one strand unlinks the other two, as they are not twisted around each other. Mathematically, a braid with that property is called a Brunnian braid.

Tassel

A tassel is a finishing feature in fabric decoration. It is a universal ornament that is seen in varying versions in many cultures around the globe.

The word "tassel" comes from the Latin "tassau", which refers to a clasp (as for the neck of a garment).

History and Use

Circa 1406 B.C.

...Tell them to make tassels on the corners of their garments throughout their generations, and to put a blue thread in the tassels of the corners. And you shall have the tassel, that you may look upon it and remember all the commandments of the LORD and do them, and that you may not follow the harlotry to which your own heart and your own eyes are inclined, and that you may remember and do all My commandments, and be holy for your God. *Numbers 15:38-40 (NKJ).*

In the West, tassels were originally a series of windings of thread or string around a suspending string until the desired curvature was attained. Decades later, turned wooden moulds, which were either covered in simple wrappings or much more elaborate coverings called "satinings", were used. This involved an intricate binding of bands of filament silk vertically around the mould by means of an internal "lacing" in the bore of the mould.

These constructions were varied and augmented with extensive ornamentations that were each assigned an idiosyncratic term by their French practitioners. In France those practitioners were called "Passementiers", and an apprenticeship of seven years was required to become a master in one of the subdivisions of the guild. The French widely exported their very artistic work, and at such low prices that no other nation developed a mature "trimmings" industry.

Tassels and their associated forms changed style throughout the years, from the small and casual of Renaissance designs, through the medium sizes and more staid designs of the Empire period, and to the Victorian Era with the largest and most elaborate. Some of these designs are returning today from the European and American artisans who may charge a thousand dollars for a single hand-made tassel.

Tassels (also called tufts) were traditionally worn by Oxford and Cambridge University undergraduates on their caps (hence a slang word - tassel for an undergraduate), those wearing gold tassels were those who had paid for the status of "gentleman-commoner", thus receiving increased social prestige and more luxurious accommodation than ordinary commoners who wore plain black tassels on their caps. Today, only the Chancellor of Oxford wears a gold tassel.

In the Middle East, tassels were worn as talismans, especially on headwear. In Egypt, Mesopotamia, and throughout the Arab world tassels were worn by children on hoods or caps to protect them from malevolent spirits and ward off demons.

Ceremonial Wear

In the US, tassels, or liripipes, are also found on mortarboards during university graduation ceremonies and possibly upon the shoes of the graduates at the ceremony. Near the conclusion of the graduation ceremony the tassel that hangs from the graduate's mortarboard is moved from the right to the left. Typically the entire graduating class does this in unison.

Creation

A tassel is made by binding plaited or otherwise gathered threads from which at one end protrudes a cord on which the tassel is hung, and which may have loose, dangling threads at the other end. Tassels are normally decorative elements, and as such one often finds them attached, usually along the bottom hem, to garments, curtains, pasties covering the nipples of burlesque performers, or other hangings.

A tassel is primarily an ornament, and was at first the casual termination of a cord to prevent unraveling with a knot. As time went on, various peoples developed variations on this, until by the 16th century in France the first Guild of Passementiers was created and documented the art of passementerie. The tassel was its primary expression, but it also included fringes (applied, as opposed to integral), ornamental cords, galloons, pompons, rosettes, and gimps as other forms. Tassels, pompons, and rosettes are *point* ornaments; the others are linear ornaments.

Tassels consist of:

- a suspending cord
- the body, which is usually made up of one or more moulds
- a skirt of fringe or other ornament.

Patchwork

Patchwork or "pieced work" is a form of needlework that involves sewing together pieces of fabric into a larger design. The larger design is usually based on repeat patterns built up with different fabric shapes (which can be different colours). These shapes are carefully measured and cut, basic geometric shapes making them easy to piece together. Precise joining by the most part with a quarter inch foot makes for a patchwork that lies flat without puckers.

Uses

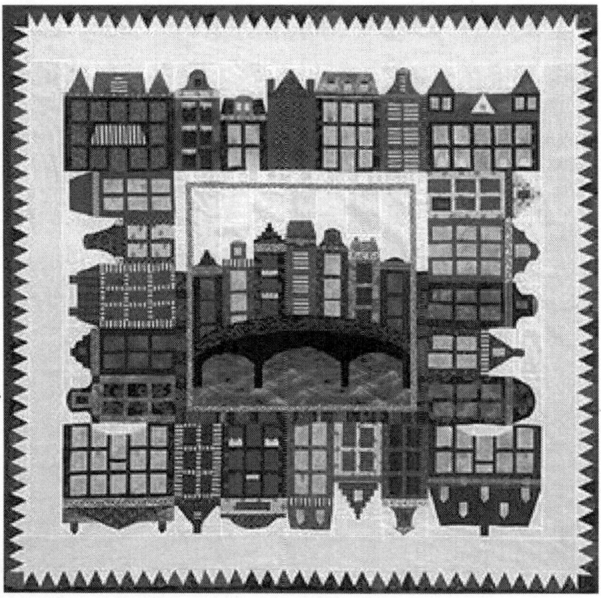

Patchwork is most often used to make quilts, but it can also be used to make bags, wall-hangings, warm jackets, cushion covers, skirts, waistcoats and other items of clothing. Some textile artists work with patchwork, often combining it with embroidery and other forms of stitchery.

When used to make a quilt, this larger patchwork or pieced design becomes the "top" of a three-layered quilt, the middle layer being the batting, and the bottom layer the backing.

To keep the batting from shifting, a patchwork or pieced quilt is often quilted by hand or machine using a running stitch in order to outline the individual shapes that make up the pieced top, or the quilting stitches may be random or highly ordered overall patterns that contrast with the patchwork composition

History

Evidence of patchwork—piecing small pieces of fabric together to create a larger piece, then quilting layers of textile together—has been found throughout history.

The earliest examples have been located in Egyptian tombs and also in early age of China about 5000 years ago. Further finds have been dated from the early Middle Ages, where layers of quilted fabric were used in the construction of armour—this kept the soldiers warm and protected. Japanese armour was made in a similar fashion.

Using this technique, quilts began to appear in households of the 11th to 13th centuries.

As the European climate became colder around this time, the incidence of the use bed quilts rose, and so developed the practice of embellishing a simple cloth through the creation of pattern and design, alongside the development of decorative quilting.

The tradition of making quilts in this fashion was taken to America by the Pilgrims.

In America

Patchwork enjoyed a widespread revival during the Great Depression as a way to recycle worn clothing into warm quilts. Even very small and worn pieces of material are suitable for use in patchwork, although crafters today more often use new 100% cotton fabrics as the basis for their designs.

In the US, patchwork declined after World War II, but was again revived during the American bicentennial.

Making

In the past, hand quilting was often done in a group around a frame. Instead of quilting, the layers are sometimes tied together at regular intervals with pieces of yarn, a practice known as tying or knotting, and which produces a "comforter".

In India stitching blanket using different small pieces of cloth is an art. It is popularly known as Kaudhi in Karnataka. Such blankets are given as gifts to new born babies in some parts of Karnataka. Also Lambani tribes wear skirts with such art

Structure

There are three traditional structures used to construct a patchwork or pieced composition: 1) the block, 2) overall, and 3) strip piecing. Traditional patchwork has identifying names based on the arrangement of colours and shapes.

Blocks

Patchwork blocks are pieced squares made up of coloured shapes that repeat specific shapes to create patterns within the square or block, of, say, light and dark, or contrasting colours (motif (textile arts)). The blocks can all repeat the same pattern, or blocks can have several different patterns.

The patchwork blocks are typically around 8–10" square (20 cm to 25 cm). They are sewn together in stacked rows to make a larger composition. Often strips of contrasting fabric forming a lattice separate the patchwork blocks from each other. Some common patchwork block names are Log Cabin, Drunkard's Path, Bear's Paw, Tulip, and Nine Patch.

A unique form of patchwork quilt is the crazy quilt. Crazy quilting was popular during the Victorian era (mid–late 19th century). The crazy quilt is made up of random shapes of luxurious fabric such as velvets, silks, and brocades and buttons, lace, and other embellishments left over from the gowns they had made for themselves.

The patchwork pieces are stitched together forming "crazy" or non-repeat, asymmetric compositions. Fancy embroidery embellishes the seam lines between the individual, pieced shapes. The crazy quilt was a status symbol, as only well-to-do women had a staff to do all the household work, and had the time to sew their crazy quilt. Traditionally, the top was left without lining or batting. Many surviving crazy quilts still have the newspaper and other foundation papers used for piecing.

Overall

Overall patchwork designs are incrementally pieced geometric shapes stitched together to form a larger random or composed design. The coloured shapes can be randomly pieced or follow a strict order to create a specific effect, e.g. value (light to dark) progressions, or checkerboard effects. Names such as Hit or Miss, Clamshell, back-stitch, needle weave, criss-cross and Starburst identify some overall patchwork structures.

Strip Piecing

Strip piecing involves stitching together pieces of fabric in repeat patterns into long strips and then stitching the strips together lengthwise. The patchwork strips can be alternated with strips of contrasting colours. A typical strip patchwork quilt is the Flying Geese pattern.

Forms

Specialised forms of patchwork include:

- Cathedral window
- Scrap piecework
- Foundation piecework or the closely related
- English paper piecework
- Seminole patchwork
- Hawaiian piecework (primarily applique)
- Stained glass window patchwork

Stained glass window patchwork is a type of patchwork which simulates the effect of stained glass in church windows. Satin fabrics simulate the coloured glass, and black bias binding tape simulates the lead.

Popularity

The 2003 Quilting in America survey estimated that the total value of the American quilting industry was $2.7 billion. International quilting exhibitions attract thousands of visitors, while countless smaller exhibitions are held every weekend in local regions. Active cyber-quilting communities abound on the web; books and magazines on the subject are published in the hundreds every year; and there are many active local quilting guilds and shops in different countries. "Quilt Art" is established as a legitimate artistic medium, with quilted works of art selling for thousands of dollars to corporate buyers and galleries.

Quilt historians and quilt appraisers are re-evaluating the heritage of traditional quilting and antique quilts, while superb examples of antique quilts are purchased for large sums by collectors and museums. The American Quilt Study Group is active in promotion of research on the history of quilting.

Trends

Today, many things are quilted using a Longarm quilting system. The system consists of a frame and a sewing machine. The patchwork, batting and backing are loaded onto the frame and in some systems each layer can be tensioned independently. No basting is usually necessary.

The frames can be up to 14' long which is big enough for a king size quilt to be tensioned ready for quilting. The sewing machine known as the Longarm machine has an extended throat space, up to 36", and it can be moved on a two-axis rail system—left and right, forwards and backwards, enabling a 360-degree movement over the surface of the quilt.

Until recently, most longarm machines were hand-guided which meant the operator had to synchronise the speed of their hands with that of the machine motor. Fast hands and slow motor meant big stitches. Slow hands and fast motor meant small stitches.

Since just after the turn of the century, most longarm machines are now sold with stitch-regulation, which means that the operator no longer has to synchronize hand speed with that of the motor. Electronics in the machine ensures the stitch length remains constant. More recently, fully computerized machines are being sold.

Fully computerized machines have been available for over 12 years. They were invented by Paul Statler but have only recently become popular.

These machines use specialised machine-driver software and CAD-type drawing packages to enable pattern digitisation and automatic quilting. An operator is still required to mind the machine and set the pattern onto the quilt.

It is thought that over 10,000 longarm quilting machines are in use today. In the US, there are many brands available and many places to obtain training and few distributors and trainers in other countries where business quilters are more likely to travel to the States for ongoing longarm training.

Passementerie

Passementerie or passementarie is the art of making elaborate trimmings or edgings (in French, passements) of applied braid, gold or silver cord, embroidery, coloured silk, or beads for clothing or furnishings.

Styles of passementerie include the tassel, fringes (applied, as opposed to integral), ornamental cords, galloons, pompons, rosettes, and gimps as other forms. Tassels, pompons, and rosettes are *point* ornaments, and the others are linear ornaments.

Overview

Passementerie worked in white linen thread is the origin of bobbin lace, and *passement* is an early French word for lace. Today, passementerie is used with clothing, such as the gold braid on military dress uniforms, and for decorating couture clothing and wedding gowns. They are also used in furniture trimming, such as the Centripetal Spring Armchair of 1849 and some lampshades, draperies, fringes and tassels.

History

In the 16th century, the Guild of Passementiers was created in France. In France practitioners of the art were called "passementiers", and an apprenticeship of seven years was required to become a master in one of the subdivisions of the guild.

The Guild documented the art of passementerie. The tassel was its primary expression, but it also included fringes (applied, as opposed to integral), ornamental cords, galloons, pompons, rosettes, and gimps as other forms. Tassels, pompons, and rosettes are *point* ornaments; the others are linear ornaments. These constructions were varied and augmented with extensive ornamentations. These constructions were each assigned an idiosyncratic term by their French practitioners.

The French widely exported their very artistic work, and at such low prices that no other nation developed a mature "trimmings" industry. Tassels and their associated forms changed style throughout the years, from the small and casual of Renaissance designs, through the medium sizes and more staid designs of the Empire period, and to the Victorian Era with the largest and most elaborate.

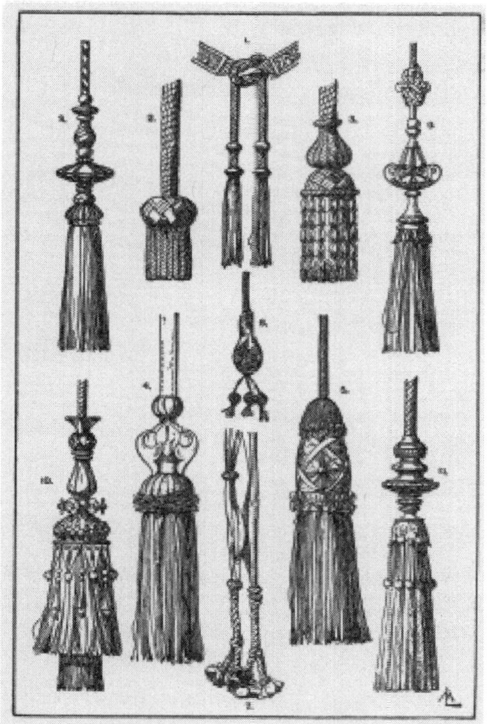

Figure: *In the West, tassels were originally a series of windings of thread or string around a suspending string until the desired curvature was attained. Decades later, turned wooden moulds, which were either covered in simple wrappings or much more elaborate coverings called "satinings", were used. This involved an intricate binding of bands of filament silk vertically around the mould by means of an internal "lacing" in the bore of the mould. A tassel is primarily an ornament, and was at first the casual termination of a cord to prevent unraveling with a knot. As time went on, various peoples developed variations on this.*

Passementerie with clothing was for a long time reserved for the elites as a sign of social distinction among royalty, aristocracy, religious, and military. Since the 18th century, the use became obsolete with the simplification of clothing.

Some of the historic designs are returning today from European and American artisans.

Plying

In the textile arts, plying is a process used to create a strong, balanced yarn. It is done by taking two or more strands of yarn that each have a twist to them and putting them together. The strands are twisted together, in the direction opposite that in which they were spun. When just the right amount of twist is added, this creates a balanced yarn, which is a yarn with no tendency to twist upon itself. Almost all store bought yarns are balanced, plied yarns.

A two-ply is thus a yarn plied from two strands, a six-ply is one from six strands, and so on. Most commercial yarns are more than a two ply. Embroidery floss is generally a six ply yarn, for example.

The creation of two-ply yarn requires two separate spools of singles and either a lazy kate or something to hold the spools in place. On a wheel, two-ply is created by taking two spools of singles, placing them on a lazy kate, tying the ends together onto the spool attached to the wheel, and spinning the wheel in the opposite direction that the singles were spun in while also feeding it onto the spool on the wheel.

On a drop spindle, two-ply is created by placing the spools on a lazy kate, tying the ends together onto the drop spindle, holding equal lengths of singles together and dropping the spindle. The weight of the drop spindle combined with the twist in the singles, causes the drop spindle to turn in the opposite direction that the singles were twisted in until the two singles are plied together.

Plying Handspun Yarns

When hand-spinning, there are two common ways to ply a balanced yarn: regular and Navajo. When spinning fleece into yarn, you must first scour the fleece, remove the vegetable matter, card or comb it, and then spin it into singles. These singles are then used to create the finished yarn in a process known as plying. The purpose of plying singles is to strengthen them so that they do not break while knitting or crocheting them.

Most spinners (who use spinning wheels) ply from bobbins. This is easier than plying from balls because there is less chance for the yarn to become tangled and knotted if it is simply unwound from the bobbins. So that the bobbins can unwind freely, they are put in a device called a Lazy Kate, or sometimes simply *kate*. The simplest lazy kate consists of wooden bars with a metal rod running between them. Most hold between three and four bobbins. The bobbin sits on the metal rod.

Other lazy kates are built with devices that create an adjustable amount of tension, so that if the yarn is jerked, a whole bunch of yarn is not wound off, then wound up again in the opposite direction. Some spinning wheels come with a built in lazy kate.

Regular Plying

Regular plying consists of taking 2 or more singles and twisting them together, the opposite way. This can be done on either a spinning wheel or a spindle. The most important thing to remember though is that the twist must go the opposite direction.

If in spinning the single the wheel was spinning clockwise (which is called a "Z" twist, as on any given side the fibres appear to cross diagonally in the same direction as the diagonal of a "Z"), in order to ply it the wheel must spin counter-clockwise (an "S" twist). This is because otherwise you are not balancing the twist, just twisting it more.

The concept is similar to when a heavily twisted piece of yarn is folded, and it twists up on itself. It is most common for singles to be spun with a "Z" twist, and then plied with an "S" twist.

When plying, the singles are kept separate, either with the fingers or with a tool. This tool can be anything from the top of a salt dispenser, and the singles threaded through the holes, or a specially carved piece of wood with holes in it. The singles are kept separate to ensure that they do not get tangled and so the tension can be controlled.

Navajo Plying

Navajo plying (also known as chain plying) consists of making large loops, similar to crocheting. Only one single is necessary, and if the single is already dyed this technique allows it to be plied without ruining the colour scheme. First make a loop about 8 inches long through the loop on the end on the leader. (A leader is the string left on the bobbin, which the new yarn is spun from.)

Start spinning all three strands together in the opposite direction than that they were spun in. When only 2 to 3 inches (76 mm) remain of the loop, pull a new loop of yarn through the loop, and continue spinning. The new loop should be around 7 inches (180 mm) long. Repeat this process until the yarn is all plied. This technique allows the spinner to try to match up thick and thin spots in the yarn, thus making for a smoother end product.

Machined Yarns

Machines that ply yarn use the 'regular' method mentioned above. The main difference is that instead of humans, gears control the intake making sure that the strands all have the same tension and the same length. Other than that, the process for plying is exactly the same.

Novelty Yarns

Many novelty yarns make use of special plying techniques to gain their special effects. By varying the tension in the strands, or the relative sizes of the strands, or many other factors different effects can be achieved. For example, when a soft, thick strand is plied against a tightly twisted thin strand, the resulting yarn spirals. Another example is bouclé, which is a yarn where one strand is held loosely and allowed to make loops on the other yarn while plying.

Speciality Styles

- Foundation piecing – also known as paper-piecing – sewing pieces of fabric onto a temporary or permanent foundation
- Shadow or Echo Quilting – Hawaiian Quilting, where quilting is done around an appliquéd piece on the quilt top, then the quilting is echoed again and again around the previous quilting line.
- Ralli Quilting – Pakistani and Indian quilting, often associated with the Sindh (Pakistan) and Gujarat (India) regions.
- Sashiko stitching – Basic running stitch worked in heavy, white cotton thread usually on dark indigo coloured fabric. It was originally used by the working classes to stitch layers together for warmth.
- Trapunto quilting – stuffed quilting, often associated with Italy.
- Machine Trapunto quilting – a process of using water soluble thread and an extra layer of batting to achieve trapunto design

and then sandwiching the quilt and re-sewing the design with regular cotton thread.

- Shadow trapunto – This involves quilting a design in fine Lawn and filling some of the spaces in the pattern with small lengths of coloured wool.
- Tivaevae or tifaifai – A distinct art from the Cook Islands.
- Watercolour Quilting – A sophisticated form of scrap quilting whereby uniform sizes of various prints are arranged and sewn to create a picture or design.
- Thread Art – A custom style of sewing where thread is layered to create the picture on the quilt.

Quilt Art

Quilt art, sometimes known as *art quilting*, is an art form that uses traditional quilting techniques to create art objects. Practitioners of quilt art create it based on their experiences, imagery, and ideas rather than traditional patterns.

Quilt art generally has more in common with the fine arts than it does with traditional quilting. This art is generally either wall hung or mounted as sculpture, though exceptions exist.

Early US and British Contributors to the Field

Because of feminism and the new craft movements of the 1960s and 1970s, quilting techniques, traditionally used by women, became prominent in the making of fine arts. The transition from traditional quilting through art quilts to quilted art was rapid; many of the most important advances in the field came in the 1970s and 1980s.

Jean Ray Laury (1928 - 2011)is cited by Robert Shaw as the "most prominent and influential of [the] early modern [American] quiltmakers." Laury was an "academically trained artist and designer who encouraged women to create their own new designs based on their own experiences, surroundings and ideas rather than traditional patterns."

Laury wrote, "There are no rules in stitchery — no single 'right' way of working."

Pauline Burbidge, a British artist, first saw old quilts in Portobello Road in London and 30 years later is still working in the medium. (McMorris p. 48)

Radka Donnell (1928 - 2013), as a former painter, used her training in her quilted works. Donnell was a feminist who eschewed the "art scene" in order to explore quilts as liberating creativity for women. As recently as 1996 she was still teaching in the field with a course on the history, theory, and techniques of quilting at Simmons College and Westfield State College in Massachusetts.

Charles and Rubynelle Counts, after studying at Berea College and elsewhere, started a crafts centre. Charles Counts designed tops which were then quilted by local artisans. Rising Fawn, the crafts centre, continued to produce quilts into the mid-1970s; the designs are little known today but are still distinctive. (Shaw, p. 49–50)

Joan Lintault produced original textile and quilted art before quilting or quilt art became a national pastime. She and Therese May, as well as the Counts, had work that was first published by Jean Ray Laury in *Quilts and Coverlets: A Contemporary Approach*, 1970. While Lintault often makes openwork tops, May is known for her embellished and painted quilts, using private symbols and figures.

Beth Gutcheon and Michael James were quilting instructors, beginning a trend which still allows quilting artists to earn income from a pursuit close to their art. Gutcheon published *The Perfect Patchwork Primer* in 1973. James' book, *The Quiltmaker's Handbook: a Guide to Design and Construction* (1978) was more technical.

These two books are often cited as the place where contemporary quilt artists began. James' follow-up book, published in 1981, *The Second Quiltmaker's Handbook: Creative Approaches to Contemporary Quilt Design* showed his work as well as photos and analyses of art by Nancy Halpern, Beth Gutcheon, Radka Donnell, Nancy Crow, Francoise Barnes, Katie Pasquini, among others. (Shaw, p. 54)

By 2010 Gutcheon had established herself as a successful novelist based in New York City. James currently serves as Professor and Chair of the Department of Textiles, Merchandising & Fashion Design at the University of Nebraska-Lincoln, the academic home of the International Quilt Study Centre & Museum, located in Quilt House.

James teaches courses in textile design and quilt studies, and continues his studio practice focused on non-traditional quilts incorporating digitally developed and digitally printed fabrics.

Nancy Crow, another influential teacher and writer of books, was instrumental in freeing quilting artists from certain preconceptions about rules. Her 1995 exhibit, *Improvisational Quilts*, was the first solo exhibition of art quilts done by the Renwick Gallery.(Shaw, p. 66)

Two other quilt artists, Molly Upton (1953 - 1977) and Susan Hoffman, exhibited with Radka Donnell in 1975 at the Carpenter Centre for the Visual Arts at Harvard University. Also in 1975 Upton and Hoffman exhibited at the Kornblee Gallery on 57th Street in New York City. In doing so, they brought quilt art to the forefront as comparable to other forms of contemporary art.

According to Robert Shaw, "Where other quilters were moving away from the traditional quilt one step at a time, seeing how far they could push the quilt format while still remaining connected to historical precedent, Hoffman and Upton largely ignored the rules and the assumed limitations of traditional quilting and simply leapt forward." (Shaw, p. 60)

Other quilt artists working in the 1970s include Terrie Hancock Mangat, Gayle Fraas and Duncan Slade, Nancy Clearwater Herman, Jan Myers-Newbury, Pamela Studstill, Joan Schultz, Yvonne Porcella, Ruth McDowell, Katherine Westphal and Rise Nagin. (McMorris, Shaw)

The Quilters Hall of Fame (QHF) is a non-profit organization dedicated to honouring those who have made outstanding contributions to the world of quilting and quilted art. Many of the quilt artists discussed here appear in their list of honourees. The organization's list of honourees can be found on its website; early in their history, they had many honourees; now it appears that they generally honour only one and sometimes no quilt artists for their list.

Important Early Exhibits in the U.S.

Although many quilts made and displayed prior to the 1970s can now be defined as art, the form was most importantly recognized as legitimate art in the 1971 Whitney exhibit, *Abstract Design in American quilts*. That exhibit of pieced quilts from the 19th and early 20th centuries, organized by Jonathan Holstein, presented the quilts on stark white walls with simple gallery labels.

Holstein organized the exhibit so that each piece could "be seen both as an isolated object and as part of a balanced flow of objects." This type of visual presentation marked a break from the traditional crowded hanging of quilts in county fairs and guild shows that had predominated throughout earlier displays. The exhibit was widely reviewed, including a glowing report by the *New York Times* art critic, Hilton Kramer.

The presentation of pieced quilts, with their emphasis on colour and geometric forms, fit perfectly into the art modes of the time. The abstract expressionists, like Mark Rothko and Barnett Newman, who used large swaths of colour on canvas, had had their moment in the 1950s. They were followed in the 1960s by such hard edge abstractionists as Frank Stella. Thus the public had already been prepared for highly coloured abstract art work; the pieced quilts in the Whitney exhibit fit into the current art scene.

The Whitney's pieced art exhibit toured the country and was followed by a quilt craze, which reached a culmination in the Bicentennial events of 1976. Many quilts were made for that event and a revival of interest in quilting techniques and materials started giving artists expanded work potential.

In addition the feminist movement of the late 60s and 70s produced a new interest in women who worked in the arts as well as formerly neglected women's work that could now be seen as art. Quilts, exhibited in galleries and museums, fit into the country's cultural and social concerns.

Other exhibits in the 1970s presented the "new type of quilt, one markedly different from its tradition-inspired counterparts." "The Art Quilt" was a travelling exhibit, sponsored by the Art Museum Association of America, debuting at the Los Angeles Municipal Art Gallery on October 1, 1986. Two other exhibits were "The New American Quilt" at The Museum of Contemporary Crafts in New York City in 1976 and "Quilt National" in 1979, the first of the still existing biennial exhibits spotlighting contemporary, generally original, designs. It too is a travelling exhibit.

Other important exhibits of the 1970s include "Bed and Board", DeCordova Museum (a museum of twentieth-century American art), Lincoln, Massachusetts, 1975; "Quilts for 76", the Boston Centre for the Arts, 1975; and "Quilted Tapestries," Kornblee Gallery, New York City, 1975.

Many annual venues now exist in which quilt art is exhibited; these include the International Quilt Festival in Houston, Texas, and elsewhere, and Quilt Visions, in Oceanside, California.

Art quilts are now part of collections in museums such as the:

- American Craft Museum, New York, New York
- Missoula Museum of the Arts, Missoula, Montana
- Los Angeles County Museum of Art, Los Angeles, California
- High Museum of Art, Atlanta, Georgia
- Muse ArtColle, Sergines, France
- Museum of the State of Pennsylvania, Harrisburg, Pennsylvania
- Renwick Gallery of the National Museum of American Art, Smithsonian Institution, Washington, D.C.
- International Quilt Study Centre & Museum, University of Nebraska, Lincoln, Nebraska
- Racine Art Museum, Racine, Wisconsin
- The Mint Museum of Craft & Design, Charlotte, North Carolina
- The Newark Museum, Newark, New Jersey
- Museum of Nebraska Art, Kearney, Nebraska
- The Rocky Mountain Quilt Museum, Golden, Colorado
- The Fuller Craft Museum, Brockton, Massachusetts
- The Indianapolis Museum of Art, Indianapolis, Indiana
- Museum of the American Quilters' Society, Paducah, Kentucky
- Ball State University Gallery of Art, Muncie, Indiana
- Shelburne Museum, Shelburne, Vermont
- Philadelphis Museum of Art, Philadelphia, Pennsylvania

Museum of the State of Pennsylvania, Harrisburg, Pennsylvania Quilted art outside the U.S. has flourished in the UK, France, Japan, Korea, New Zealand, Australia, Canada, and possibly elsewhere. More information about the art in these countries needs added to this site.

Professional Organizations

The professional organization for quilt artists in the U.S. and elsewhere is Studio Art Quilt Associates, founded in 1989. SAQA's membership overlaps with other professional organizations, such as the Surface Design Association and the International Machine Quilter.

Major exhibitions involving only quilt art are at Quilt National,in Athens, Ohio, at Quilt Visions in San Diego California, and at The National Quilt Museum in Paducah, Kentucky.

Art using quilting techniques are appropriate for all fine art venues. Many mixed media and collage art exhibitions are especially appropriate.

Making Quilt Art

A quilted work of art is generally defined as two layers of cloth held together by stitching. In most cases, a middle batting layer made of polyester, cotton, wool or silk is also incorporated.

Although quilt art originated in traditional quilting techniques, quilt artists now may use many different processes to create their artwork, including painting, dyeing, stamping, piecing, collage, printing (often incorporating a photograph printed onto fabric), applique, and other complex cloth processes.

Machine Quilting

Machine quilting is quilting made using a sewing machine to stitch in rows or patterns using select techniques to stitch through layers of fabric and batting in the manner of old-style hand-quilting. Some machines even replicate hand stitching, for example Sashiko or running stitch quilting.

While sewing machines are commonly used to piece such quilts as patchwork tops, it is rare to find a vintage quilt that was not hand quilted. Regular (domestic) sewing machines have been used to hold layers of a quilt together since they were invented, however, it wasn't until the 1990s that this productive skill became acceptable and has now replaced hand quilting in popularity.

Techniques

To begin any machine quilting, the three layers of the quilt, the quilt top, batting and backing fabric, are temporarily basted with safety pins. Stitching in a straight line is normally accomplished by replacing the normal presser foot with an even feed *walking foot* attachment. This gadget was designed to avoid puckering by advancing multiple layers at the same rate as the feed dogs of the machine. With the feed dogs up, the length of the stitch is controlled by the stitch length setting of the machine.

Free-motion Quilting

Free motion quilting is a process used to stitch the layers of a quilt together using a domestic sewing machine with the feed dogs lowered, with a *darning foot* installed. When the feed dogs are lowered they do not advance the fabric; and with the darning foot merely hovering over the layers, the operator controls the stitch length as well as the direction of the stitching line by moving the quilt with their hands.

The stitching can be made in any direction and to for curvilinear lines or straight patterns. Each design, whether drawn on the quilt top or held in the imagination of the quilter, is formed with a line of stitching that is guided by the movement of the quilt under the machine needle.

The length of each stitch is determined by the distance the quilt has been moved since the previous stitch.

Heirloom Machine Quilting

Heirloom machine quilting is a more advanced quilting technique using a sewing machine. In 1985, Harriet Hargrave coined the term *heirloom machine quilting.*

It was Hargrave's determination to use her domestic sewing machine to replicate the look of hand quilting that compelled her to originate this art. For heirloom machine quilting, the operator uses advanced free motion techniques. The scale of the work is refined, using smaller threads and needles that allow the use of detailed and complex patterns.

Quilts with heirloom machine quilting usually include background quilting which fills the negative space around the designs with dense stitching. This creates contrast between the curvilinear shapes and the flattened background space using stippling, echo quilting, repeated patterns, or geometric grids. The intricate quilted designs produce three dimensions on the surface of the quilt through the play of light and shadows. Motifs puff up, appear brighter because the high areas catch the light; while low areas recede into the depth of the shadow.

Broderie Perse

Broderie perse (French for "Persian embroidery") is a style of appliqué embroidery which uses printed elements to create a scene on the background fabric. It was most popular in Europe in the 17th century, and probably travelled from India, as there are some earlier findings there. The technique could be considered an early form of puzzle piecing.

Broderie perse can be done with any printed fabric on any ground, but it originally was worked with Chintz type fabrics. Chintz typically has clearly defined, separated motifs, which were cut out and invisibly applied onto the ground fabric.

The typical intention was to create a scene from the motifs, but the decoration could also be random. The resulting fabric was often made into bedspreads, either unlined for summer or quilted for winter. They were typically saved for special occasions, such as guest beds.

Rope

A rope is a linear collection of plies, yarns or strands which are twisted or braided together in order to combine them into a larger and stronger form. Ropes have tensile strength and so can be used for dragging and lifting, but are far too flexible to provide compressive strength. As a result, they cannot be used for pushing or similar compressive applications. Rope is thicker and stronger than similarly constructed cord, line, string, and twine.

Construction

Rope may be constructed of any long, stringy, fibrous material, but generally is constructed of certain natural or synthetic fibres. Synthetic fibre ropes are significantly stronger than their natural fibre counterparts, but also possess certain disadvantages, including slipperiness.

Common natural fibres for rope are manila hemp, hemp, linen, cotton, coir, jute, straw, and sisal. Synthetic fibres in use for rope-making include polypropylene, nylon, polyesters (e.g. PET, LCP, HDPE, Vectran), polyethylene (e.g. Dyneema and Spectra), Aramids (e.g. Twaron, Technora and Kevlar) and acrylics (e.g. Dralon).

Some ropes are constructed of mixtures of several fibres or use co-polymer fibres. Rope can also be made out of metal. Ropes have been constructed of other fibrous materials such as silk, wool, and hair, but such ropes are not generally available. Rayon is a regenerated fibre used to make decorative rope.

The twist of the strands in a twisted or braided rope serves not only to keep a rope together, but enables the rope to more evenly distribute tension among the individual strands. Without any twist in the rope, the shortest strand(s) would always be supporting a much higher proportion of the total load.

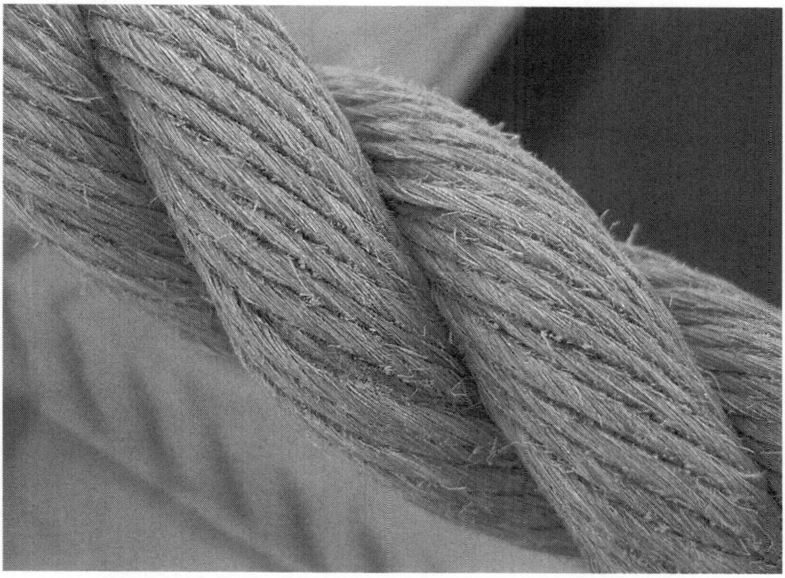

Figure: *Three-strand twisted natural fibre rope*

Usage

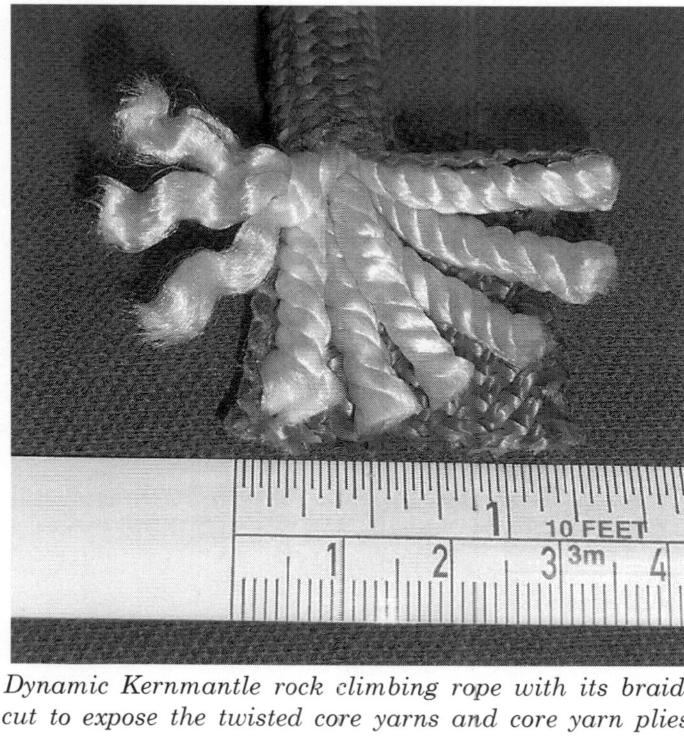

Figure: *Dynamic Kernmantle rock climbing rope with its braided sheath cut to expose the twisted core yarns and core yarn plies.*

Rope is of paramount importance in fields as diverse as construction, seafaring, exploration, sports, hangings, theatre, and communications; and has been used since prehistoric times.

In order to fasten rope, a large number of knots have been invented for countless uses. Pulleys are used to redirect the pulling force to another direction, and may be used to create mechanical advantage, allowing multiple strands of rope to share a load and multiply the force applied to the end. Winches and capstans are machines designed to pull ropes.

Rock Climbing Ropes

The modern sport of rock climbing makes extensive use of so-called "dynamic" rope, which is designed to stretch under load in an elastic manner in order to absorb the energy required to arrest a person in free fall without generating forces high enough to injure them. Such ropes normally use a kernmantle construction, as described below.

"Static" ropes, used for example in caving, rappelling, and rescue applications, are designed for minimal stretch; they are not designed to arrest free falls. The UIAA, in concert with the CEN, sets climbing-rope standards and oversees testing.

Any rope bearing a GUIANA or CE certification tag is suitable for climbing. Despite the hundreds of thousands of falls climbers suffer every year, there are few recorded instances of a climbing rope breaking in a fall, the cases that do are often attributable to previous damage to, or contamination of, the rope. Climbing ropes, however, do cut easily when under load. Keeping them away from sharp rock edges is imperative.

Rock climbing ropes come with either a designation for single, double or twin use.

A single rope is the most common and it is intended to be used by itself, as a single strand. Single ropes range in thickness from roughly 9 mm to 11 mm. Smaller ropes are lighter, but wear out faster. Double ropes are thinner ropes, usually 9mm and under, and are intended to be used as a pair.

These ropes offer a greater margin or security against cutting, since it is unlikely that both ropes will be cut, but complicate belaying and leading.

Double ropes are usually reserved for ice and mixed climbing, where there is need for two ropes to rappel or abseil. They are also popular among traditional climbers, and particularly in the UK, due to the ability to clip each rope into alternating pieces of protection; allowing the ropes to stay straighter and hence reduce rope drag. Twin ropes are not to be confused with doubles.

When using twin ropes, both ropes are clipped into the same piece of protection, treating the two as a single strand. This would be favourable in a situation where there was a high chance of a rope being cut. However new lighter-weight ropes with greater safety have virtually replaced this type of rope.

The butterfly coil is a method of carrying a rope used by climbers where the rope remains attached to the climber and ready to be uncoiled at short notice. Another method of carrying a rope is the alpine coil.

Aerial Rope

Rope is also an Aerial acrobatics circus skill, where a performer makes artistic figures on a vertical suspended rope. Tricks performed on the rope are for example drops, rolls and hangs.

History

The use of ropes for hunting, pulling, fastening, attaching, carrying, lifting, and climbing dates back to prehistoric times. It is likely that the earliest "ropes" were naturally occurring lengths of plant fibre, such as vines, followed soon by the first attempts at twisting and braiding these strands together to form the first proper ropes in the modern sense of the word.

Impressions of cordage found on fired clay provide evidence of string and rope-making technology in Europe dating back 28,000 years. Fossilized fragments of "probably two-ply laid rope of about 7 mm diameter" were found in one of the caves at Lascaux, dating to approximately 15,000 BC.

The ancient Egyptians were probably the first civilization to develop special tools to make rope. Egyptian rope dates back to 4000 to 3500 B.C. and was generally made of water reed fibres. Other rope in antiquity was made from the fibres of date palms, flax, grass, papyrus, leather, or animal hair.

The use of such ropes pulled by thousands of workers allowed the Egyptians to move the heavy stones required to build their monuments. Starting from approximately 2800 B.C., rope made of hemp fibres was in use in China. Rope and the craft of rope making spread throughout Asia, India, and Europe over the next several thousand years.

In the Middle Ages (from the 13th to the 18th centuries), from the British Isles to Italy, ropes were constructed in so-called *Ropewalks*, very long buildings where strands the full length of the rope were spread out and then *laid up* or twisted together to form the rope.

The cable length was thus set by the length of the available rope walk. This is related to the unit of length termed *cable length*. This allowed for long ropes of up to 300 yards long or longer to be made. These long ropes were necessary in shipping as short ropes would require splicing to make them long enough to use for sheets and halyards.

The strongest form of splicing is the short splice, which doubles the cross-sectional area of the rope at the area of the splice, which would cause problems in running the line through pulleys. Any splices narrow enough to maintain smooth running would be less able to support the required weight.

Leonardo da Vinci drew sketches of a concept for a ropemaking machine, but it was never built. Nevertheless, remarkable feats of construction were accomplished without advanced technology:

In 1586, Domenico Fontana erected the 327 ton obelisk on Rome's Saint Peter's Square with a concerted effort of 900 men, 75 horses, and countless pulleys and metres of rope. By the late 18th century several working machines had been built and patented.

Some rope continues to be made from natural fibres such as coir and sisal, despite the dominance of synthetic fibres such as nylon and polypropylene which have become popular since the 1950s.

Styles of Rope Construction

Laid or Twisted Rope: Laid rope, also called twisted rope, is historically the prevalent form of rope, at least in modern western history. Common twisted rope generally consists of three strands and is normally right-laid, or given a final right-handed twist.

The ISO 2 standard uses the uppercase letters S and Z to indicate the two possible directions of twist, as suggested by the direction of slant of the central portions of these two letters. The handedness of the twist is the direction of the twists as they progress away from an observer. Thus Z-twist rope is said to be right-handed, and S-twist to be left-handed.

Twisted ropes are built up in three steps. First, fibres are gathered and spun into yarns. A number of these yarns are then formed into strands by twisting.

The strands are then twisted together to lay the rope. The twist of the yarn is opposite to that of the strand, and that in turn is opposite to that of the rope. It is this counter-twist, introduced with each successive operation, which holds the final rope together as a stable, unified object.

Traditionally, a three strand laid rope is called a *plain-* or *hawser-laid*, a four strand rope is called *shroud-laid*, and a larger rope formed by counter-twisting three or more multi-strand ropes together is called *cable-laid.*

One property of laid rope is partial untwisting when used. This can cause spinning of suspended loads, or stretching, kinking, or hockling of the rope itself. An additional drawback of twisted construction is that every fibre is exposed to abrasion numerous times along the length of the rope. This means that the rope can degrade to numerous inch-long fibre fragments, which is not easily detected visually.

Twisted ropes have a preferred direction for coiling. Normal right-laid rope should be coiled *with the sun*, or clockwise, to prevent kinking. Coiling this way imparts a twist to the rope. Rope of this type must be bound at its ends by some means to prevent untwisting.

Braided Rope

Braided ropes are generally made from nylon, polyester, polypropylene or high performance fibres such as high modulus polyethylene (HMPE) and aramid. Nylon is chosen for its strength and elastic stretch properties.

However, nylon absorbs water and is 10-15% weaker when wet. Polyester is about 90% as strong as nylon but stretches less under load and is not affected by water. It has somewhat better UV resistance, and is more abrasion resistant. Polypropylene is preferred for low cost and light weight (it floats on water) but it has limited resistance to ultraviolet light, is susceptible to friction and has a poor heat resistance. Braided ropes (and objects like garden hoses, fibre optic or coaxial cables, etc.) that have no *lay*, or inherent twist, will uncoil better if coiled into *figure-8* coils, where the twist reverses regularly and essentially cancels out.

Single braid consists of an even number of strands, eight or twelve being typical, braided into a circular pattern with half of the strands going clockwise and the other half going anticlockwise. The strands can interlock with either twill or plain weave. The central void may be large or small; in the former case the term hollow braid is sometimes preferred.

Double braid, also called braid on braid, consists of an inner braid filling the central void in an outer braid, that may be of the same or different material. Often the inner braid fibre is chosen for strength while the outer braid fibre is chosen for abrasion resistance.

In solid braid the strands all travel the same direction, clockwise or anticlockwise, and alternate between forming the outside of the rope and the interior of the rope. This construction is popular for general purpose utility rope but rare in specialized high performance line.

Kernmantle rope has a core (kern) of long twisted fibres in the centre, with a braided outer sheath or mantle of woven fibres. The kern provides most of the strength (about 70%), while the mantle protects the kern and determines the handling properties of the rope (how easy it is to hold, to tie knots in, and so on). In dynamic climbing line, the core fibres are usually twisted, and chopped into shorter lengths which makes the rope more stretchy. Static kernmantle ropes are made with untwisted core fibres and tighter braid, which causes them to be stiffer in addition to limiting the stretch.

Other Types

Plaited rope is made by braiding twisted strands, and is also called *square braid*. It is not as round as twisted rope and coarser to the touch. It is less prone to kinking than twisted rope and, depending on the material, very flexible and therefore easy to handle and knot. This construction exposes all fibres as well, with the same drawbacks as described above. Brait rope is a combination of braided and plaited, a non-rotating alternative to laid three-strand ropes. Due to its excellent energy-absorption characteristics, it is often used by arborists. It is also a popular rope for anchoring and can be used as mooring warps. This type of construction was pioneered by Yale Cordage.

Endless winding rope is made by winding single strands of high-performance yarns around two end terminations until the desired break strength or stiffness has been reached. This type of rope (often specified as cable to make the difference between a braided or twined construction) has the advantage of having no construction stretch as is the case with above constructions. Endless winding is pioneered by SmartRigging and FibreMax.

Gallery of μCT/micro-CT Images and Animations

Rope made from hemp, cotton or nylon is generally stored in a cool dry place for proper storage. To prevent kinking it is usually coiled. To prevent fraying or unravelling, the ends of a rope are bound with twine (whipping), tape, or heat shrink tubing. The ends of plastic fibre ropes are often melted and fused solid.

If a load-bearing rope gets a sharp or sudden jolt or the rope shows signs of deteriorating, it is recommended that the rope be replaced immediately and should be discarded or only used for non-load-bearing tasks.

The average rope life-span is 5 years. Serious inspection should be given to line after that point. When preparing for a climb, it is important to stack the rope on the ground or a tarp and check for any "dead-spots".

Avoid stepping on rope, as this might force tiny pieces of rock through the sheath, which can eventually deteriorate the core of the rope. Ropes may be flemished into coils on deck for safety and presentation/tidiness as shown in the picture.

Line

"Rope" refers to the manufactured material. Once rope is purposely sized, cut, spliced, or simply assigned a function, the result is referred to as a "line", especially in nautical usage. Sail control lines are mainly referred to as sheets (e.g. jibsheet).

A halyard, for example, is a line used to raise and lower a sail, and is typically made of a length of rope with a shackle attached at one end. Other examples include clothesline, chalk line, anchor line ("rode"), stern line, fishing line, marline and so on.

Rug Making

Braided

Braided rugs are made by using three or more strips of fabric, usually wool, folding the raw edges to the middle and braiding them together. For an oval rug the centre braid should be one inch longer than the width-length in feet. example 2' x 4' rug centre strip would be 2’2" long. The centre braid is laced together and new strips are sewn on to make the braid longer as lacing continues.

Hooking

Traditional rug hooking is a craft in which rugs are made by pulling loops of yarn or fabric through a stiff woven base such as burlap, linen, rug warp or monks cloth. The loops are pulled through the backing material by using a latch hook mounted in a handle (usually wood) for leverage.

Rag Rugs

Rag rugs were commonly made in households up to the middle of the 20th century by using odd scraps of fabric on a background of old sacking.

Needlepunch

Using either yarn or strips of cloth, you work with the punch tool from the back side of the pattern. The Monk’s cloth backing is tightly stretched on to a frame.

Every time you punch the needle down through the backing, it makes a long thread on the right side of the rug. Then, as you lift the needle, it automatically makes it into a loop. These loops pack together to create a rug so solid that chewing dogs and clawing cats are its only enemy. As long as you use the tool correctly, it will automatically make all the loops the same length.

Sometimes referred to as “speed hooking”, this method of rug hooking is liked for its ease and speed.

Prodded

Proddy rugs are made, as the name implies, by prodding or poking strips of fabric through burlap or linen from the back side. Rag rugs made this way have many names; clippies, proddies, stobbies, pricked, in Northumberland they are called proggy mats, and in

Scotland they are called clootie mats. They were often made for more utilitarian use such as by the backdoor; their pile hiding dirt well.

Woven

Handmade and machine-made. Woven rugs include both flat rugs (for example kilims) and pile rugs. The more tightly a rug is woven or knotted, the more detailed a design can be. "It is generally believed that the density of knots determines the value of a carpet.

Afghan Carpet

An Afghan rug (or Afghan carpet) is a type of handwoven floor-covering textile traditionally made in Afghanistan. Many of the Afghan rugs are also woven by Afghan refugees who reside in Pakistan and Iran.

One of the most exotic and distinctive of all oriental rugs is the *Shindand* or *Adraskan* (named after local Afghan towns), woven in the Herat area, in western Afghanistan. Strangely elongated human and animal figures are their signature look. The carpet can be sold across Afghanistan with the most based in Mazar-e Shariff.

Another staple of Afghanistan is Baluchi rugs, most notably Baluchi prayer rugs. They are made by Afghanistan's Baloch people, also in the south-western part of the country.

Most of the weavers in Afghanistan are the Ersari Turkmen, but other smaller groups such as Chub Bash and Kizil Ayaks are also in the line of weaving rugs. In addition, Uzbeks, Kyrgyz, Kazakhs, and Arabs label their rugs according to their ethnic group.

Various vegetable, and other natural dyes are used to produce the rich colours.

The rugs are mostly of medium sizes. Many patterns and colours are used, but the traditional and most typical is that of the octagonal elephant's foot (Bukhara) print, often with a red background. The weavers also produce other trappings of the nomadic lifestyle, including tent bags and ceremonial pieces.

Gabbeh

Gabbeh carpets are a traditional variety of Persian carpet. Gabbeh is known as Gava in Kurdish and Luri and is also called Khersak in Bakhtiari. A Gabbeh a hand-woven pile rug of coarse quality and medium size (90 x 150 cm or larger) characterized by an abstract design that relies upon open fields of colour and a playfulness with geometry. This type of rug is popular among the populations of the Zagros Mountains of Iran, including Kurdish, Luri and Qashqai people. The Gabbeh is usually crafted by women.

'Gabbeh' carpet is much thicker and coarser than other Persian carpets; sometimes it is as much as one inch in depth. In fact, it is more of a variety of kilim than carpet. The word 'Gabbeh' comes from the Persian meaning raw, natural, uncut. This is a rough and primitive carpet.

Gabbeh patterns are of a very basic kind with only a limited number of decorative, mostly rectangular objects resembling mainly animals. In *Gabbeh* usually bright colours, such as yellow and red, are used. Although large fields of solid colour are used in Gabbeh designs, the colour is variegated (the colour varies throughout the rug).

Gabbehs are made of natural, handspun wool yarn and all the colours are created with natural plant dye. Due to its relative ease of production (less precise pattern, small number of knots per square centimeter, etc.) a *Gabbe* is one of the less expensive varieties of Persian carpet.

These days weavers from Pakistan are making Persian Gabbehs. For example, they are producing natural-dyed, hand-spun *Gabbeh* rugs in the Balochistan area in Pakistan. Balochistan province of Pakistan neighbours Iran and shares the Persian language/culture

Heatsetting

Heat setting is a term used in the textile industry to describe a thermal process taking place mostly in either a steam atmosphere or a dry heat environment.

The effect of the process gives fibres, yarns or fabric dimensional stability and, very often, other desirable attributes like higher volume, wrinkle resistance or temperature resistance.

Very often, heat setting is also used to improve attributes for subsequent processes.

Yarns tend to have increased torquing just after spinning, cabling or twisting. Heat setting can influence or even eliminate this tendency to undesirable torquing.

At the winding, twisting, weaving, tufting and knitting processes, an increased tendency to torquing can cause difficulties in processing the yarn.

When using heat setting for carpet yarns, desirable results include not only the diminishing of torquing but also the stabilization or fixing of the fibre thread. Both twist stabilization and stabilization of frieze effect are results of the heat setting process. Heat setting benefits staple yarns as well as bulked continuous filament (BCF) yarns.

Heat setting often causes synthetic fibres to gain volume as well. This volume growth is commonly described as "bulk development". All processes using temperature and/or moisture to give textiles one of the above mentioned attributes are known as heat setting. The term "thermal fixation" is used less frequently. In the carpet industry, the process is exclusively called "heat setting".

Crinkling Tendency

The crinkle tendency is due to the technological conditions of the spun yarn production and the physical fibre properties. Above all, the "technological conditions of the spun yarn production" means the turning moment of the thread.

A twisted thread will always try to twist when it hangs freely between two fixed points in the form of a loop. In doing this, it gives up a part of its original twist which becomes spirals whose twisting direction is opposite to the original twist direction. This development of twist in the opposite direction occurs as the twisted yarn attempts to reach equilibrium.

Twisting in the opposite direction is due to the tensions resulting from the yarn twisting that Mueller indicated in the diagram of tension and pressure. The total tension acting against the twisting is increased in relation to increased twisting due to the increasing tension and pressure of the bundle of fibres in the yarn. It may become so strong that the thread core buckles when it can no longer withstand the compressive strains.

The yarn curls, meaning that the yarn tries to reach a state of equilibrium in which twists in the opposite direction from the original twist direction balance the yarn's torque.These twists are also called negative twists. In this state of equilibrium, the inner torsional tensions cancel each other out. The thread always buckles at a spot where the cross section is small due to the unevenness of the thread. During the spinning process this spot took up more twists and is therefore subjected to higher inner tensions, which ultimately break the thread core. Although thicker yarns are less twisted than fine ones, the inner tension rises opposite to the yarn size. Smaller yarn is more weakened by steaming. Further positive aspects of steaming are the reduction of curling and, at the same time, the setting of the physical properties of closeness and extension imparted to the yarn by twisting.

The Chemical Process

There are completely different behaviours depending on the kind of yarn material. Much is known about the steaming of woolen yarns but more research is needed on the steaming behaviour of artificial fibres and cotton.

Wool

As soon as steam enters, the yarns quantity of moisture rises at once, caused by the heating of the yarn and by steam condensation. According to Speakmann the following phenomena can be seen in the stretched woolen fibre: The cystine side chains are subjected to a hydrolysis at the sulphur bridge, where cystine is dissolved into cysteine and a not yet isolated sulphonic acid.

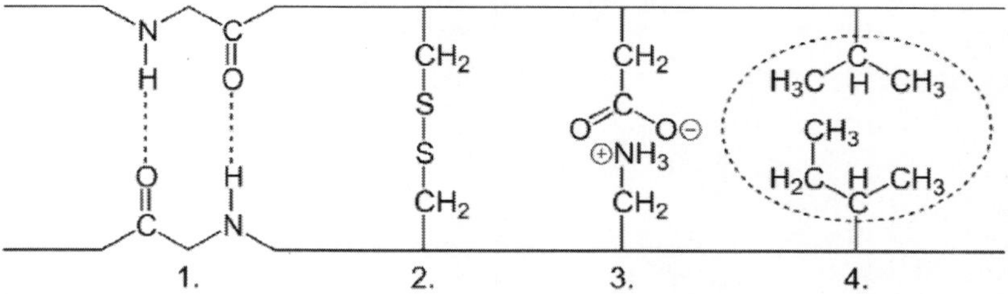

Figure: *Physical and chemical forces between two polypeptide chains*

1. Hydrogen bridges between peptide groups (polar bond)
2. Cystine bridge (covalent bond)
3. Salt bridge between two amino acids (ionic bond)
4. Hydrophobic bond between a valine and an isolyeine rest (non-polar bond)

The broken ellipse shows the part where water is displaced. An ionization can be seen at the bridges that were produced from salt liberation. Due to the increase of temperature in the fibres during steaming an oscillation of the molecules is produced which leads to the bursting of the hydrogen bridges; now residual valencies are set free which are able to saturate with the dipole water. The water then acts like a lubrication between the individual molecules.

Thus the bonds of the main chains between each other are dissolved by the side chains, the individual polypeptide chains can shift against each other and the tensions find their equilibrium. When the steaming of the yarn is continued, new side chains are formed between the individual components of the main chains.

When finally the yarn is dried, i.e. the moisture balance occurring within the yarn, salt is liberated again and hydrogen bridges are formed. Now the individual polypeptide chains can no longer be shifted against each other and the fibres regained their former closeness, however without having remarkable tensions inside.

The yarn or doubled yarn twist is set. Of course, the morphological structure of the fibres must be considered when equalizing the tensions by steaming.

Since the woolen fibre very quickly gets the temperature for breaking up the hydrogen bridges and the steam for hydrolysing the cystine bridges, a relatively quick twist modification is possible which roughly corresponds to the values of an autoclave moderated yarn; however, the steaming quality of the Steamatic steaming process is much better with reference to the evenness of moisture absorption.

Synthetic Fibre

1. amorphous fibre domains
2. crystalline fibre domains
3. bonding force

Synthetic fibres can be divided up into two fibre domains, the crystalline (organized) domain and the amorphous (unorganized) domain. In crystalline domains physical forces of attraction are acting between the closely parallel lines of polymers. These forces acting transversely to the fibre axis make up the closeness of a fibre. If tension is applied to the fibre, these forces hinder the fibre from breaking.

In contrast, the amorphous fibre domains act like links of the fibres. They are responsible for the flectional strength of the fibres. Additionally, the amorphous fibre domains make it possible for water or dye to enter.

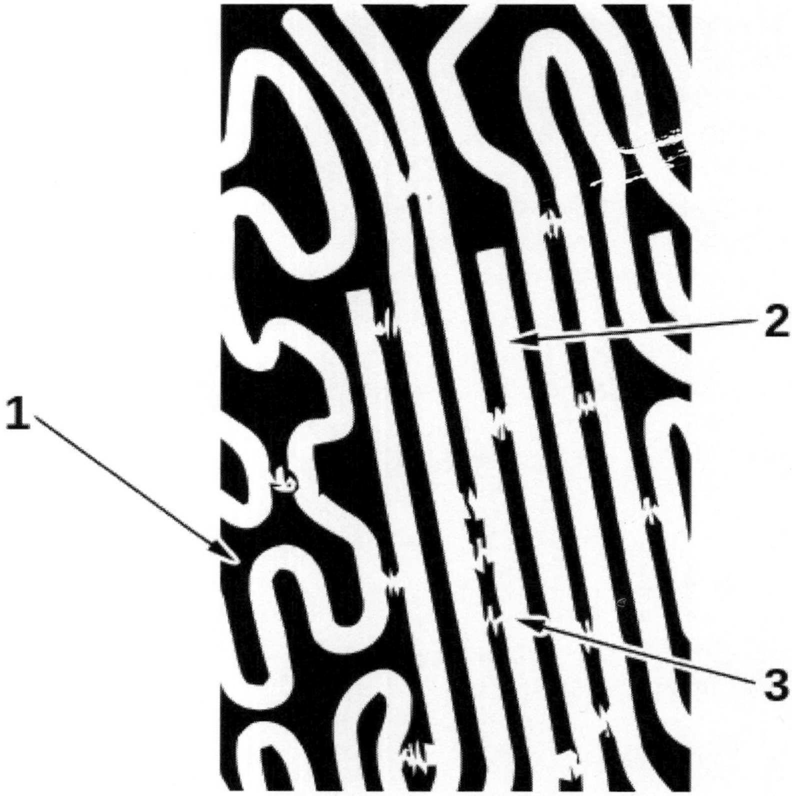

Figure: *Fibre strength and elongation*

During steaming, the heating of the fibre causes its molecules to start oscillating.

The increase of oscillation that can be influenced by the degree and the period of heating dissolves the electric bond forces in the fibre; at first in the amorphous domains, later in the crystalline ones and at last in the polymers.

As with wool, the tensions brought in by spinning are set free. During drying or cooling of the fibre, the binding forces are rebuilt without having tensions in the inner part.

The problem of synthetic fibres is that the reduction of the binding forces only takes place between the so-called deformation point (start of changing the firm - solidified - amorphous fibre domains into a visco-elastic - easily deformable state) and the distortion point (the crystalline fibre domains change into a visco-elastic state, too) which is in a relatively high temperature range.

***Table:** Glass transition temperature and deformation point of artificial fibre*

Material	*Deformation point*	*Distortion temperature*
Polyester	80-85 °C	230-240 °C
Nylon 6	80-85 °C	180-200 °C
Nylon 66	90-95 °C	220-235 °C

This is also an explanation for the fact that wool mixed with synthetic fibres is more difficult to set than pure wool. Setting synthetic fibres is only possible beyond a temperature range of 85 to 95 °C. In contrast, pure wool can set very well at these temperatures.

Cotton

In in-line steaming, cotton plays a more or less subordinate role. The exact physical or chemical process in the fibre are not well known.

Applications in the Carpet Industry

The quality of cut pile carpets is improved significantly by a reduction of inner tensions in the yarn. This essential benefit results from the effects of steaming and heatsetting.

Carpet Classification

Carpet styles are divided into two basic types. These types are loop pile carpets and cut pile carpets. Especially for cut-pile and its variations (Saxony, shag, frieze) the heat setting process is of highest importance.

Tip Definition (Pinpoint tip Definition)

Usually, when yarn is cut, the ends fray similar to the way the ends of a braid or rope would fray when they are cut and a kind of a brush forms. This fraying must be avoided in cut-pile carpets by all means. A cut pile carpet with frayed yarn ends would have a poor appearance, a shorter life cycle and ergonomic disadvantages for the "walker" as scientific research has proven.

The carpet is less elastic and doesn't absorb the steps of the user as well as a heat set carpet would. A carpet manufactured from heat set yarn is more attractive, durable and comfortable for the user. The added value of heatset carpet is significant. Normally a heat set carpet can be identified by its grainy structure, which is called "pinpoint tip definition" in the industry. The appearance of the cut pile ends is similar to pin points.

Current Heat Setting Processes

Several different heat setting processes are known in the textile industry. The most important are presented here.

Autoclave Heat Setting

The oldest heat setting process is autoclave heat setting. Mostly, it is a discontinuous process.Autoclave installations use vacuum and/ or pressure. Textile material is brought into the autoclave either on bobbins, in skeins or loose in a container. As nearly all autoclaves are exposed to certain pressures they are usually built in cylindrical shape and mounted horizontally. Most commonly, autoclaves are loaded and unloaded from the end of the cylinder but some may be loaded from one end and unloaded from the other end. Autoclaves mounted vertically exist but are less common. They are mostly used for the synthetic yarns like polyester, polyethylene, poly propylene and nylons.

Steamatic Process

For automation in link spinning/winding there is the so-called "in-line steamer". The first known process of this type is the Steamatic process by Resch. In this case the heat setting process happens in between the ring spinning and the winding machines. As soon as the ring spinning frame has finished spinning, the loaded bobbins are transported into the in-line steamer. Those bobbins are steamed there with a vacuum method and dried again within seconds. After steaming and drying, the bobbins are transported on to the winding machine where they are re-wound onto a cross-wound package.

The carpet industry currently utilizes two continuous processes, the Power-Heat-Set process and the TVP process which was derived from the autoclave technology.

Power-Heat-Set Technology

The Power-Heat-Set process, formerly known as Suessen process, was developed in the beginning of the 1970s and was the first continuous heat setting system worldwide. The process itself was revolutionary in that it was the first system not operated with saturated steam and pressure, but with a superheated steam/airmix at atmospheric pressure. Using this innovative technology, completely new carpet collections were created. In the Power-Heat-Set process, the yarns and filaments oxidize slightly on the surface due to the existing oxygen in the surrounding atmosphere and the higher temperatures. This capillary oxide film causes the complete carpet later to be more stain resistant. Dirt particles adhere less to the fibres.

Superba TVP Process

In addition to the Power-Heat-Set technology there is the SUPERBA TVP3 process which is also a continuous process. In the TVP3 process yarn is placed on a conveyor belt and inserted through a lock into a pressure tunnel that could be up to 15 m long. Inside the tunnel, it undergoes a heat setting process with saturated steam. At the end of the tunnel the yarn is taken out through a second lock. The yarn which is still hot and moist is dried and cooled after heat setting and fed to the winding process. Up to 72 yarn ends can be processed at the same time.

Process Description (Exemplary with the Power-Heat-Set Process)

In the Power-Heat-Set process yarn is heat set with superheated steam in an open system at atmospheric pressure. All the materials normally used in the carpet industry such as polyamide 6, polyamide 6.6, polypropylene, Acrylic, PET, polyester and wool can be processed.

The unprocessed yarn is provided on packages in a creel (up to 48 packages). At a speed of up to 700 m/min, the yarn is pulled off the packages and entered into the heat setting process. There are two basic ways of transportation of the yarn through the process. One way is to place the yarn in coils or a "figure pattern on a belt or to wrap it onto ropes arranged as a polygon in order to convey it through the process.

With Frieze yarns only belt conveying is utilized. Frieze is produced by a special stuffer box, the so-called Twinroll-Box (TRB). The heat setting process takes place at temperatures between 110 °C and 200 °C in a steam-air-mix.

After heat setting, the yarn is cooled and wound onto packages again at the winder. In general a heat setting machine consists of six lines at eight ends (fibres) each. A daily production of up to 10.5 tons is possible.

Knot Density

Knot density is a traditional measure for quality of handmade carpets. It refers to the number of knots per unit of surface area - typically either per square inch or per square centimeter. Number of knots per unit area is directly proportional to the quality of carpet.

For two carpets of the same age, origin, condition and design, the one with the higher number of knots will be the more valuable. Knot density is normally measured in knots per square inch (KPSI) which is simply the number of vertical knots across one inch of carpet multiplied by the number of horizontal knots in the same area. Average knot density varies between region and design. A rug could have a knot density half that of another yet still be more valuable, KPSI is only one measurement of quality and value in Persian Carpets.

Hand-tying of knots is a very labour-intensive task. An average weaver can tie almost 10,000 knots per day. More difficult patterns with an above-average knot density can only be woven by a skilful weaver, thus increasing the production costs even more.

Oriental Rugs

An authentic oriental rug is a handmade carpet that is either knotted with pile or woven without pile. By definition, oriental rugs are rugs that come from the "Orient" (East). The simple definition of the term would be rugs that come from (were made in) an Asian country such as: China and Vietnam in the east to Turkey, Maghreb countries, Cyprus and Iran in the west, the Caucasus in the north, and India in the south.

People from different cultures, countries, racial groups and religious faiths are involved in the production of oriental rugs. Oriental rugs are organized by origin: Persian rugs, Arabian rugs, Anatolian rugs, Kurdish rugs, Caucasian rugs, Central Asian rugs, Turkestanian (Turkmen, Turkoman) rugs, Chinese rugs, Tibetan rugs and Indian rugs.

In the Occident, the collecting of oriental rugs as an art form really began in the 1880s. It was confirmed by two exhibitions. The first exhibition of oriental rugs was in 1891 consisting mostly of the rugs of the Imperial House of Habsburg, but including some from private collections as well. The second, and more influential, was in London in 1892, and was capped by the sale of a single carpet for £2,500.

Tapestry

Tapestry is a form of textile art, traditionally woven on a vertical loom. However, it can also be woven on a floor loom as well. It is composed of two sets of interlaced threads, those running parallel to the length (called the warp) and those parallel to the width (called the weft); the warp threads are set up under tension on a loom, and the weft thread is passed back and forth across part or all of the warps. Tapestry is weft-faced weaving, in which all the warp threads are hidden in the completed work, unlike cloth weaving where both the warp and the weft threads may be visible. In tapestry weaving, weft yarns are typically discontinuous; the artisan interlaces each coloured weft back and forth in its own small pattern area. It is a plain weft-faced weave having weft threads of different colours worked over portions of the warp to form the design.

Most weavers use a naturally based warp thread such as linen or cotton. The weft threads are usually wool or cotton, but may include silk, gold, silver, or other alternatives.

Function

The success of decorative tapestry can be partially explained by its portability (Le Corbusier once called tapestries "nomadic murals"). Kings and noblemen could roll up and transport tapestries from one residence to another. In churches, they were displayed on special occasions. Tapestries were also draped on the walls of castles for insulation during winter, as well as for decorative display.

In the Middle Ages and renaissance, a rich tapestry panel woven with symbolic emblems, mottoes, or coats of arms called a baldachin, canopy of state or cloth of state was hung behind and over a throne as a symbol of authority. The seat under such a canopy of state would normally be raised on a dais.

The iconography of most Western tapestries goes back to written sources, the Bible and Ovid's *Metamorphoses* being two popular choices. Apart from the religious and mythological images, hunting scenes are the subject of many tapestries produced for indoor decoration.

Historical Development

Tapestries have been used since at least Hellenistic times. Samples of Greek tapestry have been found preserved in the desert of Tarim Basin dating from the 3rd century BC.

Tapestry reached a new stage in Europe in the early 14th century AD. The first wave of production originated in Germany and Switzerland. Over time, the craft expanded to France and the Netherlands. The basic tools have remained much the same.

In the 14th and 15th centuries, Arras, France was a thriving textile town. The industry specialised in fine wool tapestries which were sold to decorate palaces and castles all over Europe. Few of these tapestries survived the French Revolution as hundreds were burnt to recover the gold thread that was often woven into them. *Arras* is still used to refer to a rich tapestry no matter where it was woven.

By the 16th century, Flanders, the towns of Oudenaarde, Brussels, Geraardsbergen and Enghien had become the centres of European tapestry production. In the 17th century, Flemish tapestries were arguably the most important productions, with many specimens of this era still extant, demonstrating the intricate detail of pattern and colour embodied in painterly compositions, often of monumental scale.

In the 19th century, William Morris resurrected the art of tapestry-making in the medieval style at Merton Abbey. Morris & Co. made successful series of tapestries for home and ecclesiatical uses, with figures based on cartoons by Edward Burne-Jones.

Kilims and Navajo rugs are also types of tapestry work. In the mid-twentieth century, new tapestry art forms were developed by children at the Ramses Wissa Wassef Art Centre in Harrania, Egypt and by modern French artists under Jean Lurcat in Aubusson, France. Traditional tapestries are still made at the factory of Gobelins and a few other old European workshops, which also repair and restore old tapestries. The craft is also currently practiced by hobbyist weavers.

Jacquard Tapestries, Colour and the Human Eye

The term tapestry is also used to describe weft-faced textiles made on Jacquard looms. Before the 1990s tapestry upholstery fabrics and reproductions of the famous tapestries of the Middle Ages had been produced using Jacquard techniques but more recently, artists such as Chuck Close and the workshop Magnolia Editions have adapted the computerised Jacquard process to producing fine art.

Typically, tapestries are translated from the original design via a process resembling paint-by-numbers: a cartoon is divided into regions, each of which is assigned a solid colour based on a standard palette.

However, in Jacquard weaving, the repeating series of multicoloured warp and weft threads can be used to create colours that are optically blended – i.e., the human eye apprehends the threads' combination of values as a single colour.

This method can be likened to pointillism, which originated from discoveries made in the tapestry medium. The style's emergence in the 19th century can be traced to the influence of Michel Eugène Chevreul, a French chemist responsible for developing the colour wheel of primary and intermediary hues.

Chevreul worked as the director of the dye works at Les Gobelins tapestry works in Paris, where he noticed that the perceived colour of a particular thread was influenced by its surrounding threads, a phenomenon he called "simultaneous contrast."

Chevreul's work was a continuation of theories of colour elaborated by Leonardo da Vinci and Goethe; in turn, his work influenced painters including Eugène Delacroix and Georges-Pierre Seurat.

The principles articulated by Chevreul also apply to contemporary television and computer displays, which use tiny dots of red, green and blue (RGB) light to render colour, with each composite being called a pixel.

List of Famous Tapestries

- The Trojan War tapestry referred to by Homer in Book III of the Iliad, where Iris disguises herself as Laodice and finds Helen "working at a great web of purple linen, on which she was embroidering the battles between Trojans and Achaeans, that Ares had made them fight for her sake."

  Though the composition of the Iliad spanned a period of approximately 700 years, it is worth noting that this method of weaving was in common use in or before the eighth century BCE.
- The Cloth of St Gereon – oldest European tapestry still extant.
- The Sampul tapestry, woollen wall hanging, 3rd–2nd century BCE, Sampul, Ürümqi Xinjiang Museum.
- The Hestia Tapestry, 6th century, Egypt, Dumbarton Oaks Collection.
- The Bayeux Tapestry is an embroidered cloth — not an actual tapestry — nearly 70 metres (230 ft) long, which depicts the events leading up to the Norman conquest of England, likely made in England — not Bayeux — in the 1070s
- The Apocalypse Tapestry is the longest tapestry in the world, and depicts scenes from the Book of Revelation. It was woven

between 1373 and 1382. Originally 140 m (459 ft), the surviving 100m are displayed in the Château d'Angers, in Angers.

- The six-part piece *La Dame à la Licorne* (The Lady and the Unicorn), stored in l'Hôtel de Cluny, Paris.
- The Devonshire Hunting Tapestries, four Flemish tapestries dating from the mid-fifteenth century depict men and women in fashionable dress of the early fifteenth century hunting in a forest. The tapestries formerly belonged to the Duke of Devonshire and are now in the Victoria and Albert Museum.
- The Hunt of the Unicorn is a seven piece tapestry from 1495 to 1505, currently displayed at The Cloisters, Metropolitan Museum of Art in New York.
- The tapestries for the Sistine Chapel, designed by Raphael in 1515–16, for which the Raphael Cartoons, or painted designs, also survive.
- The Wawel Tapestries, (mid 16th century) a collection of 134 tapestries at the Wawel Castle in Kraków, Poland displaying various religious, natural, and royal themes. These famous tapestries, created in Arras, were collected by Polish Kings Sigismund I the Old and Sigismund II Augustus.
- The Valois Tapestries are a cycle of 8 hangings depicting royal festivities in France in the 1560s and 1570s
- The New World Tapestry is a 267 feet long tapestry which depicts the colonisation of the Americas between 1583 and 1648, displayed at the British Empire and Commonwealth Museum; this is not (strictly speaking) a tapestry, but is instead embroidery.
- The biggest collection of Flanders tapestry is in the Spanish royal collection, there is 8000 metres of historical tapestry from Flanders, as well as Spanish tapestries designed by Goya and others.

  There is a special museum in the Royal Palace of La Granja de San Ildefonso, and others are displayed in various historic buildings.
- The Pastoral Amusements, also known as "Les Amusements Champêtres", a series of 8 Beauvais Tapestries designed by Jean-Baptiste Oudry between 1720 and 1730.

- The Prestonpans Tapestry is a 104 metres long embroidery which tells the story of Bonnie Prince Charlie and the Battle of Prestonpans.
- Christ in Glory, (1962) for Coventry Cathedral designed by Graham Sutherland. Up until the 1990s this was the world's largest vertical tapestry.
- The Quaker Tapestry (1981–1989) is a modern set of embroidery panels that tell the story of Quakerism from the 17th century to the present day.

Sewing

Sewing is the craft of fastening or attaching objects using stitches made with a needle and thread. Sewing is one of the oldest of the textile arts, arising in the Paleolithic era. Before the invention of spinning yarn or weaving fabric, archaeologists believe Stone Age people across Europe and Asia sewed fur and skin clothing using bone, antler or ivory needles and "thread" made of various animal body parts including sinew, catgut, and veins.

Although usually associated with clothing and household linens, sewing is used in a variety of crafts and industries, including shoemaking, upholstery, sailmaking, bookbinding and the manufacturing of some kinds of sporting goods. Sewing is the fundamental process underlying a variety of textile arts and crafts, including embroidery, tapestry, quilting, appliqué and patchwork.

For thousands of years, all sewing was done by hand. The invention of the sewing machine in the 19th century and the rise of computerization in the later 20th century led to mass production of sewn objects, but hand sewing is still practised around the world. Fine hand sewing is a characteristic of high-quality tailoring, haute couture fashion, and custom dressmaking, and is pursued by both textile artists and hobbyists as a means of creative expression.

The first known use of the word sewing was in the 14th century.

History

Origins: Sewing has an ancient history estimated to begin during the Paleolithic Age. Sewing was used to stitch together animal hides for clothing and for shelter. The Inuit, for example, used sinew from caribou for thread and needles made of bone; the indigenous peoples of the American Plains and Canadian Prairies used sophisticated sewing methods to assemble tipi shelters. Sewing was combined with the weaving of plant leaves in Africa to create baskets, such as those made by Zulu weavers, who used thin strips of palm leaf as "thread" to stitch wider strips of palm leaf that had been woven into a coil. The weaving of cloth from natural fibres originated in the Middle East around 4000 BCE, and perhaps earlier during the Neolithic Age, and the sewing of cloth accompanied this development.

During the Middle Ages, Europeans who could afford it employed seamstresses and tailors. Sewing for the most part was a woman's occupation, and most sewing before the 19th century was practical. Clothing was an expensive investment for most people, and women had an important role in extending the longevity of items of clothing. Sewing was used for mending.

Clothing that was faded would be turned inside-out so that it could continue to be worn, and sometimes had to be taken apart and reassembled in order to suit this purpose. Once clothing became worn or torn, it would be taken apart and the reusable cloth sewn together into new items of clothing, made into quilts, or otherwise put to practical use.

The many steps involved in making clothing from scratch (weaving, pattern making, cutting, alterations, and so forth) meant that women often bartered their expertise in a particular skill with one another. Decorative needlework such as embroidery was a valued skill, and young women with the time and means would practise to build their skill in this area. From the Middle Ages to the 17th century, sewing tools such as needles, pins and pincushions were included in the trousseaus of many European brides.

Decorative embroidery was valued in many cultures worldwide. Although most embroidery stitches in the Western repertoire are traditionally British, Irish or Western European in origin, stitches originating in different cultures are known throughout the world today. Some examples are the Cretan Open Filling stitch, Romanian Couching or Oriental Couching, and the Japanese stitch.

The stitches associated with embroidery spread by way of the trade routes that were active during the Middle Ages. The Silk Road brought Chinese embroidery techniques to Western Asia and Eastern Europe, while techniques originating in the Middle East spread to Southern and Western Europe through Morocco and Spain. European imperial settlements also spread embroidery and sewing techniques worldwide. However, there are instances of sewing techniques indigenous to cultures in distant locations from one another, where cross-cultural communication would have been historically unlikely. For example, a method of reverse appliqué known to areas of South America is also known to Southeast Asia.

Industrial Revolution

The Industrial Revolution shifted the production of textiles from the household to the mills. In the early decades of the Industrial Revolution, the machinery produced whole cloth. The world's first sewing machine was patented in 1790 by Thomas Saint. By the early 1840s, other early sewing machines began to appear. Barthélemy Thimonnier introduced a simple sewing machine in 1841 to produce military uniforms for France's army; shortly afterward, a mob of tailors broke into Thimonnier's shop and threw the machines outof the windows, believing the machines would put them out of work. By the 1850s, Isaac Singer developed the first sewing machines that could operate quickly and accurately and surpass the productivity of a seamstress or tailor sewing by hand.

While much clothing was still produced at home by female members of the family, more and more ready-made clothes for the middle classes were being produced with sewing machines. Textile sweatshops full of poorly paid sewing machine operators grew into entire business districts in large cities like London and New York City. To further support the industry, piece work was done for little money by women living in slums. Needlework was one of the few occupations considered acceptable for women, but it did not pay a living wage. Women doing piece work from home often worked 14 hour days to earn enough to support themselves, sometimes by renting sewing machines that they could not afford to buy.

Tailors became associated with higher-end clothing during this period. In London, this status grew out of the dandy trend of the early 19th century, when new tailor shops were established around Savile Row. These shops acquired a reputation for sewing high-quality handmade clothing in the style of the latest British fashions, as well as more classic styles. The boutique culture of Carnaby Street was absorbed by Savile Row tailors during the late 20th century, ensuring the continued flourishing of Savile Row's businesses.

20th Century and Today

Sewing underwent further developments during the 20th century. As sewing machines became more affordable to the working class, demand for sewing patterns grew. Women had become accustomed to seeing the latest fashions in periodicals during the late 19th and early 20th century, increasing demand for sewing patterns yet more. American tailor and manufacturer Ebenezer Butterick met the demand with paper patterns that could be traced and used by home sewers. The patterns, sold in small packets, became wildly popular. Several pattern companies soon established themselves. Women's magazines also carried sewing patterns, and continued to do so for much of the 20th century.

This practice declined during the last decades of the 20th century, when ready-made clothing became a necessity as women joined the paid workforce in larger numbers, leaving them with less time to sew, if indeed they had an interest. Today, the low price of ready-made clothing in shops means that home sewing is confined largely to hobbyists in Western countries.

The spread of sewing machine technology to industrialized economies around the world meant the spread of Western-style sewing methods and clothing styles as well. In Japan, traditional clothing was sewn together with loose chain stitches that were removed so that the clothing could be taken apart and the assorted pieces laundered separately.

The tight-locked stitches made by home sewing machines, and the use of Western clothing patterns, led to a movement towards wearing Western-style clothing during the early 20th century. Western sewing and clothing styles were disseminated in sub-Saharan Africa by Christian missionaries from the 1830s onward. Indigenous cultures, such as the Zulu and Tswana, were indoctrinated in the Western way of dress as a sign of conversion to Christianity. First Western hand sewing techniques, and later machine sewing, spread throughout the regions where the European colonists settled. However, a recent examination of new online learning methods demonstrated that technology can be adapted to share knowledge of a culture's traditional sewing methods. Using self-paced online tutorials, a Malay sewing class learned how to tailor and sew a traditional men's *Baju Kurung* garment in 3 days, whereas a traditional Malay sewing class would have taken 5 days to teach the same information.

Advances in industrial technology, such as the development of synthetic fibres during the early 20th century, have brought profound changes to the textile industry as a whole. Textile industries in Western countries have declined sharply as textile companies compete for cheaper labour in other parts of the world.

It is estimated that every lost textile job in a Western country in recent years has resulted in 1.5 jobs being created in an outsourced country such as China. Textile workers who perform tasks with sewing machines, or do detailed work by hand, are still a vital component of the industry, however. Small-scale sewing is also an economic standby in many developing countries, where many people, both male and female, are self-employed sewers.

Garment Construction

Before sewing together an article of clothing, a pattern is generally followed to construct the garment. A pattern can be quite simple; some patterns are nothing more than a mathematical formula that the sewer calculates based on the intended wearer's measurements. Once calculated, the sewer has the measurements needed to cut the cloth and sew the garment together. At the other end of the spectrum are haute couture fashion designs. When a couture garment is made of unusual material, or has extreme proportions, the design may challenge the sewer's engineering knowledge. Complex designs are drafted and refitted dozens of times, may take around 40 hours to develop a final pattern, and require 60 hours of cutting and sewing.

Most clothing today is mass-produced, and conforms to standard sizing, based on body measurements that are intended to fit the greatest proportion of the population.

However, while "standard" sizing is generally a useful guideline, it is little more than that, because there is no industry standard that is "both widely accepted and strictly adhered to in all markets".

Elements of Garment Sewing

Sewers working on a simple pattern need only a few sewing tools: measuring tape, needle, thread, cloth, and sewing shears. More complex patterns done on a sewing machine may only need a few more simple tools to get the job done, but there are an ever-growing variety of helpful sewing aids available, such as presser foot attachments for sewing ruffles, or hem repair glue.

When the sewer has gathered the necessary tools to tackle a pattern, there are several elements of garment construction that are part of the process. Patterns will specify whether to cut on the grain or a bias cut. Construction stitches include edgestitching, understitching, staystitching and topstitching; seam types include the plain seam, zigzag seam, flat fell seam, French seam, and many others.

Supporting materials, such as interfacing, interlining or lining, or fusing, may be used as well, to give the fabric a more rigid or durable shape. Volume can be added with elements such as pleats, or reduced with the use of darts.

Sewing machines are now made for a broad range of specialised sewing purposes, such as quilting machines, computerized machines for embroidery, and various sergers for finishing raw edges of fabric.

Stitch

In the textile arts, a stitch is a single turn or loop of thread or yarn. Stitches are the fundamental elements of sewing, knitting, embroidery, crochet, and needle lace-making, whether by hand or machine. A variety of stitches, each with one or more names, are used for specific purposes.

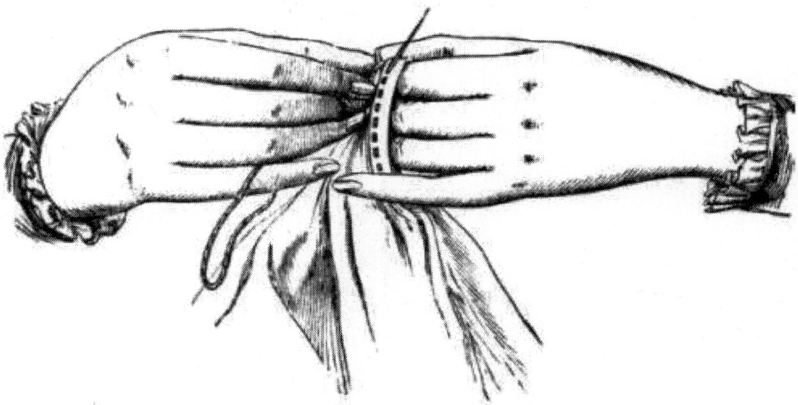

Figure: *Hand-stitches.*

Sewing, Embroidery, and Lace

All stitches made with a sewing needle with an "eye" or hole are variations on seven basic stitches:

- Running stitch
- Backstitch

- Overcast stitch
- Cross stitch
- Buttonhole or blanket stitch
- Chain stitch
- Knot stitch

These stitches and their variations are named according to the position of the needle and direction of sewing (*running stitch*, *backstitch*), the form or shape of the stitch (*chain stitch*, *feather stitch*) or the purpose of the stitch (tailor's tack, *hem stitch*).

Sewing machine stitches are classified by their structure:

- Chain stitch, made with one thread
- Lockstitch, made with two threads
- Overlock, made with one to four threads
- Coverstitch, made with two or four threads (a twine)

Fancy machine stitches mimic traditional hand stitches using variations on the basic stitches.

Knitting

In knitting, a stitch is a single loop of yarn, secured to the loops beside it to form a row or *course* of stitches and to the loops above and below it to form a *wale*. In securing the previous stitch in a wale, the next stitch can pass through the previous loop either from below or above. If the former, the stitch is denoted as a knit stitch or a plain stitch; if the latter, as a purl stitch. The two stitches are related in that a knit stitch seen from one side of the fabric appears as a purl stitch on the other side.

Crochet

In crochet, stitches are made by pulling a loop of thread through the work with a crochet hook. Crochet stitches are named based on their structure. In the English-speaking crochet world, basic stitches have different names that vary by country. The differences are usually referred to as UK/US or British/American.

3

Textile Printing

Textile printing is the process of applying colour to fabric in definite patterns or designs. In properly printed fabrics the colour is bonded with the fibre, so as to resist washing and friction.

Textile printing is related to dyeing but, whereas in dyeing proper the whole fabric is uniformly covered with one colour, in printing one or more colours are applied to it in certain parts only, and in sharply defined patterns.

In printing, wooden blocks, stencils, engraved plates, rollers, or silkscreens can be used to place colours on the fabric.

Colourants used in printing contain dyes thickened to prevent the colour from spreading by capillary attraction beyond the limits of the pattern or design.

Traditional textile printing techniques may be broadly categorised into four styles:

- Direct printing, in which colourants containing dyes, thickeners, and the mordants or substances necessary for fixing the colour on the cloth are printed in the desired pattern.
- The printing of a mordant in the desired pattern prior to dyeing cloth; the colour adheres only where the mordant was printed.
- Resist dyeing, in which a wax or other substance is printed onto fabric which is subsequently dyed. The waxed areas do not accept the dye, leaving uncoloured patterns against a coloured ground.

- Discharge printing, in which a bleaching agent is printed onto previously dyed fabrics to remove some or all of the colour.

Resist and discharge techniques were particularly fashionable in the 19th century, as were combination techniques in which indigo resist was used to create blue backgrounds prior to block-printing of other colours.

Most modern industrialised printing uses direct printing techniques.

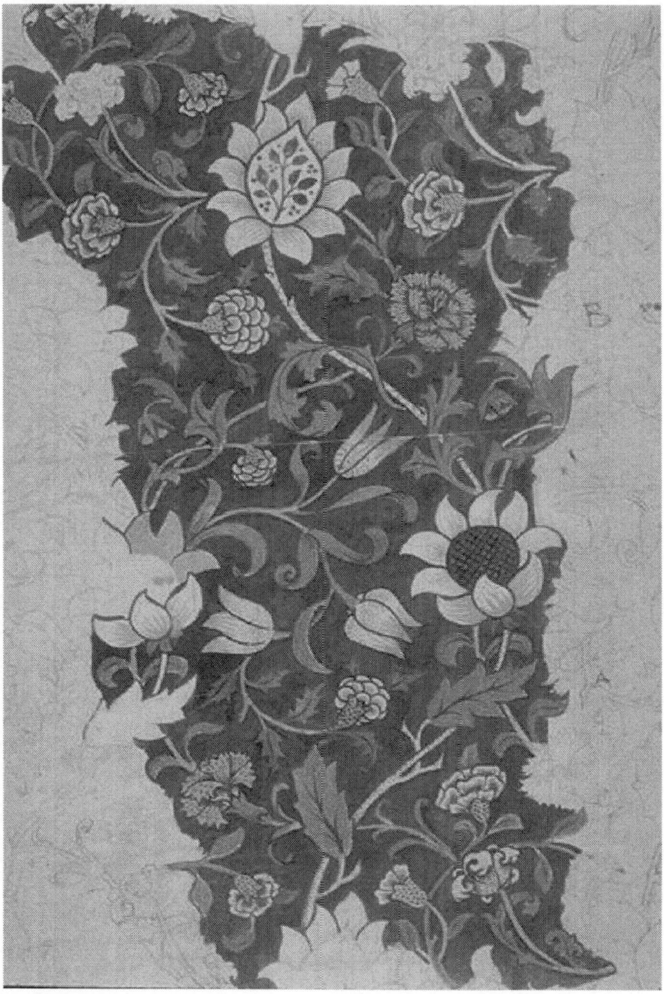

Figure: *Design for a hand woodblock printed textile, showing the complexity of the blocks used to make repeating patterns.* Evenlode *by William Morris, 1883.*

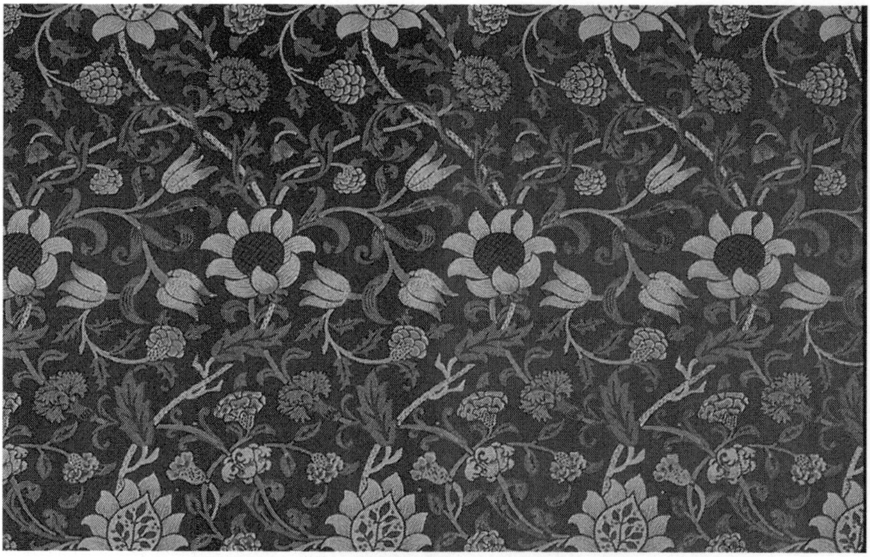

Figure: Evenlode *block-printed fabric.*

Origins

Woodblock printing is a technique for printing text, images or patterns used widely throughout East Asia and probably originating in China in antiquity as a method of printing on textiles and later paper.

As a method of printing on cloth, the earliest surviving examples from China date to before 220.

Textile printing was known in Europe, via the Islamic world, from about the 12th century, and widely used. However, the European dyes tended to liquify, which restricted the use of printed patterns. Fairly large and ambitious designs were printed for decorative purposes such as wall-hangings and lectern-cloths, where this was less of a problem as they did not need washing.

When paper became common, the technology was rapidly used on that for woodcut prints. Superior cloth was also imported from Islamic countries, but this was much more expensive.

The Incas of Peru, Chile and the Aztecs of Mexico also practiced textile printing previous to the Spanish Invasion in 1519; but owing to the imperfect character of their records before that date, it is impossible to say whether they discovered the art for themselves, or, in some way, learned its principles from the Asiatics.

During the later half of the 17th century the French brought directly by sea, from their colonies on the east coast of India, samples of Indian blue and white resist prints, and along with them, particulars of the processes by which they had been produced, which produced washable fabrics.

Technology

Textile printing was introduced into England in 1676 by a French refugee who opened works, in that year, on the banks of the Thames near Richmond. Curiously enough this is the first print-works on record; [This is an old story from a reference in the late 1800s but it has never been proven and is generally not believed to be the case any more. There are no French names on the list of fabric printers and dyers at that time.

Later a few French Huguenots arrived but that was after the British had a flourishing calico printing industry established.] but the nationality and political status of its founder are sufficient to prove that printing was previously carried on in France.

In Germany, too, textile printing was in all probability well established before it spread to England, for, towards the end of the 17th century, the district of Augsburg was celebrated for its printed linens, a reputation not likely to have been built up had the industry been introduced later than 1676.

As early as the 1630s, the East India Company was bringing in printed and plain cotton for the English market. By the 1660s British printers and dyers were making their own printed cotton to sell at home, printing single colours on plain backgrounds; less colourful than the imported prints, but more to the taste of the British. Designs were also sent to India for their craftspeople to copy for export back to England.

There were many dyehouses in England in the latter half of the 17th century, Lancaster being one area and on the River Lea near London another. Plain cloth was put through a prolonged bleaching process which prepared the material to receive and hold applied colour; this process vastly improved the colour durability of English calicoes and required a great deal of water from nearby rivers. Again, there were many dyehouses, the one I am most familiar with was that started by John Meakins, a London Quaker who lived in Cripplegate.

When he died, he passed his dyehouse to his son-in-law Benjamin Ollive, Citizen and Dyer, who moved the dye-works to Bromley Hall where it remained in the family until 1823, known as [Benjamin Ollive and Company] Ollive & Talwin, Joseph Talwin & Company, Talwin & Foster... Samples of their fabrics and designs can be found in many museums in England and the United States, including the Victoria and Albert Museum in London and the Smithsonian Copper-Hewett in New York.

On the continent of Europe the commercial importance of calico printing seems to have been almost immediately recognized, and in consequence it spread and developed there much more rapidly than in England, where it was neglected and practically at a standstill for nearly ninety years after its introduction.

During the last two decades of the 17th century and the earlier ones of the 18th new works were started in France, Germany, Switzerland and Austria; but it was only in 1738 that calico printing was first, practiced in Scotland, and not until twenty-six years later that Messrs Clayton of Bamber Bridge, near Preston, established in 1764 the first print-works in Lancashire, and thus laid the foundation of the industry.

At the present time calico printing is carried on extensively in every quarter of the globe, and it is pretty safe to say that there is scarcely a civilized country in either hemisphere where a print-works does not exist.

From an artistic point of view most of the pioneer work in calico printing was done by the French; and so rapid was their advance in this branch of the business that they soon came to be acknowledged as its leading exponents. Their styles of design and schemes of colour were closely followed-even deliberately copied by all other European printers; and, from the early days of the industry down to the latter half of the 20th century, the productions of the French printers in Jouy, Beauvais, Rouen, Alsace-Lorraine, &c., were looked upon as representing all that was best in artistic calico printing.

This reputation was established by the superiority of their earlier work, which, whatever else it may have lacked, possessed in a high degree the two main qualities essential to all good decorative work, viz., appropriateness of pattern and excellency of workmanship. If, occasionally, the earlier designers permitted themselves to indulge in somewhat bizarre fancies, they at least carefully refrained from any attempt to produce those pseudo-realistic effects the undue straining after which in later times ultimately led to the degradation of not only French calico printing design, but of that of all other European nations who followed their lead.

The practice of the older craftsmen, at their best, was to treat their ornament in a way at once broad, simple and direct, thoroughly artistic and perfectly adapted to the means by which it had to be reproduced.

The result was that their designs were characterized, on the one hand, by those qualities of breadth, flatness of field, simplicity of treatment arid pureness of tint so rightly prized by the artist; and, on the other, by their entire freedom from those meretricious effects of naturalistic projection and recession so dear to the modern mind and so utterly opposed to the principles of applied art.

Methods of Printing

There are seven distinct methods at present in use for producing coloured patterns on cloth:

Hand Block Printing

This process, though considered by some to be the most artistic, is the earliest, simplest and slowest of all methods of printing.

In this process, a design is drawn on, or transferred to, a prepared wooden block. A separate block is required for each distinct colour in the design.

A blockcutter carves out the wood around the heavier masses first, leaving the finer and more delicate work until the last so as to avoid any risk of injuring it during the cutting of the coarser parts. When finished, the block presents the appearance of flat relief carving, with the design standing out.

Fine details are very difficult to cut in wood, and, even when successfully cut, wear down very rapidly or break off in printing. They are therefore almost invariably built up in strips of brass or copper, bent to shape and driven edgewise into the flat surface of the block. This method is known as coppering.

To print the design on the fabric, the printer applies colour to the block and presses it firmly and steadily on the cloth, ensuring a good impression by striking it smartly on the back with a wooden mallet. The second impression is made in the same way, the printer taking care to see that it fits exactly to the first, a point which he can make sure of by means of the pins with which the blocks are provided at each corner and which are arranged in such a way that when those at the right side or at the top of the block fall upon those at the left side or the bottom of the previous impression the two printings join up exactly and continue the pattern without a break.

Each succeeding impression is made in precisely the same manner until the length of cloth is fully printed. When this is done it is wound over the drying rollers, thus bringing forward a fresh length to be treated similarly.

If the pattern contains several colours the cloth is usually first printed throughout with one, then dried, and printed with the second, the same operations being repeated until all the colours are printed.

Block printing by hand is a slow process it is, however, capable of yielding highly artistic results, some of which are unobtainable by any other method.

Perrotine Printing

The perrotine is a block-printing machine invented by Perrot of Rouen in 1834, and practically speaking is the only successful mechanical device ever introduced for this purpose. For some reason or other it has rarely been used in England, but its value was almost immediately recognized on the Continent, and although block printing of all sorts has been replaced to such an enormous extent by roller printing, the perrotine is still largely employed in French, German and Italian works.

The construction of this ingenious machine is too complex to describe here without the aid of several detailed drawings, but its mode of action is roughly as follows:

Three large blocks (3 ft. long by 3 to 5 in. wide), with the pattern cut or cast on them in relief, are brought to bear successively on the three faces of a specially constructed printing table over which the cloth passes (together with its backing of printers blanket) after each impression.

The faces of the table are arranged at right angles to each other, and the blocks work in slides similarly placed, so that their engraved faces are perfectly parallel to the tables. Each block is moreover provided with its own particular colour trough, distributing brush, and woolen colour pad or sieve, and is supplied automatically with colour by these appliances during the whole time that the machine is in motion.

The first effect of starting the machine is to cause the colour sieves, which have a reciprocating motion, to pass over, and receive a charge of colour from, the rollers, fixed to revolve, in the colour troughs. They then return to their original position between the tables and the printing blocks, coming in contact on the way with the distributing brushes, which spread the colour evenly over their entire surfaces.

At this point the blocks advance and are gently pressed twice against the colour pads (or sieves) which then retreat once more towards the colour troughs. During this last movement the cloth to be printed is drawn forward over the first table, and, immediately the colour pads are sufficiently out of the way, the block advances and, with some force, stamps the first impression on it.

The second block is now put into gear and the foregoing operations are repeated for both blocks, the cloth advancing, after each impression, a distance exactly equal to the width of the blocks. After the second block has made its impression the third comes into play in precisely the same way, so that as the cloth leaves the machines it's fully printed in three separate colours, each fitting into its proper place and completing the pattern.

If necessary the forward movement of the cloth can be arrested without in any way interfering with the motion of the block, san arrangement which allows any insufficiently printed impression to be repeated in exactly the same place with a precision practically impossible in hand printing.

For certain classes of work the perrotine possesses great advantages over the hand-block; for not only is the rate of production greatly increased, but the joining up of the various impressions to each other is much more exacting fact, as a rule, no sign of a break in continuity of line can be noticed in well-executed work. On the other hand, however, the perrotine can only be applied to the production of patterns containing not more than three colours nor exceeding five inches in vertical repeat, whereas hand block printing can cope with patterns of almost any scale and continuing any number of colours. All things considered, therefore, the two processes cannot be compared on the same basis: the perrotine is best for work of a utilitarian character and the hand-block for decorative work in which the design only repeats every 15 to 20 in. and contains colours varying in number from one to a dozen. -

Engraved Copperplate Printing

The printing of textiles from engraved copperplates was first practiced in the United Kingdom by Thomas Bell in 1770. The presses first used were of the ordinary letterpress type, the engraved plate being fixed in the place of the type.

In later improvements the well-known cylinder press was employed; the plate was inked mechanically and cleaned off by passing under a sharp blade of steel; and the cloth, instead of being laid on the plate, was passed round the pressure cylinder. The plate was raised into frictional contact with the cylinder and in passing under it transferred its ink to the cloth.

The great difficulty in plate printing was to make the various impressions join up exactly; and, as this could never be done with any certainty, the process was eventually confined to patterns complete in one repeat, and was made obsolete by roller printing.

Roller Printing, Cylinder Printing, or Machine Printing

This elegant and efficient process was patented and worked by Bell in 1785 only fifteen years after his application of the engraved plate to textiles. Bell's first patent was for a machine to print six colours at once, but, owing probably to its incomplete development, this was not immediately successful, although the principle of the method was shown to be practical by the printing of one colour with perfectly satisfactory results. The difficulty was to keep the six rollers, each carrying a portion of the pattern, in perfect register with each other. This defect was soon overcome by Adam Parkinson of Manchester, and in 1785, the year of its invention, Bells machine with Parkinson's improvement was successfully employed by Messrs Livesey, Hargreaves and Company of Bamber Bridge, Preston, for the printing of calico in from two to six colours at a single operation.

The advantages possessed by roller printing over other contemporary processes were three: firstly, its high productivity, 10,000 to 12,000 yards being commonly printed in one day of ten hours by a single-colour machine; secondly, by its capacity of being applied to the reproduction of every style of design, ranging from the fine delicate lines of copperplate engraving and the small repeats and limited colours of the perrotine to the broadest effects of block printing and to patterns varying in repeat from I to 80 in.; and thirdly, the wonderful exactitude with which each portion of an elaborate multicolour pattern can be fitted into its proper place without faulty joints at its points of repetition.

Stencil Printing

The art of stenciling is not new. It has been applied to the decoration of textile fabrics from time immemorial by the Japanese, and, of late years, has found increasing employment in Europe for certain classes of decorative work on woven goods for furnishing purposes.

The pattern is cut out of a sheet of stout paper or thin metal with a sharp-pointed knife, the uncut portions representing the part that is to be reserved or left uncoloured. The sheet is now laid on the material to be decorated and colour is brushed through its interstices.

It is obvious that with suitable planning an all over pattern may be just as easily produced by this process as by hand or machine printing, and that moreover, if several plates are used, as many colours as plates may be introduced into it. The peculiarity of stenciled patterns is that they have to be held together by ties, that is to say, certain parts of them have to be left uncut, so as to connect them with each other, and prevent them from falling apart in separate pieces.

For instance, a complete circle cannot be cut without its centre dropping out, and, consequently, its outline has to be interrupted at convenient points by ties or uncut portions. Similarly with other objects. The necessity for ties exercises great influence on the design, and in the hands of a designer of indifferent ability they may be very unsightly. On the other hand, a capable man utilizes them to supply the drawing, and when thus treated they form an integral part of the pattern and enhance its artistic value whilst complying with the conditions and the process.

For single-colour work a stenciling machine was patented in 1894 by S. H. Sharp. It consists of an endless stencil plate of thin sheet steel that passes continuously over a revolving cast iron cylinder.

Between the two the cloth to be ornamented passes and the colour is forced on to it, through the holes in the stencil, by mechanical means.

Screen-printing

Screen printing is by far the most used technology today. Two types exist: rotary screen printing and flat (bed) screen printing. A blade squeezes the printing paste through openings in the screen onto the fabric.

Digital Textile Printing

Digital textile printing, often referred to as direct to garment printing, DTG printing, and digital garment printing is a process of printing on textiles and garments using specialized or modified inkjet technology. Inkjet printing on fabric is also possible with an inkjet printer by using fabric sheets with a removable paper backing.

Today major inkjet technology manufacturers can offer specialized products designed for direct printing on textiles, not only for sampling but also for bulk production. Since the early 1990s, inkjet technology and specially developed water-based ink (known as dye-sublimation or disperse direct ink) has offered the possibility of printing directly onto polyester fabric.

This is mainly related to visual communication in retail and brand promotion (flags, banners and other point of sales applications). Printing onto nylon and silk can be done by using an acid ink. Reactive ink is used for cellulose based fibres, such as cotton and linen. Using inkjet technology in digital textile printing allows for single pieces, mid-run production and even long-run alternatives to screen printed fabric.

Other Methods of Printing

Although most work is executed throughout by one or other of the seven distinct processes mentioned above, combinations of them are frequently employed. Sometimes a pattern is printed partly by machine and partly by block; and sometimes a cylindrical block is used along with engraved copper-rollers in the ordinary printing machine. The block in this latter case is in all respects, except that of shape, identical with a flat wood or coppered block, but, instead of being dipped in colour, it receives its supply from an endless blanket, one part of which works in contact with colour-furnishing rollers and the other part with the cylindrical block. This block is known as a surface or peg roller. Many attempts have been made to print multicolour patterns with surface rollers alone, but hitherto with little success, owing to their irregularity in action and to the difficulty of preventing them from warping. These defects are not present in the printing of linoleum in which opaque oil colours are used, colours that neither sink into the body of the hard linoleum nor tend to warp the roller.

'*Inkjet Printing on Fabric*' is a way anyone can print on fabric using their home printer. Specially treated Cotton, as well as various types of Bamboo and Silk fabric sheets, are available in various sizes. The fabric sheets have a paper backing which enable the fabric to go through the inkjet printer. Family photos printed on fabric are used to make memory quilts, pillows, notebook covers, wall hangings, ornaments and many other products. The printed fabric is dipped in water to set the ink after the inkjet ink dries, making it washable. Print on Fabric paper-backed inkjet sheets are available on Amazon and other websites.

The printing of yarns and warping is extensively practiced. It is usually carried on by a simple sort of surface printing machine and calls for no special mention.

Lithographic printing, too, has been applied to textile fabrics with somewhat qualified success. Its irregularity and the difficulty of printing all over patterns to repeat properly, have restricted its use to the production of decorative panels, equal in size to that of the plate or stone, and complete in themselves.

Pad printing has been recently introduced to textile printing for the specific purpose of printing garment tags (care labels).

Preparation of Cloth for Printing

Goods intended for calico printing ought to be exceptionally well-bleached, otherwise stains, and other serious defects, are certain to arise during subsequent operations.

The chemical preparations used for special styles will be mentioned in their proper places; but a general prepare, employed for most colours that are developed and fixed by steaming only, consists in passing the bleached calico through a weak solution of sulphated or turkey red oil containing from 21/2 per cent, to 5 per cent, of fatty acid. Some colours are printed on pure bleached cloth, but all patterns containing alizarine red, rose and salmon shades, are considerably brightened by the presence of oil, and indeed very few, if any, colours are detrimentally affected by it.

Apart from wet preparations the cloth has always to be brushed, to free it from loose nap, flocks and dust that it picks up whilst stored. Frequently, too, it has to be sheared by being passed over rapidly revolving knives arranged spirally round an axle, which rapidly and effectually cuts off all filaments and knots, leaving the cloth perfectly smooth and clean and in a condition fit to receive impressions of the most delicate engraving.

Some figured fabrics, especially those woven in checks, stripes and crossovers, require very careful stretching and straightening on a special machine, known as a stenter, before they can be printed with certain formal styles of pattern which are intended in one way or another to correspond with the cloth pattern.

Finally, all descriptions of cloth are wound round hollow wooden or iron centres into rolls of convenient size for mounting on the printing machines.

Preparation of Colours

The art of making colours for textile printing demands both chemical knowledge and extensive technical experience, for their ingredients must not only be properly proportioned to each other, but they must be specially chosen and compounded for the particular style of work in hand.

For a pattern containing only one colour any mixture may be used so long as it fulfills all conditions as to shade, quality and fastness; but where two or more colours are associated in the same design each must be capable of undergoing without injury the various operations necessary for the development and fixation of the others.

All printing pastes whether containing colouring matter or not are known technically as colours, and are referred to as such in the sequence.

Colours vary considerably in composition. The greater number of them contain all the elements necessary for the direct production and fixation of the colour-lake. Some few contain the colouring matter alone and require various after-treatments for its fixation; and others again are simply mordants thickened. A mordant is the metallic salt or other substance that combines with the colouring principle to form an insoluble colour-lake, either directly by steaming, or indirectly by dyeing.

All printing colours require thickening, for the twofold object of enabling them to be transferred from colour-box to cloth without loss and to prevent them from running or spreading beyond the limits of the pattern.

Selecting Thickening Agents

The printing thickeners used depend on the printing technique and fabric and dyestuff used. Typical thickening agents are starch derivatives, flour, gum arabic, guar gum derivatives, tamarind, sodium alginate, sodium polyacrylate, gum Senegal and gum tragacanth, British gum or dextrine and albumen.

Hot water soluble tickening agents as native starch are made into pastes by boiling in double or jacketed pans, between the inner and outer casings of which either steam or water may be made to circulate, for boiling and cooling purposes. Mechanical agitators are also fitted in these pans to mix the various ingredients together, and to destroy lumps and prevent the formation of lumps, keeping the contents thoroughly stirred up during the whole time they are being boiled and cooled to make a smooth paste. Most thickening agents used today are cold soluble and require only extensive stirring.

Starch Paste

This is made from wheat starch, cold water, and olive oil, and boiled for thickening. Non modified Starch was the most extensively used of all the thickenings. It is applicable to all but strongly alkaline or strongly acid colours. With the former it thickens up to a stiff unworkable jelly, while mineral acids or acid salts convert it into dextrine, thus diminishing its viscosity or thickening power. Acetic and formic acids have no action on it even at the boil. Today mostly modified carboxymethylated cold soluble starches are used which have a stable viscosity and are easier to rinse out of the fabric and give reproducible "short" pasty rheology.

Flour paste is made in a similar way to starch paste. At the present time it is rarely used for anything but the thickening of aluminium and iron mordants. In the impressive textile traditions of Japan, several techniques using starch paste resists of rice flour have been perfected over several centuries.

Gums

Gum arabic and gum Senegal are both very old thickenings, but their expense prevents them from being used for any but pale delicate tints. They are especially useful thickenings for the light ground colours of soft muslins and sateens on account of the property they possess of dissolving completely out of the fibres of the cloth in the washing process after printing and have a long flowing, viscous rheology, giving sharp print and good penetration in the cloth. Today guar gum and tamarind derivates offer a cheaper alternative.

British gum or dextrin is prepared by heating starch. It varies considerably in composition sometimes being only slightly roasted and consequently only partly converted into dextrine, and at other times being highly torrefied, and almost completely soluble in cold water and very dark in colour.

Its thickening power decreases and its gummy nature increases as the temperature at which it is roasted is raised. The lighter coloured gums or dextrines will make a good thickening with from 2 to 3 lb of gum to one gallon of water, but the darkest and most highly calcined require from 6 to lb per gallon to give a substantial paste. Between these limits all qualities are obtainable.

The darkest qualities are very useful for strongly acid colours, and with the exception of gum Senegal, are the best for strongly alkaline colours and discharges. Like the natural gums, neither light nor dark British gums penetrate as well into the fibre of the cloth so deeply as pure starch or flour, and are therefore unsuitable for very dark strong colours.

Gum tragacanth, or Dragon, is one of the most indispensable thickening agents possessed by the textile printer. It may be mixed in any proportion with starch or flour and is equally useful for pigment colours and mordant colours. When added to starch paste it increases its penetrative power, adds to its softness without diminishing its thickness, makes it easier to wash

Out of the fabric and produces much more level colours than starch paste alone. Used by itself it is suitable for printing all kinds of dark grounds on goods that are required to retain their soft clothy feel. A tragacanth mucilage may be made either by allowing it to stand a day or two in contact with cold water or by soaking it for twenty-four hours in warm water and then boiling it up until it is perfectly smooth and homogeneous. If boiled under pressure it gives a very fine, smooth mucilage (not a solution proper), much thinner than if made in the cold.

Starch always leave on the printed cloth somewhat harsh in feel (unless modified carboxymethylated starches are used) but are well suited to obtain very dark colours. Gum Senegal, gum arabic or modified guar gum thickening are yielding beautifully clear and perfectly even tints comparing to starch, but give lighter colours and are washed away too much during the rinsing or washing of the printed fabric and are thus less suited for very dark colours. (The gums are apparently preventing the colours from combining fully with the fibres.)

So a printing stock solution is mostly a combination of modified starch and gum stock solutions usually made by dissolving 6 or 8 lb of either in one gallon of water.

Albumen

Albumen is both a thickening and a fixing agent for insoluble pigments such as chrome yellow, the ochres, vermilion and ultramarine. Albumen is always dissolved in the cold, a process that takes several days when large quantities are required. The usual strength of the solution is 4 lb per gallon of water for blood albumen, and 6 lb per gallon for egg albumen.

The latter is expensive and only used for the lightest shades. For most purposes one part of albumen solution is mixed with one part of tragacanth mucilage, this proportion of albumen being found amply sufficient for the fixation of all ordinary pigment colours. In special instances the blood albumen solution is made as strong as 50 per cent, but this is only in cases where very dark colours are required to be absolutely fast to washing. After printing, albumen thickened colours are exposed to hot steam, which coagulates the albumen and effectually fixes the colours.

Printing Thickeners and the Dye System

Combinations of cold water soluble carboxymethylated starch, guar gum and tamarind derivatives are most commonly used today in disperse screen printing on polyester, for cotton printing with reactive dyes alginates are used, sodium polyacrylates for pigment printing and with vat dyes on cotton only carboxymethylated starch is used.

Printing Paste Preparation

Formerly colours were always prepared for printing by boiling the thickening agent, the colouring matter and solvents, &c., together, then cooling and adding the various fixing agents. At the present time, however, concentrated solutions of the colouring matters and other adjuncts are often simply added to the cold thickenings, of which large quantities are kept in stock.

Colours are reduced in shade by simply adding more stock (printing) paste. For example, a dark blue containing 4 oz. of methylene blue per gallon may readily be made into a pale shade by adding to it thirty times its bulk of starch paste or gum, as the case may be. Similarly with other colours.

Before printing it is very essential to strain or sieve all colours in order to free them from lumps, fine sand, &c., which would inevitably damage the highly polished surface of the engraved rollers and result in bad printing. Every scratch on the surface of a roller prints a fine line in the cloth, and too much care, therefore, cannot be taken to remove, as far as possible, all grit and other hard particles from every colour.

The straining is usually done by squeezing the colour through filter cloths as artisanal fine cotton, silk or industrial woven nylon. Fine sieves can also be employed for colours that are used hot or are very strongly alkaline or acid.

Silk Printing

The colours and methods employed are the same as for wool, except that in the case of silk no preparation of the material is required before printing and the ordinary dry steaming is preferable to damp steaming.

Both acid and basic dyes play an important role in silk printing, which for the most part is confined to the production of articles for wearing apparel dress goods, handkerchiefs, scarves, articles for which bright colours are in demand. Alizarine and other mordant colours are mainly used, or ought to be, for any goods that have to resist repeated washings and prolonged exposure to light. In this case the silk frequently requires to be prepared in alizarine oil, after which it is treated in all respects like cotton steamed, washed and soaped the colours used being the same.

Silk is especially adapted to discharge and reserve effects. Most of the acid dyes can be discharged in the same way as when they are dyed on wool; and reserved effects are produced by printing mechanical resists, such as waxes and fats, on the cloth and then dyeing it up in cold dye-liquor.

The great affinity of the silk fibre for basic and acid dyestuffs enables it to extract colouring matter from cold solutions, and permanently combine with it to form an insoluble lake. After dyeing, the reserve prints are washed, first in cold water to get rid of any colour not fixed on the fibre, and then in hot water or benzene, to dissolve out the resisting bodies.

As a rule, after steaming, silk goods are only washed in hot water, but, of course, those printed entirely in mordant dyes will stand soaping, and indeed require it to brighten the colours and soften the material. (E. K.)

COLOURHUE silk dyes do not require heat setting or steaming. They strike instantly, allowing user to dye colour upon colour. They are concentrated and should be diluted with water before dyeing. Intended mostly for silk scarf dyeing, they may also be used on silk clothing and other projects. They also will dye bamboo, rayon, linen, and some other natural fabrics like hemp and wool to a lesser extent, but will not set on cotton.

Weaving

Weaving is a method of fabric production in which two distinct sets of yarns or threads are interlaced at right angles to form a fabric or cloth. The other methods are knitting, lace making, felting, and braiding or plaiting.

The longitudinal threads are called the warp and the lateral threads are the weft or filling. (*Weft* or *woof* is an old English word meaning "that which is woven".) The method in which these threads are inter woven affects the characteristics of the cloth.

Cloth is usually woven on a loom, a device that holds the warp threads in place while filling threads are woven through them. A fabric band which meets this definition of cloth (warp threads with a weft thread winding between) can also be made using other methods, including tablet weaving, back-strap, or other techniques without looms.

The way the warp and filling threads interlace with each other is called the weave. The majority of woven products are created with one of three basic weaves: plain weave, satin weave, or twill. Woven cloth can be plain (in one colour or a simple pattern), or can be woven in decorative or artistic designs.

Figure: *A plain weave: image of warp and weft*

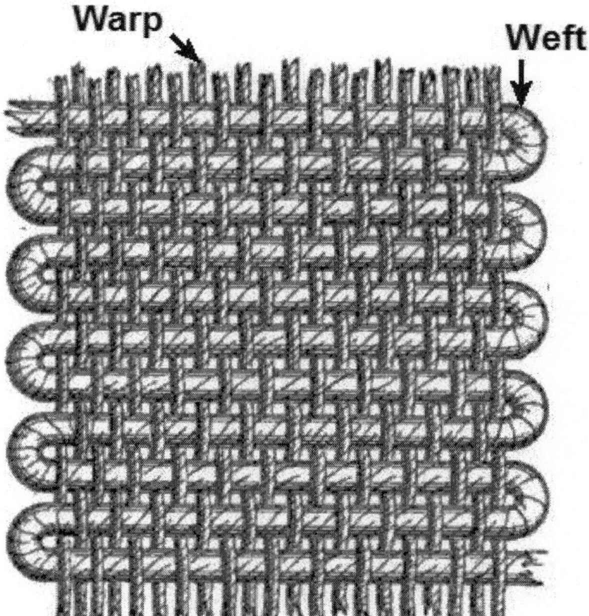

Figure: *Warp and weft in plain weaving*

Process and Terminology

In general, weaving involves using a loom to interlace two sets of threads at right angles to each other: the warp which runs longitudinally and the weft (older *woof*) that crosses it.

One warp thread is called an end and one weft thread is called a pick. The warp threads are held taut and in parallel to each other, typically in a loom. There are many types of looms.

Weaving can be summarized as a repetition of these three actions, also called the primary motion of the loom.

- Shedding: where the ends are separated by raising or lowering heald frames (heddles) to form a clear space where the pick can pass
- Picking:where the weft or pick is propelled across the loom by hand, an air-jet, a rapier or a shuttle.
- Beating-up or battening: where the weft is pushed up against the fell of the cloth by the reed.

The warp is divided into two overlapping groups, or lines (most often adjacent threads belonging to the opposite group) that run in two planes, one above another, so the shuttle can be passed between them in a straight motion.

Then, the upper group is lowered by the loom mechanism, and the lower group is raised (shedding), allowing to pass the shuttle in the opposite direction, also in a straight motion. Repeating these actions form a fabric mesh but without beating-up, the final distance between the adjacent wefts would be irregular and far too large.

The secondary motion of the loom are the:

- Let off Motion: where the warp is let off the warp beam at a regulated speed to make the filling even and of the required design
- Take up Motion: Takes up the woven fabric in a regulated manner so that the density of filling is maintained

The tertiary motions of the loom are the stop motions: to stop the loom in the event of a thread break. The two main stop motions are the

- warp stop motion
- weft stop motion

The principal parts of a loom are the frame, the warp-beam or weavers beam, the cloth-roll (apron bar), the heddles, and their mounting, the reed. The warp-beam is a wooden or metal cylinder on the back of the loom on which the warp is delivered.

The threads of the warp extend in parallel order from the warp-beam to the front of the loom where they are attached to the cloth-roll. Each thread or group of threads of the warp passes through an opening (eye) in a heddle.

The warp threads are separated by the heddles into two or more groups, each controlled and automatically drawn up and down by the motion of the heddles. In the case of small patterns the movement of the heddles is controlled by "cams" which move up the heddles by means of a frame called a harness; in larger patterns the heddles are controlled by a dobby mechanism, where the healds are raised according to pegs inserted into a revolving drum.

Where a complex design is required, the healds are raised by harness cords attached to a Jacquard machine. Every time the harness (the heddles) moves up or down, an opening (shed) is made between the threads of warp, through which the pick is inserted. Traditionally the weft thread is inserted by a shuttle.

On a conventional loom, the weft thread is carried on a pirn, in a shuttle that passes through the shed. A handloom weaver could propel the shuttle by throwing it from side to side with the aid of a picking stick.

The "picking¡ on a power loom is done by rapidly hitting the shuttle from each side using an overpick or underpick mechanism controlled by cams 80-250 times a minute. When a pirn is depleted, it is ejected from the shuttle and replaced with the next pirn held in a battery attached to the loom. Multiple shuttle boxes allow more than one shuttle to be used. Each can carry a different colour which allows banding across the loom.

The rapier-type weaving machines do not have shuttles, they propel the weft by means of small grippers or rapiers that pick up the filling thread and carry it halfway across the loom where another rapier picks it up and pulls it the rest of the way. Some carry the filling yarns across the loom at rates in excess of 2,000 metres per minute.

Manufacturers such as Picanol have reduced the mechanical adjustments to a minimum, and control all the functions through a computer with a graphical user interface.Other types use compressed air to insert the pick. They are all fast, versatile and quiet.

The warp is sized in a starch mixture for smoother running. The loom warped (loomed or dressed) by passing the sized warp threads through two or more heddles attached to harnesses. The power weavers loom is warped by separate workers. Most looms used for industrial purposes have a machine that ties new warps threads to the waste of previously used warps threads, while still on the loom, then an operator rolls the old and new threads back on the warp beam. The harnesses are controlled by cams, dobbies or a Jacquard head.

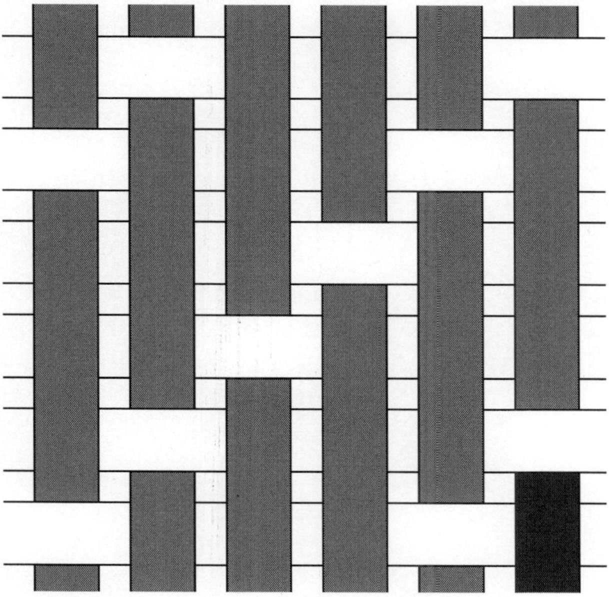

Figure: *A 3/1 twill, as used in denim*

The raising and lowering sequence of warp threads in various sequences gives rise to many possible weave structures:

- plain weave: plain, and hopsacks, poplin, taffeta, poult-de-soie, pibiones and grosgrain.
- twill weave: these are described by weft float followed by warp float, arranged to give diagonal pattern. 2/1 twill, 3/3 twill, 1/2 twill. These are softer fabrics than plain weaves.,
- satin weave: satins and sateens,
- complex computer-generated interlacings.
- pile fabrics : such as velvets and velveteens

Both warp and weft can be visible in the final product. By spacing the warp more closely, it can completely cover the weft that binds it, giving a *warp faced* textile such as repp weave. Conversely, if the warp is spread out, the weft can slide down and completely cover the warp, giving a *weft faced* textile, such as a tapestry or a Kilim rug. There are a variety of loom styles for hand weaving and tapestry.

History

There are some indications that weaving was already known in the Paleolithic era. An indistinct textile impression has been found at Pavlov, Moravia. Neolithic textiles are well known from finds from the advanced civilisation preserved in the pile dwellings in Switzerland. One extant fragment from the Neolithic was found in Fayum, at a site dated to about 5000 BCE.

This fragment is woven at about 12 threads by 9 threads per cm in a plain weave. Flax was the predominant fibre in Egypt at this time (3600 BCE) and continued popularity in the Nile Valley, though wool became the primary fibre used in other cultures around 2000 BCE.

By biblical times, weaving was known in all the great civilisations, but no clear line of causality has been established. Early looms required two people to create the shed, and one person to pass through the filling. Early looms wove a fixed length of cloth, but later ones allowed warp to be wound out as the fell progressed. The weavers were often children or slaves. Weaving became simpler when the warp was sized.

Islamic World

In 700 AD, horizontal looms and vertical looms could be found in many parts of Asia, Africa and Europe. One of the innovations of the Islamic Golden Age was the pit-treadle loom where pedals were added to operate heddles. The first such devices appeared in Syria, Iran and Islamic parts of East Africa, where "the operator sat with his feet in a pit below a fairly low-slung loom.". Islam required the faithful to cover themselves from neck to ankle, increasing the demand for cloth.

In Africa, the rich would dress in cotton while the poorer would wear wool. By 1177, it was further developed in Moorish Spain, where the mechanism was raised higher above the ground on a more substantial frame. The idea was adopted by Christian woollen weavers, particularly in Flanders. This became the standard European loom, it had the great advantage that the weavers hands were free to pass the shuttle, while the monotonous job of operating the heddles was done by the feet.

Medieval Europe

The predominant fibre was wool, followed by linen and nettlecloth for the lower classes. Cotton was introduced to Sicily and Spain in the 800s. When Sicily was captured by the Normans, they took the technology to Northern Italy and then the rest of Europe. Silk fabric production was reintroduced towards the end of this period and the more sophisticated silk weaving technoiques were applied to the other staples.

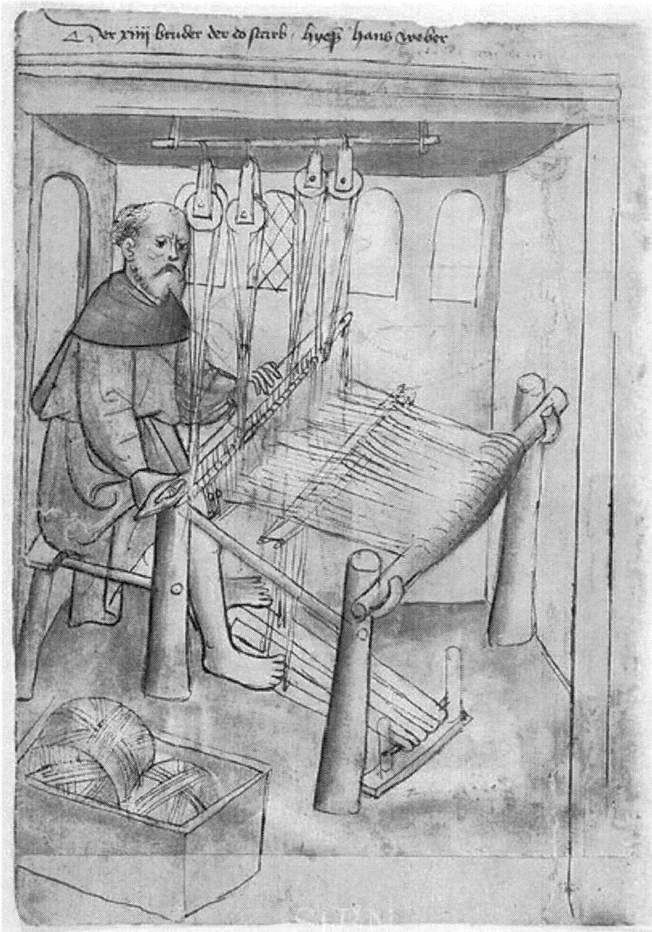

Figure: *Weaver, Nürnberg, c. 1425*

The weaver worked at home and marketed his cloth at fairs. Warp-weighted looms were commonplace in Europe before the introduction of horizontal looms in the 10th and 11th centuries. Weaving became an urban craft and to regulate their trade, craftsmen applied to establish a guild.

These initially were merchant guilds, but developed into separate trade guilds for each skill. The cloth merchant who was a member of a city's weavers guild was allowed to sell cloth; he acted as a middleman between the tradesmen weavers and the purchaser. The trade guilds controlled quality and the training needed before an artisan could call himself a weaver.

By the 13th century, an organisational change took place, and a system of putting out was introduced. The cloth merchant purchased the wool and provided it to the weaver, who sold his produce back to the merchant. The merchant controlled the rates of pay and economically dominated the cloth industry.

The merchants' prosperity is reflected in the wool towns of eastern England; Norwich, Bury St Edmunds and Lavenham being good examples. Wool was a political issue. The supply of thread has always limited the output of a weaver. About that time, the spindle method of spinning was replaced by the great wheel and soon after the treadle-driven spinning wheel. The loom remained the same but with the increased volume of thread it could be operated continuously.

The 14th century saw considerable flux in population. The 13th century had been a period of relative peace; Europe became overpopulated. Poor weather led to a series of poor harvests and starvation.

There was great loss of life in the Hundred Years War. Then in 1346, Europe was struck with the Black Death and the population was reduced by up to a half. Arable land was labour-intensive and sufficient workers no longer could be found. Land prices dropped, and land was sold and put to sheep pasture.

Traders from Florence and Bruges bought the wool, then sheep-owning landlords started to weave wool outside the jurisdiction of the city and trade guilds. The weavers started by working in their own homes then production was moved into purpose-built buildings. The working hours and the amount of work were regulated. The putting-out system had been replaced by a factory system.

Huguenot Weavers

Huguenot Weavers, Calvinists, fleeing from religious persecution migrated from mainland Europe to Britain around 1685. They came from Flanders and the great silk weaving cities of France such as Lyon and Tours and settled firstly in Canterbury; then some 13,050 moved to Spitalfields in London. Others moved further to the silk weaving town ofMacclesfield. Their arrival challenged the English cotton, woolen and worsted weavers, who consequently learned the Huguenots superior techniques.

Weaving in the American Colonies (1500-1800)

Colonial America was heavily reliant on Great Britain for manufactured goods of all kinds. British policy was to encourage the production of raw materials in colonies. The Wool Act 1699 restricted the export of Colonial wool. As a result many people wove cloth from the locally produced fibres. The colonists also used wool, cotton and flax (linen) for weaving, though hemp could be made into serviceable canvas and heavy cloth. They could get one cotton crop each year; until the invention of the cotton gin it was a labour-intensive process to separate the seeds from the fibres.

A plain weave was preferred as the added skill and time required to make more complex weaves kept them from common use. Sometimes designs were woven into the fabric but most were added after weaving using wood block prints or embroidery.

Industrial Revolution

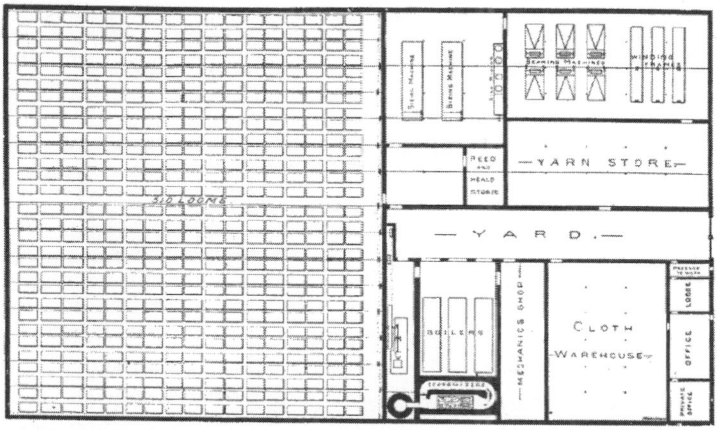

Figure: *By 1892, most cotton weaving was done in similar weaving sheds, powered by steam.*

Before the Industrial Revolution, weaving was a manual craft and wool was the principal staple. In the great wool districts a form of factory system had been introduced but in the uplands weavers worked from home on a putting-out system.

The wooden looms of that time might be broad or narrow; broad looms were those too wide for the weaver to pass the shuttle through the shed, so that the weaver needed an expensive assistant (often an apprentice). This ceased to be necessary after John Kay invented the flying shuttle in 1733.

The shuttle and the picking stick sped up the process of weaving. There was thus a shortage of thread or a surplus of weaving capacity. The opening of the Bridgewater Canal in June 1761 allowed cotton to brought into the Manchester, an area rich in fast flowing streams that could be used to power machinery. Spinning was the first to be mechanised (spinning jenny, spinning mule), and this led to limitless thread for the weaver.

Edmund Cartwright was the first to attempt to mechanise weaving from 1785. He built a factory at Doncaster and obtained a series of patents between 1785 and 1792. In 1788, his brother Major John Cartwight built Revolution Mill at Retford (named for the centenary of the Glorious Revolution).

In 1791, he licensed his loom to the Grimshaw brothers of Manchester, but their Knott Mill burnt down the following year (possibly a case of arson). Edmund Cartwight was granted a reward of £10,000 by Parliament for his efforts in 1809. However, success in power-weaving also required improvements by others, including H. Horrocks of Stockport.

Only during the two decades after about 1805, did power-weaving take hold. At that time there were 250,000 hand weavers in the UK. Textile manufacture was one of the leading sectors in the British Industrial Revolution, but weaving was a comparatively late sector to be mechanised. The loom became semi-automatic in 1842 with Kenworthy and Bulloughs Lancashire Loom.

The various innovations took weaving from a home-based artisan activity (labour intensive and man-powered) to steam driven factories process. A large metal manufacturing industry grew to produce the looms, firms such as Howard & Bullough of Accrington, and Tweedales and Smalley and Platt Brothers. Most power weaving took place in weaving sheds, in small towns circling Greater Manchester away from the cotton spinning area.

The earlier combination mills where spinning and weaving took place in adjacent buildings became rarer. Wool and worsted weaving took place in West Yorkshire and particular Bradford, here there were large factories such as Lister's or Drummond's, where all the processes took place. Both men and women with weaving skills emigrated, and took the knowledge to their new homes in New England, to places like Pawtucket and Lowell.

Woven 'grey cloth' was then sent to the finishers where it was bleached, dyed and printed. Natural dyes were originally used, with synthetic dyes coming in the second half of the 19th century. The need for these chemicals was an important factor in the development of the chemical industry.

The invention in France of the Jacquard loom in about 1803, enabled complicated patterned cloths to be woven, by using punched cards to determine which threads of coloured yarn should appear on the upper side of the cloth. The jacquard allowed individual control of each warp thread, row by row without repeating, so very complex patterns were suddenly feasible. Samples exist showing calligraphy, and woven copies of engravings. Jacquards could be attached to handlooms or powerlooms.

The Role of the Weaver

A distinction can be made between the role and lifestyle and status of a handloom weaver, and that of the powerloom weaver and craft weaver. The perceived threat of the power loom has led to disquiet and industrial unrest. Well known protests movements such as the Luddites and the Chartists had hand loom weavers amongst their leaders. In the early 19th century power weaving became viable. Richard Guest in 1823 made a comparison of the productivity of power and hand loom weavers:

A very good Hand Weaver, a man twenty-five or thirty years of age, will weave two pieces of nine-eighths shirting per week, each twenty-four yards long, and containing one hundred and five shoots of weft in an inch, the reed of the cloth being a forty-four, Bolton count, and the warp and weft forty hanks to the pound, A Steam Loom Weaver, fifteen years of age, will in the same time

Weave Seven Similar Pieces.

He then speculates about the wider economics of using powerloom weavers:...it may very safely be said, that the work done in a Steam Factory containing two hundred Looms, would, if done by hand Weavers, find employment and support for a population of more than two thousand persons.

Hand Loom Weavers

Hand loom weavers were mainly men- due to the strength needed to batten. They worked from home sometimes in a well lit attic room. The women of the house would spin the thread they needed, and attend to finishing. Later women took to weaving, they obtained their thread from the spinning mill, and working as outworkers on a piecework contract. Over time competition from the power looms drove down the piece rate and they existed in increasing poverty.

Power Loom Weavers

Power loom workers were usually girls and young women. They had the security of fixed hours, and except in times of hardship such as in the cotton famine regular income. They were paid a wage and a piece work bonus. Even when working in a combined mill, weavers stuck together and enjoyed a tight-knit community. The women usually minded the four machines and kept the looms oiled and clean. They were assisted by 'little tenters', children who on a fixed wage ran errands and did small tasks. They learnt the job of the weaver by watching. Often they would be half timers, carrying a green card which teacher and overlookers would sign to say they had turned up at the mill in the morning and in the afternoon at the school.

At fourteen or so they come full-time into the mill, and started by sharing looms with an experienced worker where it was important to learn quickly as they would both be on piece work. Serious problems with the loom were left to the tackler to sort out. He would inevitably be a man, as were usually the overlookers.

The mill had its health and safety issues, there was a reason why the women tied their hair back with scarves. Inhaling cotton dust caused lung problems, and the noise was causing total hearing loss. Weavers would mee-maw as normal conversation was impossible. Weavers used to 'kiss the shutttle' that is suck thread though the eye of the shuttle- this left a foul taste in the mouth due to the oil which was also carcinogenic.

Craft Weavers

Arts and Crafts was an international design philosophy that originated in England and flourished between 1860 and 1910 (especially the second half of that period), continuing its influence until the 1930s. Instigated by the artist and writer William Morris (1834–1896) during the 1860s and inspired by the writings of John Ruskin (1819–1900), it had its earliest and most complete development in the British Isles but spread to Europe and North America.

It was largely a reaction against mechanisation and the philosophy advocated of traditional craftsmanship using simple forms and often medieval, romantic or folk styles of decoration. Hand weaving was highly regard and taken up as a decorative art. Female students at the Bauhaus which adopted some of its philosophy, were directed to study in the Weaving Workshop. The weaver was thus a student of art, and yet again predominantly female. With the growth of leisure in the late 20th century, weaving became a popular pastime.

Wire Weavers

Weaving is not just confined to traditional materials such as Yarn and thin woods. Wire weaving is a technique used by jewellers around the world. Often regional traditional weaving techniques are interpreted into wire form to create art work, jewellery and occasional items of apparel.

Not to be confused with wire wrapping, wire weaving follows traditional on and off loom weaving techniques. Well renowned artists and design houses include Mary Lee Hu, Stuart Golder, Yuri Ichihashi, Knitted & Kitted, Boucheron and Kazumi Nagano. Wires are generally drawn out to extremely fine strands and consist of a wide range of precious metals such as Gold, Silver and Copper.

Examples of this work are displayed in a number of notable gallaries including the Victoria & Albert Museum in London and the Facere Gallery.

Other Cultures

Andean Civilizations: Whereas European cloth-making generally created ornamentation through "suprastructural" means—by adding embroidery, ribbons, brocade, dyeing, and other elements onto the finished woven textile—pre-Columbian Andean weavers created elaborate cloth by focusing on "structural" designs involving manipulation of the warp and weft of the fabric itself. Andeans used "tapestry techniques; double-, triple- and quadruple-cloth techniques; gauze weaves; warp-patterned weaves; discontinuous warp or scaffold weaves; and plain weaves" among many other techniques, in addition to the suprastructural techniques listed above.

American Southwest

Textile weaving, using cotton dyed with pigments, was a dominant craft among pre-contact tribes of the American southwest, including various Pueblo peoples, the Zuni, and the Ute tribes. The first Spaniards to visit the region wrote about seeing Navajo blankets. With the introduction of Navajo-Churro sheep, the resulting woolen products have become very well known.

By the 18th century the Navajo had begun to import yarn with their favorite colour, Bayeta red. Using an upright loom, the Navajos wove blankets worn as garments and then rugs after the 1880s for trade. Navajo traded for commercial wool, such as Germantown, imported from Pennsylvania.

Under the influence of European-American settlers at trading posts, Navajos created new and distinct styles, including "Two Gray Hills" (predominantly black and white, with traditional patterns), "Teec Nos Pos" (colourful, with very extensive patterns), "Ganado" (founded by Don Lorenzo Hubbell), red dominated patterns with black and white, "Crystal" (founded by J. B. Moore), Oriental and Persian styles (almost always with natural dyes), "Wide Ruins," "Chinlee," banded geometric patterns, "Klagetoh," diamond type patterns, "Red Mesa" and bold diamond patterns. Many of these patterns exhibit a fourfold symmetry, which is thought to embody traditional ideas about harmony, or *hózhó*.

Amazonia

In Native Amazonia, densely woven palm-bast mosquito netting, or tents, were utilized by the Panoans, Tupinambá, Western Tucano, Yameo, Záparoans, and perhaps by the indigenous peoples of the central Huallaga River basin (Steward 1963:520). Aguaje palm-bast (Mauritia flexuosa, Mauritia minor, or swamp palm) and the frond spears of the Chambira palm (Astrocaryum chambira, A.munbaca, A.tucuma, also known as Cumare or Tucum) have been used for centuries by the Urarina of the Peruvian Amazon to make cordage, net-bags hammocks, and to weave fabric. Among the Urarina, the production of woven palm-fibre goods is imbued with varying degrees of an aesthetic attitude, which draws its authentication from referencing the Urarina's primordial past. Urarina mythology attests to the centrality of weaving and its role in engendering Urarina society. The post-diluvial creation myth accords women's weaving knowledge a pivotal role in Urarina social reproduction. Even though palm-fibre cloth is regularly removed from circulation through mortuary rites, Urarina palm-fibre wealth is neither completely inalienable, nor fungible since it is a fundamental medium for the expression of labour and exchange. The circulation of palm-fibre wealth stabilizes a host of social relationships, ranging from marriage and fictive kinship (*compadrazco*, spiritual compeership) to perpetuating relationships with the deceased.

Yarn

Yarn is a long continuous length of interlocked fibres, suitable for use in the production of textiles, sewing, crocheting, knitting, weaving, embroidery, and ropemaking. Thread is a type of yarn intended for sewing by hand or machine. Modern manufactured sewing threads may be finished with wax or other lubricants to withstand the stresses involved in sewing. Embroidery threads are yarns specifically designed for hand or machine embroidery.

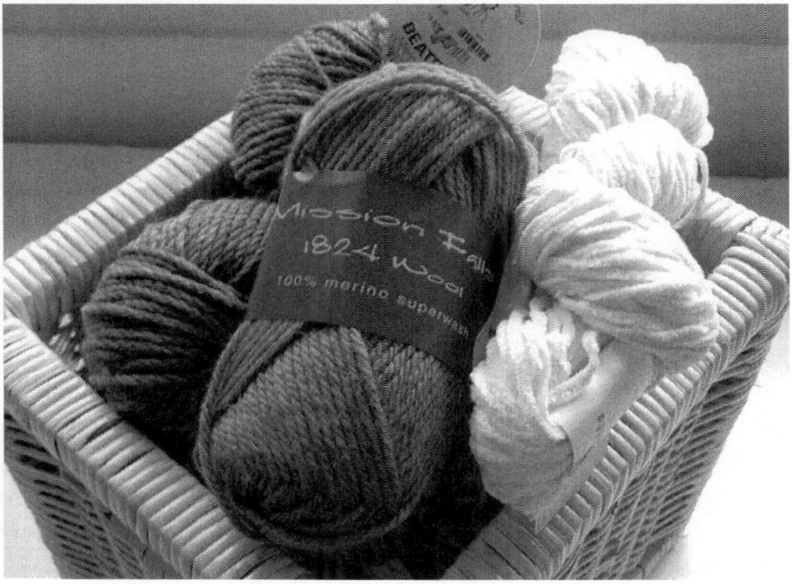

Figure: *Yarn*

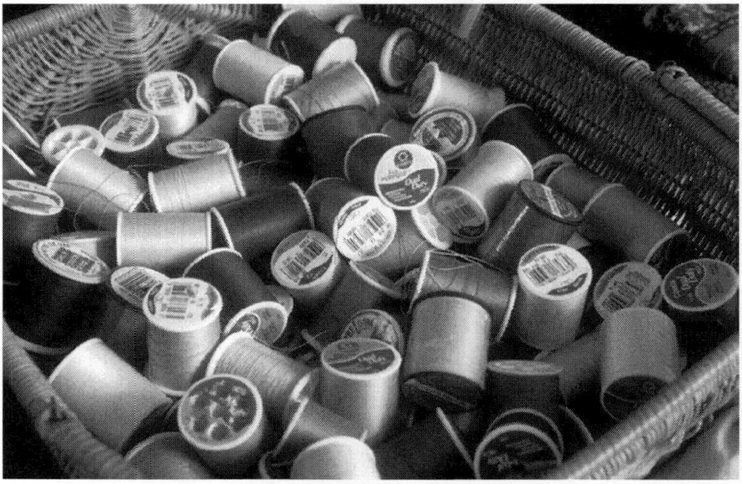

Figure: *Spools of thread*

The word yarn comes from Middle English, from the Old English *gearn*, akin to Old High German's *garn* yarn, Greek's *chordç* string, and Sanskrit's *hira* band.

Materials

Yarn can be made from any number of natural or synthetic fibres.

Natural Fibres

The most common plant fibre is cotton, which is typically spun into fine yarn for mechanical weaving or knitting into cloth. The most commonly used animal fibre is wool harvested from sheep. For hand knitting and hobby knitting, thick, wool yarns are frequently used.

Other animal fibres used include alpaca, angora, mohair, llama, cashmere, and silk. More rarely, yarn may be spun from camel, yak, possum, qiviut, cat, dog, wolf, rabbit, or buffalo hair, and even turkey or ostrich feathers. Natural fibres such as these have the advantage of being slightly elastic and very breathable, while trapping a great deal of air, making for a fairly warm fabric. Also the "yarn" can be made out of the Cameron tree.

Other natural fibres that can be used for yarn include linen and cotton. These tend to be much less elastic, and retain less warmth than the animal-hair yarns, though they can be stronger in some cases. The finished product will also look rather different from the woollen yarns. Other plant fibres which can be spun include bamboo, hemp, corn, nettle, and soy fibre.

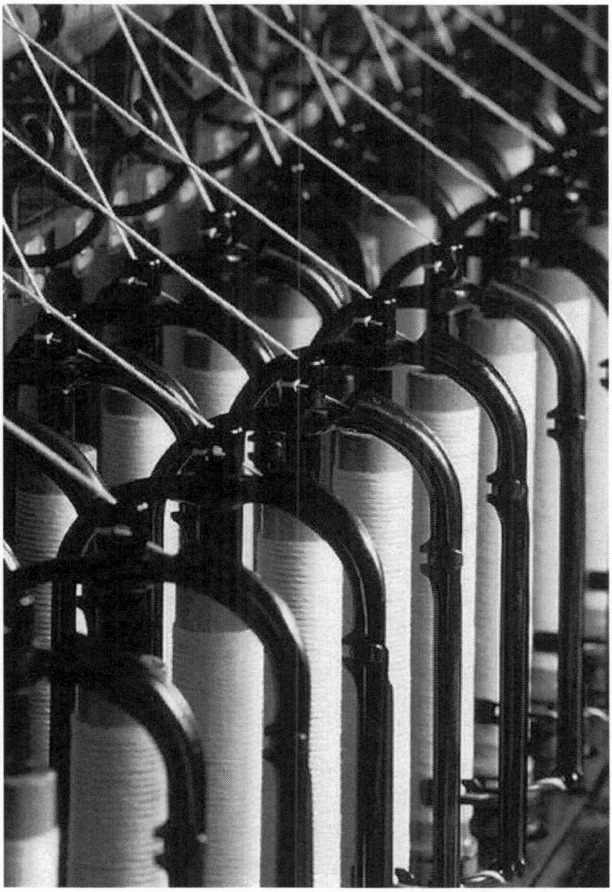

Figure: *Cotton being spun*

Comparison of Material Properties

In general, natural fibres tend to require more careful handling than synthetics because they can shrink, felt, stain, shed, fade, stretch, wrinkle, or be eaten by moths more readily, unless special treatments such as mercerization or superwashing are performed to strengthen, fix colour, or otherwise enhance the fibre's own properties.

Protein yarns (i.e., hair, silk, feathers) may also be irritating to some people, causing contact dermatitis, hives, wheezing, or other reactions.

Plant fibres tend to be better tolerated by people with sensitivities to the protein yarns, and allergists may suggest using them or synthetics instead to prevent symptoms.

Some people find that they can tolerate organically grown and processed versions of protein fibres, possibly because organic processing standards preclude the use of chemicals that may irritate the skin.

When natural fibres are burned, they tend to singe and have a smell of burnt hair; synthetic yarns tend to melt.

Noting how an unidentified fibre strand burns and smells can assist in determining if it is natural or synthetic.

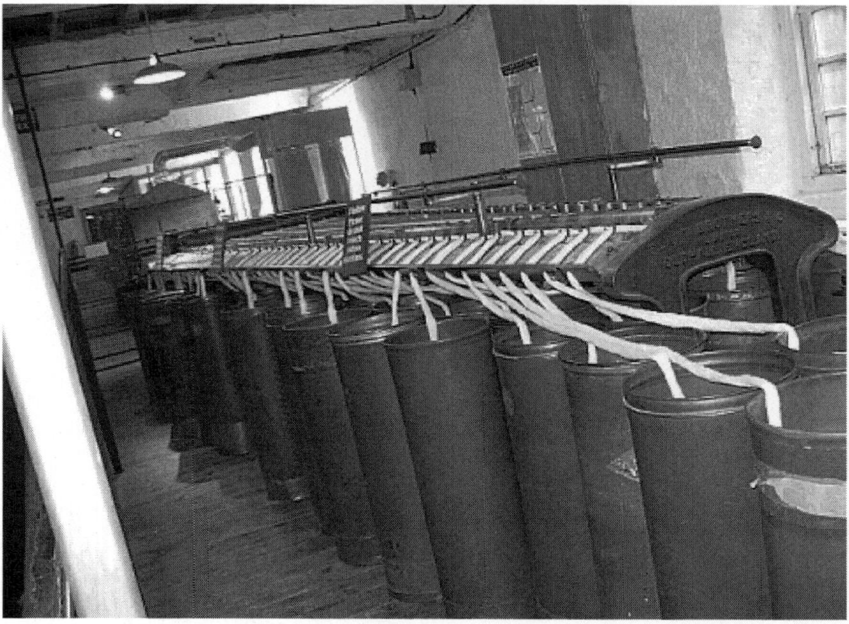

Figure: *A full restored and operative primary-level spinning machine taking freshly carded cotton tails from barrels and spinning them into yarn at the Quarry Bank Mill in the UK.*

Synthetic yarns, because of their construction as long, extruded strands, do not pill the way natural yarns can.

Yarns combining synthetic and natural materials inherit the properties of each parent, according to the proportional composition.

Synthetics are added to lower cost, increase durability, add unusual colour or visual effects, provide machine washability and stain resistance, reduce heat retention or lighten garment weight.

Structure

Spun yarn is made by twisting or otherwise bonding staple fibres together to make a cohesive thread, or "single."

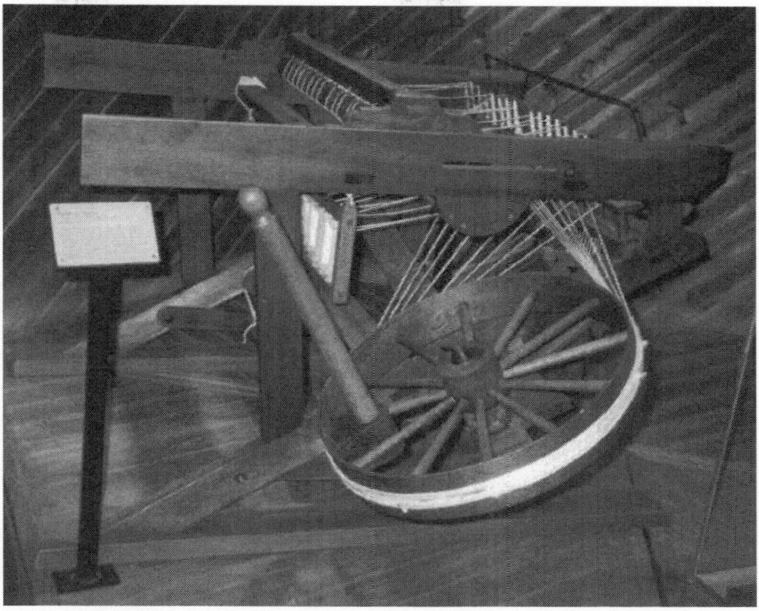

Figure: *A Spinning Jenny, spinning machine which was significant in the beginning of the Industrial Revolution*

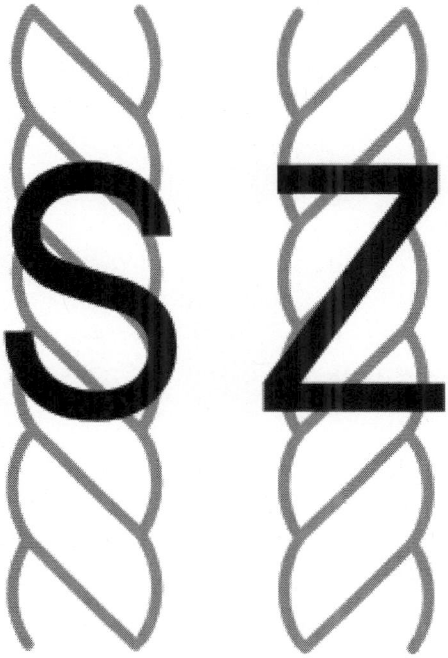

Figure: *S- and Z-twist yarn*

Twisting fibres into yarn in the process called spinning can be dated back to the Upper Paleolithic, and yarn spinning was one of the very first processes to be industrialized.

Spun yarns may contain a single type of fibre, or be a blend of various types. Combining synthetic fibres (which can have high strength, lustre, and fire retardant qualities) with natural fibres (which have good water absorbency and skin comforting qualities) is very common.

The most widely used blends are cotton-polyester and wool-acrylic fibre blends. Blends of different natural fibres are common too, especially with more expensive fibres such as alpaca, angora and cashmere. Bamboo yarn is a less expensive yarn that is a recent innovation.

Yarns are selected for different textiles based on the characteristics of the yarn fibres, such as warmth (wool), light weight (cotton or bamboo), durability (nylon is added to sock yarn, for example), or softness (cashmere, alpaca). Acrylic yarn is the least expensive.

Yarns are made up of a number of singles, which are known as plies when grouped together. These singles of yarn are twisted together (plied) in the opposite direction to make a thicker yarn. Depending on the direction of this final twist, the yarn will be known as *s twist* or *z twist*. For a single, the direction of the final twist is the same as its original twist.

Filament yarn consists of filament fibres (very long continuous fibres) either twisted together or only grouped together. Thicker monofilaments are typically used for industrial purposes rather than fabric production or decoration. Silk is a natural filament, and synthetic filament yarns are used to produce silk-like effects. Texturized yarns are made by a process of air texturizing (sometimes referred to as *taslanizing*), which combines multiple filament yarns into a yarn with some of the characteristics of spun yarns.

Colour

Yarn may be used undyed, or may be coloured with natural or artificial dyes. Most yarns have a single uniform hue, but there is also a wide selection of variegated yarns:

- Heathered or tweed: yarn with flecks of different coloured fibre
- Ombre: variegated yarn with light and dark shades of a single hue

- Multicoloured: variegated yarn with two or more distinct hues (a "parrot colourway" might have green, yellow and red)
- Self-striping: yarn dyed with lengths of colour that will automatically create stripes in a knitted or crocheted object
- Marled: yarn made from strands of different-coloured yarn twisted together, sometimes in closely related hues

Measurement

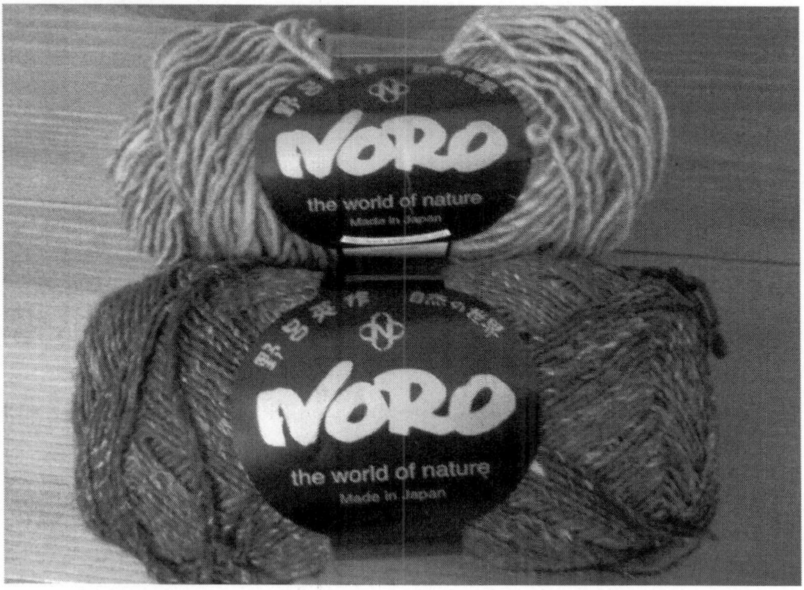

Figure: *A comparison of yarn weights (thicknesses): the top skein is aran weight, suitable for knitting a thick sweater or hat. The manufacturer's recommended knitting gauge appears on the label: 8 to 10 stitches per inch using size 4.5 to 5.1 mm needles. The bottom skein is sock weight, specifically for knitting socks. Recommended gauge: 5 to 7 stitches per inch, using size 3.6 to 4.2 mm needles. These yarns are manufactured in Japan and have variegated colours in a random-dyed pattern.*

Yarn quantities are usually measured by weight in ounces or grams. In the United States, Canada and Europe, balls of yarn for handcrafts are sold by weight. Common sizes include 25 g, 50 g, and 100 g skeins. Some companies also primarily measure in ounces with common sizes being three-ounce, four-ounce, six-ounce, and eight-ounce skeins. These measurements are taken at a standard temperature and humidity, because yarn can absorb moisture from the air. The actual length of the yarn contained in a ball or skein can vary due to the inherent heaviness of the fibre and the thickness of the strand; for instance, a 50 g skein of lace weight mohair may contain several hundred metres, while a 50 g skein of bulky wool may contain only 60 metres.

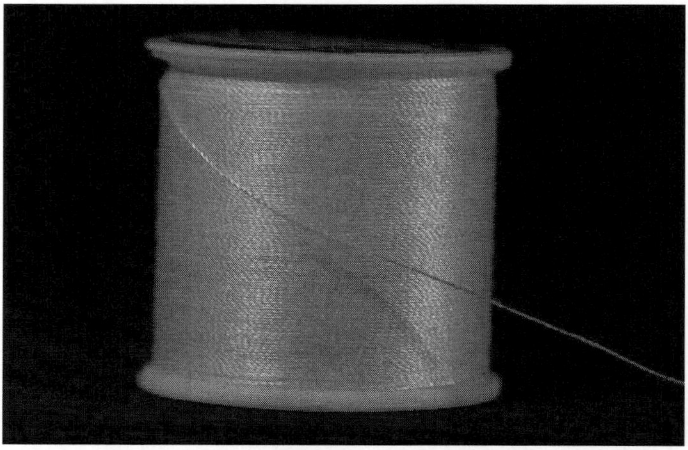

Figure: *Spool of all purpose sewing thread, closeup shows texture of 2 ply, Z twist, mercerized cotton with polyester core.*

There are several thicknesses of yarn, also referred to as weight. This is not to be confused with the measurement and/or weight listed above. The Craft Yarn Council of America is making an effort to promote a standardized industry system for measuring this, numbering the weights from 1 (finest) to 6 (heaviest). Some of the names for the various weights of yarn from finest to thickest are called lace, fingering, sport, double-knit (or DK), worsted, aran (or heavy worsted), bulky, and super-bulky. This naming convention is more descriptive than precise; fibre artists disagree about where on the continuum each lies, and the precise relationships between the sizes.

A more precise measurement of yarn weight, often used by weavers, is wraps per inch (WPI). The yarn is wrapped snugly around a ruler and the number of wraps that fit in an inch are counted.

Labels on yarn for handicrafts often include information on gauge, known in the UK as tension, which is a measurement of how many stitches and rows are produced per inch or per cm on a specified size of knitting needle or crochet hook. The proposed standardization uses a four-by-four inch/ten-by-ten cm knitted or crocheted square, with the resultant number of stitches across and rows high made by the suggested tools on the label to determine the gauge.

In Europe, textile engineers often use the unit tex, which is the weight in grams of a kilometre of yarn, or decitex, which is a finer measurement corresponding to the weight in grams of 10 km of yarn. Many other units have been used over time by different industries.

Some yarn retail stores try to help the customer choose yarn by attaching a sample knitted square to the shelf holding each display of a particular weight of yarn, sometimes provided by the manufacturer. These samples are knit in the industry standard four-by-four inch / ten-by-ten centimetre gauge. Samples help the buyer by showing them the texture and thickness of the finished knit fabric.

Crochet Thread

Crochet thread is specially formulated thread usually made from mercerized cotton for crafting decorative crochet items such as doilies or filet crochet. Crochet thread produces fabric of fine gauge that may be stiffened with starch.

Differences From Yarn and Sewing Thread

Crochet thread is almost always produced from cotton and has a denser pile and smaller diameter than ordinary yarn. Most crochet threads are thicker in diameter than sewing thread. Crochet thread can withstand considerable stresses from pulls with sharp hooks.

Crochet manufacturing conventions treat thread and yarn quite differently: manufacturers designate different sizing scales for thread and yarn. Thread is generally packaged on spools instead of skeins or hanks and is offered for sale in a separate section from ordinary yarns or threads. Crochet hooks for use with thread are also sized according to a different scale from yarn hooks. Thread hooks are also manufactured differently from yarn hooks: modern yarn hooks are usually aluminium or plastic, while thread hooks are made of steel and have smaller hook heads and shorter shanks.

The division between yarn and thread is somewhat arbitrary: crochet thread at its thickest is similar in diameter and behaviour to fine cotton yarn. The largest sizes of thread crochet hooks overlap with the smallest sizes of yarn crochet hooks.

Sizing

Crochet thread comes in sizes from 3 to 100, although historically it came in much finer sizes, down to 200. Diameter is inversely proportional to number, so size 3 is nearly as thick as yarn and size

100 is as fine as sewing thread. Thread may also be categorized by number of plies and size 10 thread is known as *bedspread weight*. Smaller sizes (40 and up) are rarely used anymore.

Embroidery Thread

Embroidery thread is yarn that is manufactured or hand-spun specifically for embroidery and other forms of needlework.

Threads for hand embroidery include:

- Crewel yarn is a fine 2-ply yarn of wool or, less often, a wool-like acrylic.
- Embroidery floss or stranded cotton is a loosely twisted, slightly glossy 6-strand thread, usually of cotton but also manufactured in silk, linen, and rayon.

  Cotton floss is the standard thread for cross-stitch. Extremely shiny rayon floss is characteristic of Brazilian embroidery. Historically, stranded silk embroidery threads were described as sleaved or sleided in the sixteenth century.
- Filoselle is a historical term for embroidery floss made using the left-over waste from reeled silk.
- Matte embroidery cotton or French *coton à broder* is a matte-finish (not glossy) twisted 5-ply thread.
- Medici or *broder medici* is a fine, light-weight wool thread formerly manufactured by DMC Group.
- Perle cotton, pearl cotton, or French *coton perlé* is an S-twisted, 2-ply thread with high sheen, sold in five sizes or weights (No. 3, 5, 8, 12 and 16 (Finca), with 3 being the heaviest and 16 the finest).
- Persian yarn is a loosely twisted 3-strand yarn of wool or acrylic, often used for needlepoint.
- Tapestry yarn or tapestry wool is a tightly twisted 4-ply yarn.

Threads for machine embroidery are usually of polyester or rayon (less often cotton or silk).

Threads, like textiles, can contain compounds that may be harmful to humans. Many dyes have been shown to be allergenic and in some cases carcinogenic. Testing for the presence of these dyes, and other additives can be done at many commercial laboratories.

Certification to the Oeko-tex standard may also be applied for. This tests the component for over 100 different chemicals and certifies the component according to human ecological safety.

ISO 2

ISO 2 is an international standard for direction of twist designation for yarns, complex yarns, slivers, slubbings, rovings, cordage, and related products. The convention of using these two letters to unambiguously designate twist direction was already used in the cordage industry by 1957.

The standard uses capital letters S and Z to indicate the direction of twist, as suggested by the direction of slant of the central portions of these two letters. The handedness of the twist is the direction of the twists as they progress away from an observer. Thus Z-twist is said to be right-handed, and S-twist to be left-handed.

Yarn Bombing

Yarn bombing, yarnbombing, yarn storming, guerrilla knitting, urban knitting or graffiti knitting is a type of graffiti or street art that employs colourful displays of knitted or crocheted yarn or fibre rather than paint or chalk.

Method and Motivation

While yarn installations – called yarn bombs or yarnstorms – may last for years, they are considered non-permanent, and, unlike other forms of graffiti, can be easily removed if necessary. Nonetheless, the practice is still technically illegal in some jurisdictions, though it is not often prosecuted vigorously.

While other forms of graffiti may be expressive, decorative, territorial, socio-political commentary, advertising or vandalism, yarn bombing was initially almost exclusively about reclaiming and personalizing sterile or cold public places.

It has since developed with groups graffiti knitting and crocheting worldwide, each with their own agendas and public graffiti knitting projects being run.

History

The practice is believed to have originated in the U.S. with Texas knitters trying to find a creative way to use their leftover and unfinished knitting projects, but it has since spread worldwide.

The start of this movement has been attributed to Magda Sayeg, 37, from Houston, who says she first got the idea in 2005 when she covered the door handle of her boutique with a custom-made cozy. Houston artist Bill Davenport was creating and exhibiting crochet-covered objects in Houston in the 1990s, and the *Houston Press* stated that "Bill Davenport could be called the grand old man of Houston crocheted sculpture."

Artist Shanon Schollian was knitting stump cozies in 2002 for clear cuts in Oregon. The Knit Knot Tree by the Jafagirls in Yellow Springs, Ohio gained international attention in 2008.

The movement moved on from simple 'cozies' with the innovation of the 'stitched story'. The concept has been attributed to Lauren O'Farrell (who creates her street art under the graffiti knitting name Deadly Knitshade), from London, UK, who founded the city's first graffiti knitting collective Knit the City.

The 'stitched story concept' uses handmade amigurumi creatures, characters and items to tell a narrative or show a theme. This was first recorded with the Knit the City collective's "Web of Woe" installation in August 2009.

The Knit the City collective were also the first to use O'Farrell's term 'yarnstorming' to describe their graffiti knitting, as an alternative to the more popular term 'yarnbombing'.

Yarn bombing's popularity has spread throughout the world. In Oklahoma City the Collected Thread store yarn bombed the Plaza District of the city on 9 September 2011 to celebrate their three-year anniversary as a functioning shop. and in Australia a group called the Twilight Taggers refer to themselves as 'fibre artists'. Joann Matvichuk of Lethbridge, Alberta founded International Yarnbombing Day, which was first observed on 11 June 2011.

African

The earliest surviving sub-Saharan African textiles are cloth fragments and parchment fragments that date to the ninth century BC from sites at Igbo Ukwu of the Igbo people of Nigeria. Some twelfth century cloth fragments date from the Tellem caves in Mali. Surviving thirteenth century samples originate from Benin City in Nigeria.

African textiles are a part of African cultural heritage that came to America along with the slave trade. As many slaves were skilled in the weaving, this skill was used as another form of income for the slave owner.

In most of Africa the weavers were men while the women spun the thread. The weavers in many of the countries were part of a caste-like group and sometimes slaves to noble families. In Yoruba compounds were used where master weavers would teach all the boys weaving and all the girls would learn to spin and dye the yarn. And children did some jobs too, like providing fabric and also weaved at a very young age of 4.

Some examples of African textiles are:

- Aso oke fabric - woven by Yoruba people
- Adire- tie-dye produced by Yoruba people
- Kente cloth - woven by Ashanti and Ewe people
- Barkcloth - produced by the Buganda tribe
- Mudcloth- produced by the Bambara tribe
- Kitenge - produced from Kenya and other regions of East Africa

Cultural Significance

Weaving has many spiritual and mythical meaning behind it. One, is that from the Dogons who believe that each stage of spinning and weaving thread is a symbolic analogy to human reproduction and resurrection. With this, they believe that the processes of spinning and weaving could only be done in daylight hours. To work at night would be to weave silence and darkness into the cloth. The colour of the cloth can also have some spiritual meaning. In one tribe a white cloth used by healing women is thought to be linked to water spirits. Although there are many meanings to the designs on the cloth very few are directly represented on the cloth itself.

Textiles were also used as a form of identity with each tribe having their own unique patterns which also made it easy to spot outsiders. Many different types of patterns were formed in places that specialized in weaving. Kings would request several types of cloth to show their prestige and importance. Kings would even compare themselves by how many robes they had and what they were made out of.

Weaving and the textiles were and still are very important to the African culture. The textiles included both men and women and the cloth they made was unique to their tribe through the patterns and spiritual meanings behind them. the designs also had aztec designs in Many centuries ago, hair from animals was woven to insulate and protect homes.

Hair, along with fibres from various plants and trees, were used to create bedding, blankets, clothing, and wall, window and door hangings. As textiles became more sophisticated, they were also used as currency for trading.

Many of the ancient designs and weaving methods are used today and remain an important part of African lifestyles. The main method of decorating cloth throughout Africa is the dyeing of thread or completed cloths.

Although there were a small range of locally produced plant dyes that allowed weavers in most areas to produce a few shades of brown, green, yellow, and in some cases red, by far the most important dye in Africa has been indigo.

The vast majority of cloth produced on the continent over the centuries was simple designs produced by combining the natural white (and sometimes beige) of the cotton fibres with stripes of various shades of indigo blue. Depending on the relative density of the warp and weft threads, the resulting cloths could have stripes down the strip (warp- faced) or across the strip (weft-faced.) They mostly wore the skin of the animal and some times wove the fur into a piece of clothing. The women wove the fabric and textiles.

Andean

Andean textiles represent a continuing textile tradition spanning at least ten thousand years. Fibrework has been found in Guitarrero Cave, Peru dates back to 8000 BCE. Beginning with non-loom, twined cotton fabric, this textile tradition expanded to include alpaca and llama wool. Today Andean weavers are known worldwide for their skills and rich traditions.

Origins

The Norte Chico civilization were the earliest known users of textiles in the Andes. They wove them of cotton. They were also the first to use the Quipu. The Quipu is a series of knotted strings that were used for accounting, using base 10, and also possibly as a binary logographic system of writing.

Quilted Armour

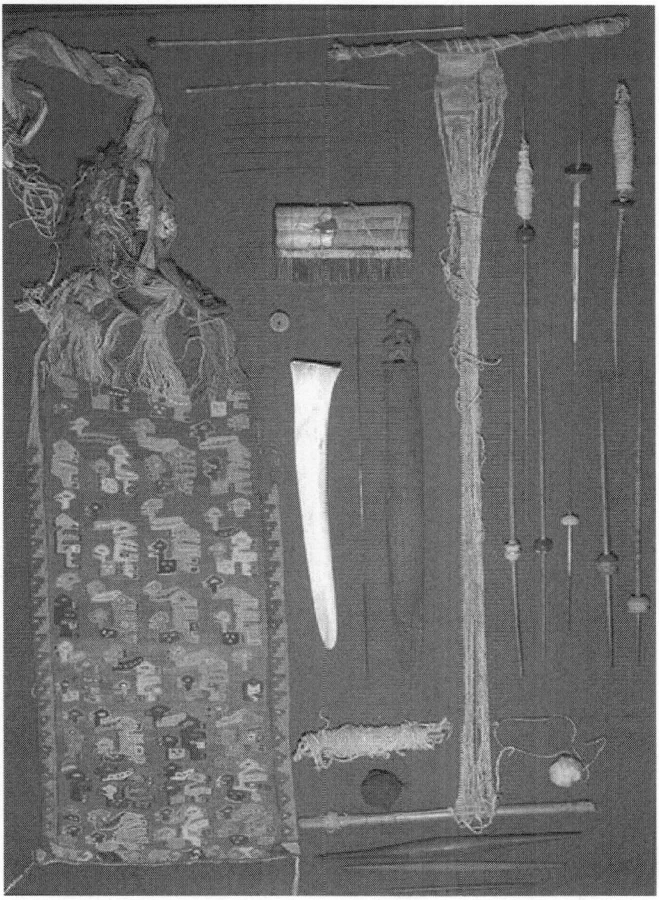

Figure: *Chancay weaving implement 1000-1400 CE, Lombards Museum*

Quilted armour of the Andeans was much lighter, more comfortable, and almost as protective as European steel plate armour.

Loom

The Andeans used the back strap loom. The Andeans had very advanced technology in textile technology, about as advanced as Eurasians were in metal technology.

Australian Aboriginal

Australian Aboriginal fibrecraft refers to the various ways Australian Aborigines created fibres traditionally. Materials used depended on where the people lived in Australia.

Bark

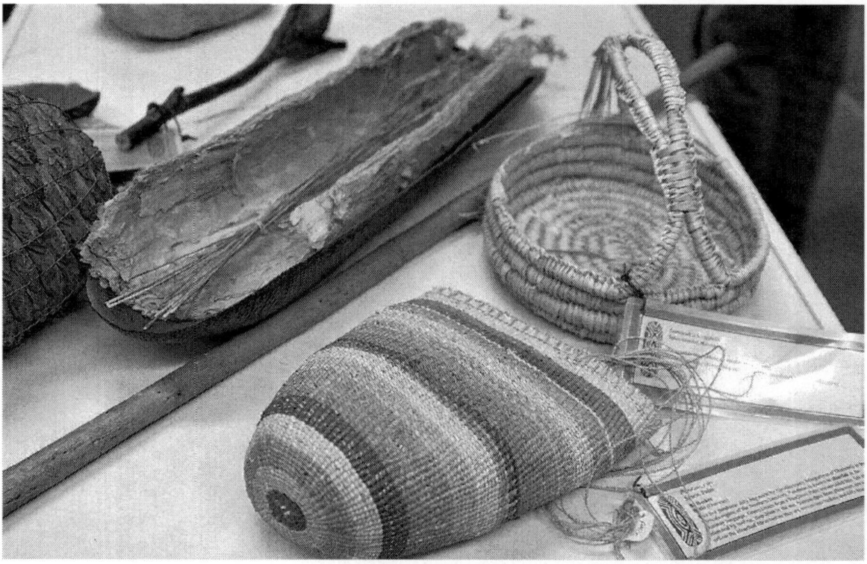

Figure: *Baskets were often made from twisted bark fibres*

Bark was used by many people across the continent. This technology is still used today to produce baskets, which are particularly popular in the tourism industry. Kurrajong bark is a popular bark, as is the bark of river wattles, sand figs, banyans, burney vines and peanut trees.

In the north, the more tightly woven styles were made, whereas in the south, a looser stringed bag, popularly known as a dilly bag was made.

Hair

Hairstring was an important textile traditionally made by Australian Aborigines.

People, particularly the women, cut their hair regularly using quartz or flint knives. This hair was never wasted. It was spun into long threads of yarn on a spindle rolled on the thigh and then plaited to about the thickness of 8 ply wool.

Purposes for the string were manifold. These included making the head ring for resting the coolamon, headbands to keep the hair off the face, spear-making (securing the head to the shaft), and even balls for ball games.

A general-purpose belt was made of the string, from which things could be hung, such as small game like goannas in order to free the hands on long walks and hunts.

Among some groups, including the Pitjantjajara, a small modesty apron was made of the string for young girls to wear when they reached puberty. People in Central Australia today may talk of a girl having her "string broken", which can mean sexual abuse, or having sex when she is not ready.

Among some tribes, adults wore a loincloth-like pubic covering, which also hung from the waist belt. This was made either of the string itself, or of other material, including paperbark. In the Kimberley region of Western Australia, the men wore pearl shells as a pubic covering, which they call *Riji*, and which are considered extremely sacred.

The string could be dyed various shades using dyes such as ochre.

Some string was only worn for ceremony, such as skirts worn by the women.

String Games

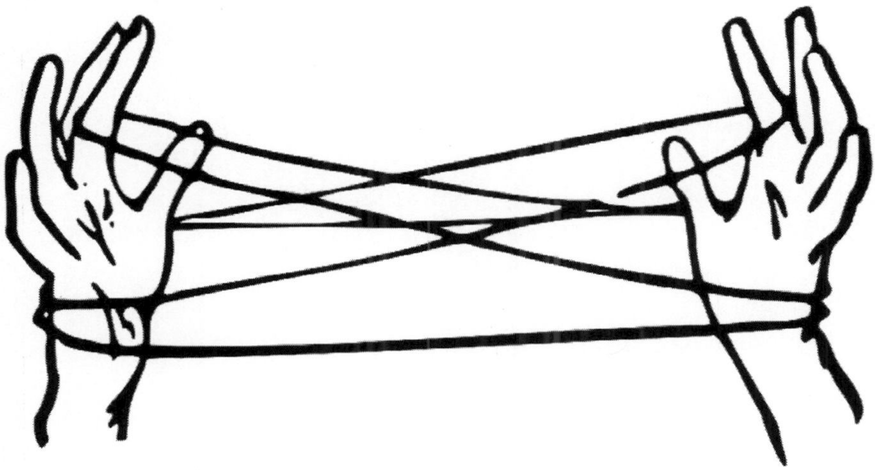

Figure: *Cat's Cradle*

Many Aboriginal groups traditionally made many shapes out of the string (cat's cradle). A researcher once watched and photographed a young Aboriginal woman from Yirrkala make over 200 separate string figures. Each one involved complicated movements of her fingers and thumbs. She was able to remember the correct sequence of finger movements for nearly every figure she made, with only an occasional mistake which she quickly corrected. As she made each figure she gave it a name. Some examples included *dangurang* — a lobster, *bapa* — lightning, *matjur* — an ibis flying into a tree and *gapu* — the ripples on a pool.

The Bangarra Dance Theatre's 2005 production of CLAN incorporated traditional desert string games into one of their performances, creating intricate patterns as they thread themselves through long, elastic strings.,

Grasses

Grasses were combined with the hair to create a tougher fibre. This varied depending on the area in Australia. In the arid areas, it was spinifex, whereas in the Top End, it was palms such as pandanus.

Pandanus and sand-palm are used in areas such as the Daly River region and Arnhem Land to weave carry baskets, dilly string bags, wall hangings, floor mats and fish-nets. The women of Peppimenarti and Oenpelli are famous for such weaving, however each community has their own distinct styles and techniques.

Hmong

Hmong textile art (RPA:*Paj ntau* or *Paj ntaub*, or "flower cloth" in the Hmong language; sometimes transliterated as pa ntau) consists of textile arts traditionally practiced by Hmong people. Closely related to practices of other ethnic minorities in China, the embroidery consists of bold geometric designs often realized in bright, contrasting colours. Different patterns and techniques of production are associated with geographical regions and cultural subdivisions within the global Hmong community.

For example, White Hmong are typically associated with reverse appliqué while Green Mong are more associated with batik. Since the mass exodus of Hmong refugees from Laos following the end of the Secret War, major stylistic changes occurred, strongly influenced by the tastes of the Western marketplace. Changes included more subdued colours and the invention of a new form of *paj ndau* often referred to as "story cloths."

These cloths, ranging in size up to several square feet, use figures to represent stories from Hmong history and folklore in a narrative form. Today, the practice of embroidery continues to be passed down through generations of Hmong people and *paj ndau* remain important markers of Hmong ethnicity.

Traditionally, *paj ndau* were applied to skirts worn for courtship during New Year festivals, as well as baby-carriers, and men's collars. The core visual elements of "layered bands of appliqué, triangles, squares tilted and superimposed on contrasting, squares, lines and dots, spirals, and crosses." The use of border patterns may show the influence of Chinese embroidery techniques.

Refugee Experience

When communist forces took control of Laos in 1975, Hmong people who supported the Royal Lao Government and fought for the American CIA during the Secret War were singled out for retribution. Tens of thousands of Hmong people escaped into Thailand as part of a mass exodus of 300,000 refugees.

Once in Thailand, most spent several years in overcrowded refugee camps awaiting resettlement. Dependent on relief agencies for subsistence, many Hmong people began selling handicrafts to improve their standard of living. As early as 1976, NGOs, like the Christian and Missionary Alliance, coordinated with Hmong women to sell their needlework abroad. In Laos, only rare moments of free time were spent on embroidery to adorn pieces of clothing for important rituals. Now with time to spare in the camps, women produced purses, bed spreads, and toaster covers which were shipped to relatives abroad who could sell them and send money back.

Men also contributed to the endeavour by creating drawings that could be transferred to cloths. In the 1960s, missionaries had taught men to draw illustrations for the folktales used in literacy primers. Cloths featuring elaborate and fantastic narratives sold well overseas and production grew. Eventually, themes from recent Hmong history, including the flight from Laos, were incorporated in the "story cloths," providing a historical record that did not require literacy for interpretation.

Indigenous Peoples of the Americas

Textile arts of indigenous peoples of the Americas are decorative, utilitarian, ceremonial, or conceptual artworks made from plant, animal, or synthetic fibres by native peoples of both North and South America.

Textile arts and fibre arts include fabric that is flexible woven material, as well as felt, bark cloth, knitting, embroidery, featherwork, skin-sewing, beadwork, and similar media. Textile arts are one of the earliest known industries. Basketry is associated with textile arts.

While humans have created textiles since the dawn of culture, many are fragile and disintegrate rapidly. Ancient textiles are preserved only by special environmental conditions. The oldest known textiles in the Americas is some early fibrework found in Guitarrero Cave, Peru dating back to 10,1000 to 9,080 BCE.

The oldest known textiles in North America are twine and plain weave fabrics preserved in a peat pond at the Windover Archaeological Site in Florida, the earliest dating to 6,000 BCE.

Cultural Regions

Andes:

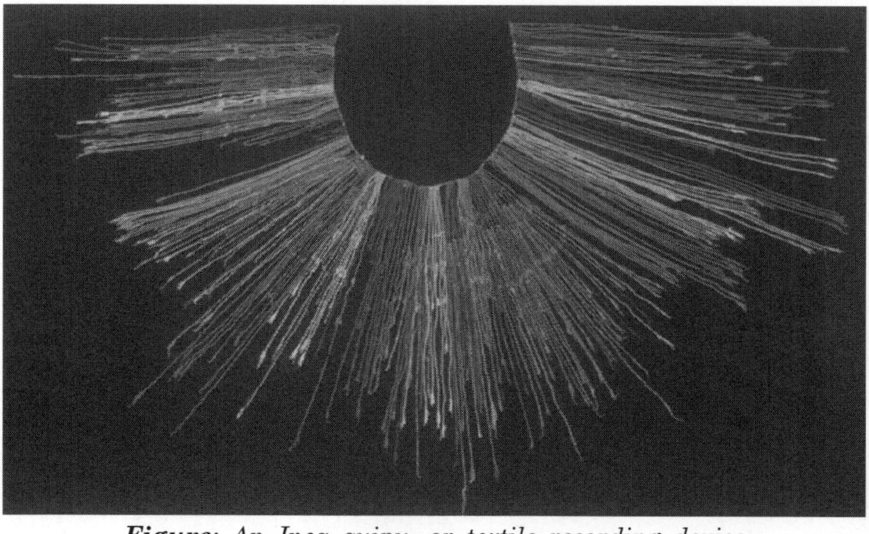

Figure: *An Inca quipu, or textile recording device*

As previously mentioned, fragments of rope and textiles dating back between 12,100 to 11,080 years ago have been unearthed from Guitarrero Cave in Peru. Because of the extremely dry conditions of the desert sands, twined textiles from the Norte Chico civilization in Peru have survived, dating back to 2500-1800 BCE. Cotton and wool from alpaca, llamas, and vicuñas have been woven into elaborate textiles for thousands of years in the Andes and are still important parts of Quechua and Aymara culture today. Coroma in Antonio

Quijarro Province, Bolivia is a major centre for ceremonial textile production. An Aymara elder from Coroma said, "In our sacred weavings are expressions of our philosophy, and the basis for our social organization... The sacred weavings are also important in differentiating one community, or ethnic group, from a neighbouring group..." Aguayos are clothes woven from camelid fibres with geometric designs that Andean women wear and use for carrying babies or goods.

Circum-Caribbean

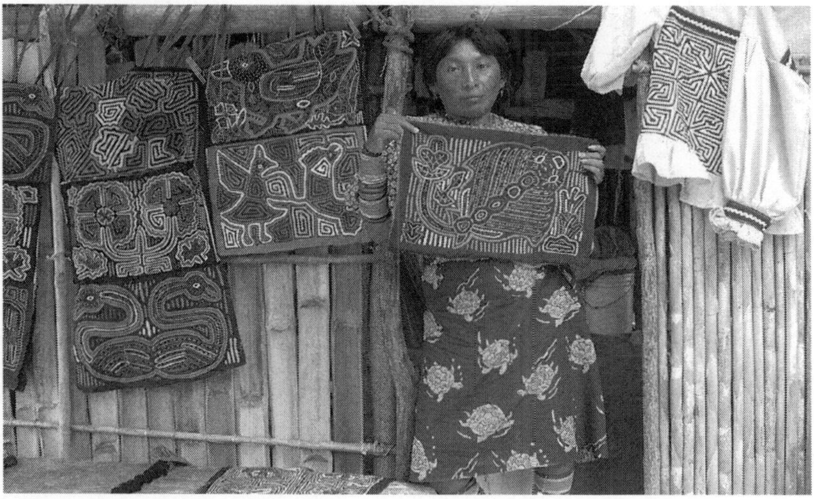

Figure: *Kuna woman with molas, San Blas Islands, Panama.*

Kuna tribal members of Panama and Colombia are famous for their molas, cotton panels with elaborate geometric designs created by a reverse appliqué technique. Designs originated from traditional skin painting designs but today exhibit a wide range of influences, including pop culture. Two mola panels form a blouse, but when a Kuna woman is tired of a blouse, she can dissemble it and sell the molas to art collectors.

Mesoamerica

Mayan women have woven cotton with backstrap looms for centuries, creating items such as *huipils* or traditional blouses. Elaborate Maya textiles featured representations of animals, plants, and figures from oral history. Organizing into weaving collectives have helped Mayan women earn better money for their work and greatly expand the reach of Mayan textiles in the world.

Southeastern Woodlands

Pieces of 7,000 to 8,000 year-old fabric have been found with human burials at the Windover Archaeological Site in Florida. The burials were in a peat pond. The fabric had turned into peat, but was still identifiable. Many bodies at the site had been wrapped in fabric before burial. Eighty-seven pieces of fabric were found associated with 37 burials. Researchers have identified seven different weaves in the fabric.

One kind of fabric had 26 strands per inch (10 strands per centimeter). There were also weaves using two-strand and three-strand wefts. A round bag made from twine was found, as well as matting. The yarn was probably made from palm leaves. Cabbage palm, saw palmetto and scrub palmetto are all common in the area, and would have been so 8,000 years ago.

Seminole seamstresses, upon gaining access to sewing machines in the late 19th century and early 20th centuries, invented an elaborate appliqué patchwork tradition. Seminole patchwork, for which the tribe is known today, came into full flower in the 1920s.

Northeastern Woodlands

Great Lakes and Prairie tribes are known for their ribbonwork, found on clothing and blankets. Strips of silk ribbons are cut and appliquéd in layers, creating designs defined by negative space. The colours and designs might reflect the clan or gender of the wearer. Powwow and other dance regalia from these tribes often feature ribbonwork. These tribes are also known for their fingerwoven sashes. Experimental contemporary textile artists include Martha Gradolf (Winnebago), whose work is overtly political in nature.

Oasisamerica

Pueblo men weave with cotton on upright looms. Their mantas and sashes are typically made for ceremonial use for the community, not for outside collectors. Navajo rugs are woven by Navajo women today from Navajo-Churro sheep or commercial wool. Designs can be pictorial or abstract, based on traditional Navajo. Spanish, Oriental, or Persian designs. 20th century Navajo weavers include Clara Sherman and Hosteen Klah, who co-founded the Wheelwright Museum of the American Indian. Valencia, Joseph and Ramona Sakiestewa (Hopi) and Melissa Cody (Navajo) explore non-representational abstraction and use experimental materials in their weaving.

Northwest Coast

Traditional textiles of Northwest Coast tribes are enjoying a dramatic revival. Chilkat weaving and ravenstail weaving are regarded as some of the most difficult weaving techniques in the world. A single Chilkat blanket can take an entire year to weave. In both techniques, dog, mountain goat, or sheep wool and shredded cedar bark are combined to create textiles featuring curvilinear formline designs. Tlingit weaver Jennie Thlunaut (1982–1986) was instrumental in this revival. Button blankets are wool blankets embellished with mother-of-pearl buttons worn on significant occasions, such as potlatches.

Korean

Korean fabric arts are craft of making fabric and textiles produced by the people on the Korean Peninsula. They have a long history, which includes fabrics such as guksa, nobang, sha, jangmidan, Korean-made jacquard, brocade and satin. Or crafts such as the Korean quilts known as bojagi, Korean embroidery, Korean knots, Korean clothing and the rarer arts of Korean blinds weaving and Korean paper clothing.

Mâori

Mâori traditional textiles are the indigenous textiles of the Mâori people of New Zealand. The organisation Te Roopu Raranga Whatu o Aotearoa, the national Mâori weavers' collective aims to preserve and foster the skills of making and using these materials.

Fibres and Dyes

Mâori made textiles from a number of plants, including harakeke, wharariki, tî kôuka, tôî, pingao, kiekie and toetoe—although the paper mulberry was introduced by Mâori, who knew it as aute, it seems not to have thrived and bark cloth (tapa) was always rare.

The prepared fibre (muka) of the New Zealand flax (*Phormium tenax*) became the basis of most clothing. The flax leaves were split and woven into mats, ropes and nets but clothing was often made from the fibre within the leaves. The leaves were stripped using a mussel shell, dressed by soaking and pounding with stone pounders (patu muka) to soften the fibre, spun by rolling the thread against the leg and woven. The fibre within the flax is called muka.

Colours for dyeing muka were sourced from indigenous materials. Paru (mud high in iron salts) provided black, raurekau bark made yellow, and tânekaha bark made a tan colour. The colours were set by rolling the dyed muka in alum (potash).

Garments

There were two main types of garments -

- A knee length kilt-like garment worn around the waist and secured by a belt
- And a rectangular garment worn over the shoulders. This might be a cape-like garment or a long cloak-like garment of finer quality.

Men's belts were known as tatua and women's as tu. The man's belt was usually the more ornate. Belts were usually made of flax but occasionally other materials were used such as kiekie and pingao. Flax belts were often plaited in patterns with black and white stripes. The belts tied with a string tie. Women often wore a belt composed of many strands of plaited fibre.

Weaving Process

The weaving process (whatu) for clothing was performed not with a loom and shuttle but with the threads being manipulated and tied with fingers. A strong thread is fastened tautly in a horizontal position between two or four upright weaving sticks (turuturu). To this thread (tawhiu) are attached the upper ends of the warp or vertical threads (io). The warp is arranged close together. The weaving process consisted of working in cross-threads from left to right. The closer these threads are together, the tighter the weave, and the finer the garment.

In the case of fine garments four threads are employed in the forming of each aho. The weaver passes two of these threads on either side of the first io or vertical thread, enclosing it. In the continuing the process the two pairs of threads are reversed, those passing behind the first vertical thread would be brought in front of the next one, then behind the next and so on. Each of the down threads would be enclosed between two or four cross-threads every half inch or so.

Pake / Hieke

To meet the cold and wet conditions of the New Zealand winter, a rain cloak called pake or hieke was worn. It was made from tags of raw flax or *Cordyline* partly scraped and set in close rows attached to the muka or plaited fibre base.

A type of garment known as a pake karure was made of two-ply closed strands of hukahuka (twisted or rolled cord or tag) interspersed with occasional black-dyed two-ply open type karure (loosely twisted) muka thread cord. Garments such as these were worn interchangeably either around the waist as a piupiu, or across the shoulder as a cape. These types of garments are thought to pre-date European contact, later becoming a more specialised form during the mid to later nineteenth century, which continues today in the standardised form of the piupiu.

Piupiu

Piupiu are a kind of grass skirt. The waistband is plaited or in some cases made from *tâniko*. The body of the piupiu is usually made from flax leaves that are carefully prepared with the *muka* or flax fibre exposed in some sections to cause geometric patterns to emerge. The unscraped leaves will curl naturally into tubes as the leaves dry, and make a percussion sound when the wearer sways or moves. The geometric patterns can be emphasised through dyeing as the dye will soak more into the exposed fibres rather than the dried raw leaf.

The Captain of HMS New *Zealand*, a battlecruiser built in 1911 by the government of New Zealand for the defence of the British Empire and which took an active part in three battles of the First World War, wore into battle a piupiu (as well as a hei-tiki, Mâori traditional pendant). The crew attributed to this the *New Zealand* being a "lucky ship" which sustained no casualties during the entire war.

Fine Cloaks

There were a number of different types of fine cloaks including korowai, kaitaka, kahu huruhuru and kahu kurî, all woven from muka (prepared harakeke fibre) using the Tâniko style.

Korowai

Korowai are finely woven cloaks covered with muka tassels (hukahuka). Hukahuka are made by the miro (twist thread) process of dying the muka (flax fibre) and rolling two bundles into a single cord which is then woven into the body of the cloak. There are many different types of korowai that are named depending on the type of hukahuka used as the decoration. Korowai karure have tassels (hukahuka) that appear to be unravelling. Korowai ngore have hukahuka that look like pompoms. Korowai hihima had undyed tassels.

Korowai seem to have been rare at the time of Captain Cook's first visit to New Zealand because they do not appear in drawings made by his artists.

But by 1844, when George French Angas painted historical accounts of early New Zealand, korowai with their black hukahuka had become the most popular style. Hukahuka on fine examples of korowai were often up to thirty centimetres long and when made correctly would move freely with every movement of the wearer. Today, many old korowai have lost their black hukahuka due to the dying process speeding up the deterioration of the muka.

Kaitaka

Kaitaka are cloaks of finely woven muka (*Phormium tenax*) fibre. Kaitaka are among the more prestigious forms of traditional Maori dress. They are made from muka (flax fibre), which is in turn made from those varieties of *Phormium tenax* that yield the finest quality fibre characterised by a silk-like texture and rich golden sheen. Kaitaka are usually adorned with broad tâniko borders at the remu (bottom) and narrow tâniko bands along the kauko (sides).

The ua (upper border) is plain and undecorated, and the kaupapa (main body) is usually unadorned. There are several sub-categories of kaitaka: parawai, where the aho (wefts) run horizontally; kaitaka paepaeroa, where the aho run vertically; kaitaka aronui or patea, where the aho run horizontally with tâniko bands on the sides and bottom borders; huaki, where the aho run horizontally with taniko bands on the sides and two broad taniko bands, one above the other, on the lower border; and huaki paepaeroa, which has vertical aho with double tâniko bands on the lower border.

Kahu Huruhuru

Fine feather cloaks called kahu huruhuru were made of muka fibre with bird feathers woven in to cover the entire cloak. These feather cloaks became more common during between 1850 and 1900, when cloaks were evolving in their production. Some early examples include kahu kiwi (kiwi feather cloak), which used the soft brown feathers of the kiwi (*Apteryx* spp). Kahu kiwi were regarded as the most prestigious form of kahu huruhuru. Other kahu huruhuru incorporated the green and white feathers of the kererû (New Zealand pigeon: *Hemiphaga novaeseelandiae*) and blue feathers from the tûî (*Prosthemadera novaeseelandiae*).

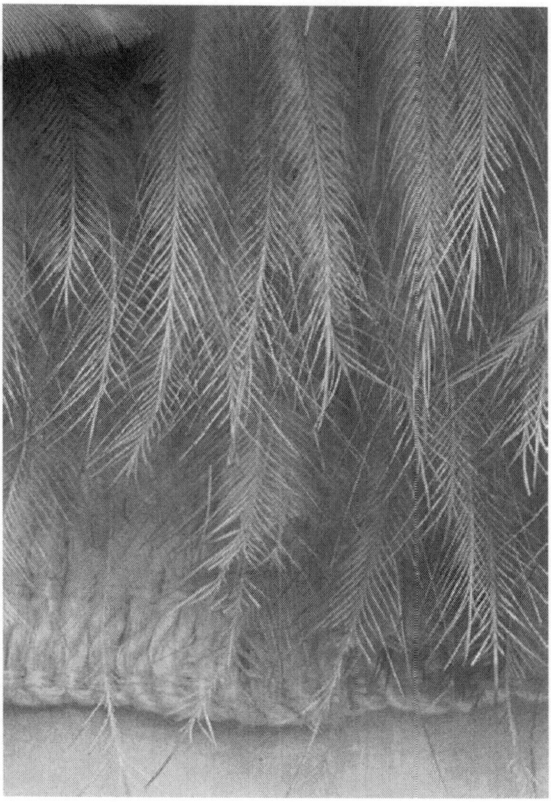

Figure: *Detail of the bottom edge of a kahu kiwi, showing the distinctive hair-like nature of the kiwi feathers.*

Kahu kurî

A particularly rare type of cloak is the kahu kurî, made from strips of dog skin with hair attached taken from the now extinct kurî (Mâori dog).

The main body of the cloak is made up of strips of white-haired dog skin of various lengths, which are sewn onto the kaupapa (main body) of the cloak with fine bone needles to form a tightly woven muka (flax fibre) foundation called pukupuku.

The pukupuku weaving technique uses the whatu-aho-patahi (single pair twine) method, which is very similar to the decorative geometric tâniko (fine embroidery or weaving in a geometric pattern) border designs usually seen on the kaitaka (fine flax cloak) class of cloak, and forms a thick and heavy protective garment. The awe (the tassels that fringe the outside length of the cloak) is likely to have been taken from the underside of the dog's tail. The kurupatu (plaited hem on the cloak edge) is entirely separate to the main kaupapa and made by threading separate strips together to form a length of collar that has been sewn onto the neck of the finished garment.

Kahu kurî are garments possessing great mana (status) and were highly prized heirlooms. Each garment had its own personal name and its history was carefully preserved right up to the time they passed out of Maori ownership.

However, most are in museum collections around the world and have lost their provenance. The possession of a kahu kurî immediately identified the owner as a rangatira (chief) or someone who possessed prestige and position within the hapû (family) or iwi (tribe). They were often exchanged between people of rank on important ceremonial occasions and affirmed both the mana of the giver and the recipient. Kahu kurî were made largely between 1500 and 1850, and it is thought that production had ceased altogether by the early nineteenth century.

There are several different varieties of kahu kurî and some tribal variation in the application of the descriptive terms of these types. Some of the types recorded include topuni, ihupuni, awarua, kahuwaero, mahiti, and puahi, but the construction technique remains essentially the same.

Tâniko

Tâniko (or taaniko) refers to any ornamental border typically found on mats and clothes. Tâniko patterns are very geometric in form because they can be reduced down to small coloured squares repeated on a lattice framework. These base square forms, articulated in the hands of a weaver, constitute the larger diamond and triangle shapes that are visible in all traditional weaving crafts.

Pâtiki or pâtikitiki (flounder/flat fish: *Rhombosolea plebeia*) designs are based on the lozenge or diamond shape of the flounder. They can be quite varied within the basic shape.

The kaokao (side or rib) pattern is formed by zigzag lines that create chevrons. These can be horizontal or vertical, open with paces or closed repetitive lines. The design is sometimes interpreted as the arms of warriors caught in haka (fierce rhythmic dance) action.

The niho taniwha (taniwha tooth) pattern is a notched-tooth design found on all types of objects, mats, woven panels, belts, and clothing.

The poutama is a stepped design signifying the growth of man, striving ever upwards.

Tahekeheke (striped) designs refer to any distinct vertical patterning.

The whetû (stars), purapura whetû (weaving pattern of stars) or roimata (teardrop) pattern is a geometric design using two colours and alternating between them at every stitch. This design is associated with the survival of an iwi (tribe), hapû (sub-tribe), or whânau (extended family), the idea being that it is vital to have a large whanau, just as there are many stars in the Milky Way.

Mayan

Maya textiles are the clothing and other textile arts of the Maya peoples, indigenous peoples of the Yucatán Peninsula in Mexico, Guatemala, Honduras, El Salvador and Belize. Women have traditionally created textiles in Maya society, and textiles were a significant form of ancient Maya art and religious beliefs.

Process

In woven textiles, the first step is preparing fibre, which can come from plants, such as cotton or maguey, or animals, such as wool from sheep. The loose fibres are spun into threads by hand, with spindles, a long stick-like device for holding the thread, and whorls, a weight held on the spindle to increase its motion.

In the pre-Columbian era, Mayan women exclusively wove with backstrap looms, that use sticks and straps worn around one's waist to create tension. After European contact, treadle looms were introduced, although backstrap looms continue to be popular. Bone picks were used before contact and were unique in that they had different designs for most families and were usually passed on from generation to generation with the elite having the most expensive and beautiful.

Materials

Ancient Maya women had two natural types of cotton to work with, one white and the other light brown, both of which were commonly dyed. The preparation of cotton for spinning was very burdensome, as it had to be washed and picked clean of seeds.

Elite women were also given the opportunity to work with the most expensive feathers and pearl beads. However, women of the elite not only had to prepare the best clothing for their families, but they also had to be talented in weaving tapestry, brocade, embroidery, and tie-dyeing for tribute to other families and rulers. Weavers had three different natural dyes to work with. Women also worked with maguey. Maguey was of major value as a cordage material used for horse gear, nets, hammocks and bags.

Pre Contact Attire

In the Maya civilization, a man's typical dress was a cotton breechcloth wrapped around his waist and sometimes a sleeveless shirt, either white or dyed in colours. A woman typically wore a *traje*, which combined a *huipil* and a *corte*, a woven wraparound skirt that reached her ankles. The *traje* was held together with a *faja* or sash worn at the waist. Both women and men wore sandals.

When the weather was temperate, Mayan clothing was needed less as protection from the elements and more for personal adornment. Maya clerics and other dignitaries wore elaborate outfits with jewellery.

Maya farmers wore minimal clothing. Men wore plain loincloths or a band of cloth winded around their waists. Some wore moccasins made of deerhide. Women possessed two items of clothing: a length of ornamented material with holes made for the arms and head, known as a *kub*. Both genders wore a heavier rectangle of cloth, as a manta, that functioned as an overwrap on cool days, and as blanket at night. The manta also served as a blind across the door.

Huipil

The most prevalent and influential aspect of women's clothing in ancient times is the *huipil*, which is still prominent in Guatemalan and Mexican culture today. The *huipil* is a loose rectangular garment with a hole in the middle for the head made from lightweight sheer cotton.

The huipil is usually white with colourful cross-stripping and zigzag designs woven into the cloth using the brocade technique still commonly used today. The *huipil* could be worn loose or tucked into a skirt; this depends on the varying lengths of the *huipil*. *Huipils* were important displaying one's religion and tribal affiliation. Different communities tended to have different designs, colours, lengths as well as particular huipils for ceremonial purposes. It was uncommon and often disgraceful to wear a huipil design from another community within one's village; although, it was a sign of respect to wear a community's *huipil* when visiting another village. Although, women were not just limited to their community's design. Instead the design offered an outline for what women were required to have and within the community design women were allowed creativity to make theirs different from others often to express praise to different *kiuggkes* animals around the collar.

Hair Sash

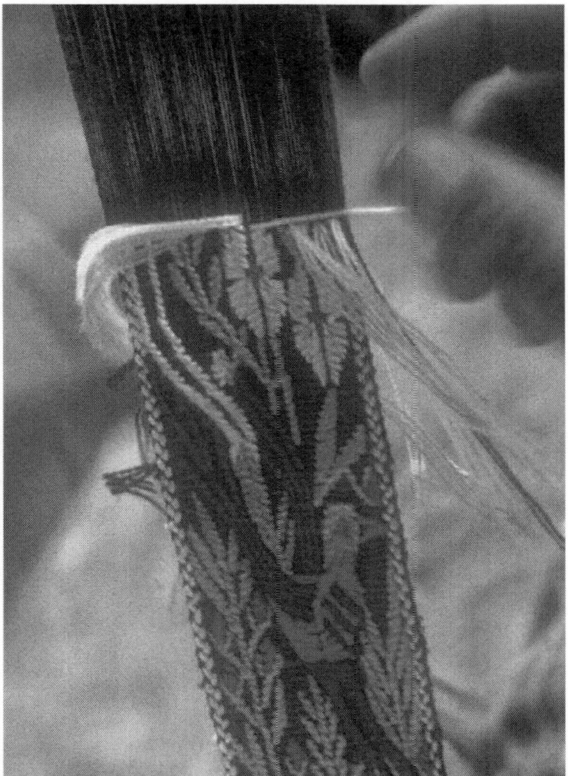

Figure: *Detail of hair sash being brocaded on a Jakaltek Maya backstrap loom.*

The hair sash is often the only part of the traditional outfit that is still locally woven by women on a backstrap loom. Each ethnic group not only has their own way of wearing the hair sash interlaced or wrapped around their long hair, but colours, motifs, widths, and the manner of setting up the loom and incorporating the geometric and figurative designs into the cloth are distinct. Elaborate hair sashes woven of finer thread with more complex imagery are worn on special occasions.

Ideological Aspects

The Maya believed that clothing could transform a person and a person could transform the garment and is expressed through it, so naturally clothing was of great cultural significance. They would often make textiles to enhance religious power; the most common way of doing this was dressing for the maize gods. Women and men would wear a net over-skirt made of jade, the colour of life, which represented their high place in society.

In order to dress as a maize deity and manipulate the regeneration of the maize plant they would weave serpents onto *huipils* to symbolize lightning. The lightning god is the god believed to have created maize on the top of Mt. Sustenance. Mayan elite would also wear a shark shell belt and a jade-netted collar to the maize deity costume. Other significant costumes consisted of wearing many quetzal and eagle feathers on headdresses to represent and elite's power in blue and green tones, which represented the fifth direction, the centre of celestial, terrestrial and the underworld levels of the cosmos. Kings would also wear jaguar skin skirts, which signified their connection between the sky and the earth.

Mexican

Textiles of Mexico have a long history. The making of fibres, cloth and other textile goods has existed in the country since at least 1400 BCE. Fibres used during the pre-Hispanic period included those from the yucca, palm and maguey plants as well as the use of cotton in the hot lowlands of the south.

After the Spanish conquest of the Aztec Empire, the Spanish introduced new fibres such as silk and wool as well as the European foot treadle loom. Clothing styles also changed radically. Fabric was produced exclusively in workshops or in the home until the era of Porfirio Díaz (1880s to 1910), when the mechanization of weaving was introduced, mostly by the French. Today, fabric, clothes and other textiles are both made by craftsmen and in factories. Handcrafted goods include pre-Hispanic clothing such as huipils and sarapes, which are often embroidered. Clothing, rugs and more are made with natural and naturally dyed fibres. Most handcrafts are produced by indigenous people, whose communities are concentrated in the centre and south of the country in states such as Mexico State, Oaxaca and Chiapas. The textile industry remains important to the economy of Mexico although it has suffered setback due to competition by cheaper goods produced in countries such as China, India and Vietnam.

History

Pre-Hispanic Period: The oldest known fabric fragments in Mexico have been found in the arid north of the country in states such as Coahuila, Chihuahua and Durango and date to approximately between 1800 and 1400 BCE. In pre-Hispanic times, the most common woven fibres in dry areas were from the yucca and palm trees, with cotton grown in the hot humid areas near the coast. It was unknown to the Aztecs until they conquered cotton growing areas and began demanding it as tribute. Then, only the upper classes were permitted to wear it. Given the important status cotton cloth had, it is often used as money. For some ceremonial garments, amate or bark paper was used.

Each of the sedentary Mesoamerican cultures had a god of weaving. Women were often buried with woven items they had made. Cortés mentions the Aztecs' skill in weaving in one of this letters to the king of Spain, in very favorable terms.

Colonial Era

After the Spanish conquest of the Aztec Empire, the production of cloth and the wearing of clothes in Mesoamerica changed drastically. Most pre-Hispanic forms of dress and body adornment were banned by the Spanish as "uncivilized." Indigenous, European and Asian fabrics influenced Mexican cloth production by the mid colonial period. The Spanish did not favor the native cotton, nor did they find the material produced on traditional backstrap looms wide enough. New techniques and materials were introduced. Spanish modes of dress, itself a mixture of European, Asia Minor and Egyptian influences, were introduced as well. At first wool and silk fabric was imported, then sheep and silkworms as well as European foot pedal looms all by the late 1530s. By 1580, Mexico had become one of the most productive areas for wool and silk cloth. Most of the production was concentrated in the present day states of Oaxaca, Tlaxcala and Puebla. At first Spanish weavers dominated production, but they were soon replaced by native weavers who were making material cheaper. Instead of prohibiting Indian made fabric, European weavers decided instead to hire them, creating workshops.

While the indigenous weavers were not paid much, the Spanish owners did make money. These workshops eventually produced enough fabric for both internal consumption and for export to Spain, the Philippines, Central America and Peru. Silk cloth production was particularly dominant from 1540 to 1580; However, the end of this period, the yearly Manila Galleon was regularly bringing cheaper silk from Asia.

While cotton cloth was not favored by the Europeans, it was still made and offered as tribute to Spanish overlords. Commercializing the fibre was difficult as the plant grows in the lowlands near the oceans and not near the manufacturing areas in the highlands, and transportation costs were high. Large cotton weaving workshops were not founded until the second half of the 17th century.

Eventually, the production of this fabric as well as wool fabric filled the gap left by the disappearance of Mexican silk fabric production. Wool fabric remained important because it was favored by the upper tiers of colonial society, and because sheep could be raised near major weaving areas, such as Puebla, Querétaro, Valladolid, Acámbaro, and San Miguel de Allende.

19th Century to Present

In times past, fabric and clothing were made to last for decades, but today fabric is much cheaper and much of what clothing is bought is soon thrown away. This is mostly due to the mechanization of weaving, which has made fabric inexpensive. In Mexico, as in other parts of the world, the introduction of modern transportation and communications brought about major changes in the production and distribution of goods and in firms' management and structure.

In the 19th century, industrialization affected textile production with the introduction of steam-powered machines and the efforts of French immigrants from Barcelonnette, who began to arrive in Mexico in the early 19th century. The mass production of textiles, especially cotton textiles, developed earlier than in other countries outside of

Western Europe and the United States, nearing the same level as in England in the mid-18th century despite social unrest at that time. Mechanization of cloth production began in the 1830s; however, high internal taxes among states kept production facilities small and unconsolidated.

While Mexican production lagged behind that of Europe, certain regions of the country such as La Laguna, in the modern states of Durango and Coahuila, became important producers of cotton fabric. The most widely produced fabric was called "manta," a natural cotton favored by many indigenous groups.

The development of steamship lines and railroad networks allowed Mexico-produced fabrics to be exported. The consolidation of power by Porfirio Díaz in the 1880s opened up business opportunities and made foreign investment possible. By the end of the 19th century, textile production and distribution was the country's largest manufacturing sector, mostly controlled by French immigrants.

The immigrants worked together, forming the "Barcelonnette network." They started off with small textile mills and dry goods stores, which eventually grew into large factories and department stores, including Palacio de Hierro, which still exists.

These French immigrants consolidated textile operations by the end of the 19th century, and by the start of the Mexican Revolution changed their power source from steam to electricity. They also changed textile mills from mostly family-owned organizations to more modern enterprises with professional managers and stock sold on exchanges.

The sewing machine appeared in the early 20th century and became widely used to join fabric and for embroidery . This led to another level of textile production: finished clothing.

Craft and Indigenous Textiles Today

Indigenous Tradition: Textiles is one of Mexico's more important crafts as it represents the continuation of tradition as well as its fusion with modern designs and techniques. Both pre-Hispanic and colonial era style textiles are still made in Mexico. In addition, many of the textile factories use machines based on old foot pedal looms from the colonial period. There are basically four types of fibres used for fabric production:

- Vegetable products such as cotton
- Animal products such as wool and silk

- Minerals such as gold and silver thread
- Synthetics.

Raw materials for textiles fall into two groups: smooth fibres such as silk, cotton, and wool, introduced to the American continent by the conquistadors; and hard fibres native to Mexico such as ixtle, lechuguilla, reeds, palm, twigs, and willow. In indigenous regions of Mexico, women are responsible for clothing the community, a process which often begins with harvesting natural fibres and then spinning, dyeing, and weaving textiles. In various parts of Mexico, both native backstrap looms and pedal-driven looms of European origin are used to weave principally cotton and wool.

Most handcrafted textiles are produced by the sixty or so indigenous ethnic groups in Mexico, who mostly live in rural areas in the centre and south of the country. In these textiles, traditional indigenous designs, and in some cases techniques still survive. One common technique in craft fabric is brocade, which allows for raised designs to be woven into the cloth.

Most indigenous textiles are made at home by women and used for clothing, home use, decorative use and ceremonial use. Items include those that are hand woven, hand embroidered, knitted and more. Clothing is one of the ways that these groups distinguish themselves from each other and the world at large.

Some of these garments include the huipil, the quechquemitl, tilmas, sandals and rebozos. A number of ethnic groups, such as the Nahua in central Mexico commercialize their original and traditional creations as well as produce them for domestic consumption. People in coastal areas continue to plant cotton, spin it, dye it with natural elements such as indigo.

Indigenous Clothing

Most of the pre-Hispanic clothing that survives is for women. These include "enredos", or wrap dresses, fajas, or cloth belts, huipils, a type of tunic, quechquemitl, which is a kind of rectangular or square short poncho. The last was originally worn directly on the upper body of a woman but today it is worn over a blouse. Loose-fitting sack dresses, called huipils in Oaxaca and guanengos in Michoacán, are often heavily embroidered with straight stitching, cross stitching and tucks with floral and geometric motifs.

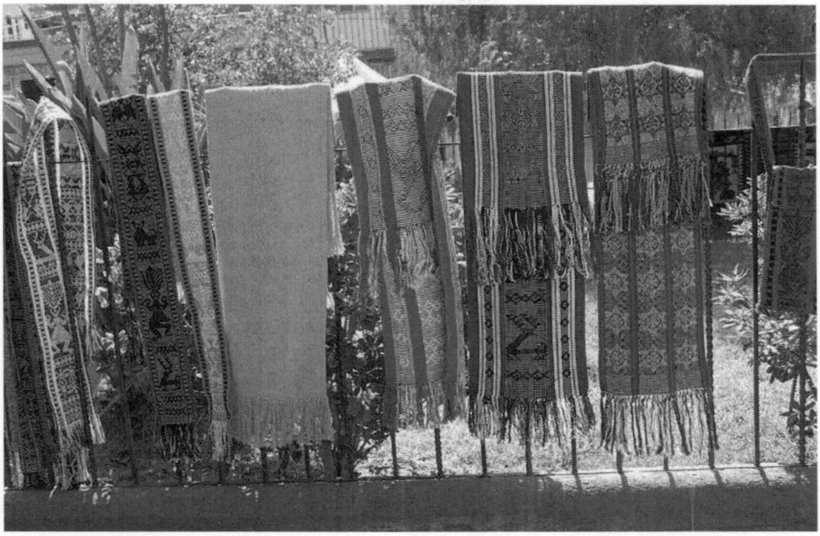

Figure: *Rebozos and "fajas" or sash/belts for sale in Zaachila, Oaxaca*

A widely used garment in both indigenous and mixed race communities is the rebozo.

This is a long rectangular shawl used both as a wrap and as a means to carry children or heavy objects tied onto the body. The rebozo came about during the colonial period, not in the pre-Hispanic era.

The rebozo is a synthesis of three historical influences, the pre-Hispanic "mámatl," the Spanish mantilla and the "repacejo," an Oriental garment. This is a long rectangular piece of cloth with long fringes at both ends.

Most rebozos are made with multicoloured designs woven into the pieces using threads of different colours. Those of a single colour are usually made of yarn or thread that has been tie-dyed to produce colour variations in the final piece. This latter style is called "jaspe" or jasper and are usually woven on backstrap looms.

The rebozo has been produced mostly in central Mexico since the colonial period, with some of the best known producers in Mexico State and Michoacan. Tenancingo is one of the best known producers of craft rebozos, usually made of cotton but wool is also used.

Traditional rebozos in the Lake Pátzcuaro area are often of white and blue over a black background and may be embroidered in tiny cross stitch.

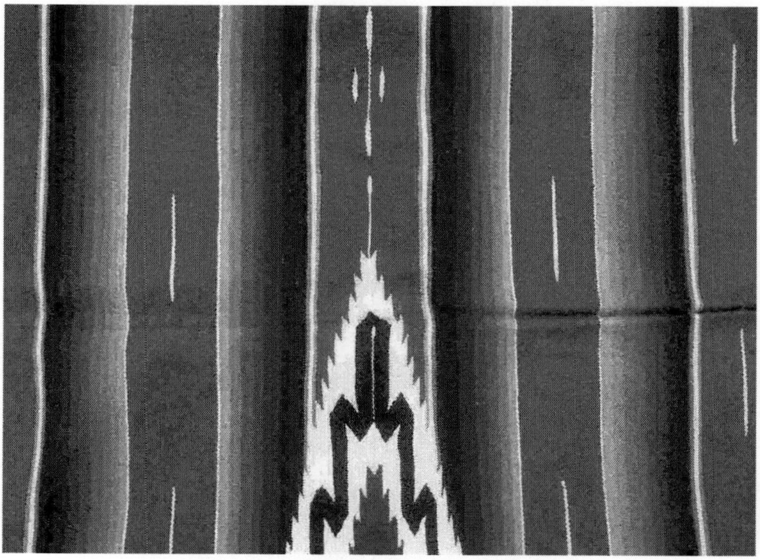

Figure: *Portion of a sarape*

Few pre-Hispanic male clothing pieces survive since many Mesoamerican males went about nude or semi nude, causing Spanish authorities to force them to adopt European shirts and pants early. This early colonial style shirts and pants have changed little in indigenous communities and are now identified with indigenous groups, especially the Tarahumara in Chihuahua, the Tacuates in Oaxaca and the Tzeltals in Chiapas.

Many male garments are heavily embroidered in multiple colours. Since indigenous pants lack pockets, many men carry decorated bags called morals. The only pre-Hispanic male garment to survive is the sarape, which is used only in certain areas of Mexico.

In addition to clothing, other items are woven such as bedspreads, blankets, hats, cinches and knapsacks. The designs for these are most often woven into the fabric itself, but embroidered stars, border designs, deer, and other can be seen as well. These items may be made with various fibres include those derived from the maguey plant.

Embroidery

One of the most distinctive aspects of indigenous handcrafted textiles is the use of embroidery. Indigenous motifs found on garments range from geometric pattens, zig-zag, spirals, moons, crosses and stepped frets. Thin cloth belts that wrap around the waist (fajillas) are common in a number of indigenous groups and are richly embroidered. The borders are often adorned with zig-zag edging, such as those of the Huichols. The Otomis use a moon pattern on these belts along with their morrals or carrying bags, and the Tarahumara tend to decorate theirs with triangular designs.

Many of the embroidery patterns of the huipils in Oaxaca, also show pre-Hispanic influence. Flower designs are popular for embroidering women's clothing among the Otomis, Nahuas, Huastecs, Huichols and others. Spirals and curved designs appear with frequency especially in the centre and south of the country.

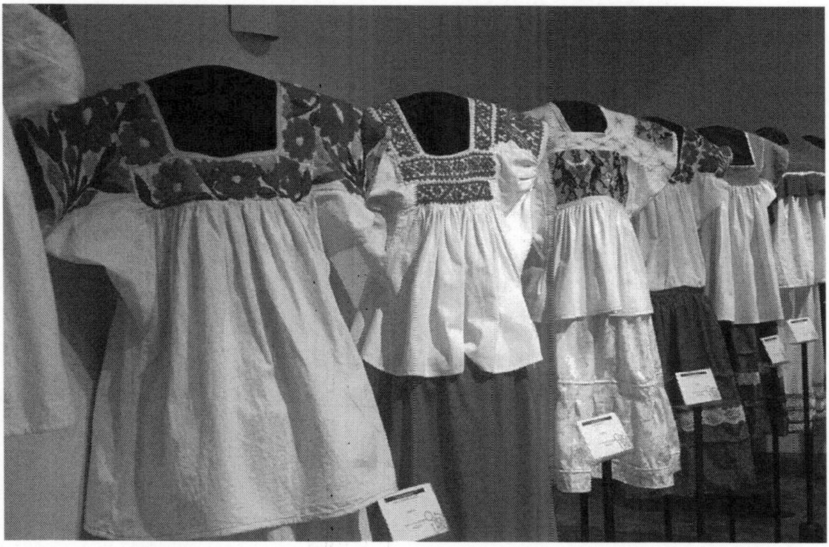

Figure: *Embroidered blouses from the La Huasteca region of Hidalgo.*

In addition to flowers, other themes from nature in woven and embroidered designs include plants, animals such as squirrels, rabbits, deer, armadillos, doves, hummingbirds, pelicans, seagulls and fish. Mazahua embroidered belts are known for their zoomorphic designs and those of Santo Tomás Jalieza tend to have images of large plumed birds. The cloth napkins of San Mateo del Mar have images of aquatic birds such as pelicans and seagulls, with those of the Tacuates of Santiago Zacatepec have borders with many diminutive animals such as centipedes, scorpions, birds, iguanas, cats, foxes and more.

Human figures appear with relative frequency as well. They feature prominently on the embroidered napkins of San Juan Colourado and as Danza de la Pluma dancers on the cloth belts of Santo Tomás

Jalieza. Patriotic symbols such as two-headed eagles, the three colours of the Mexican flag and the eagle with serpent crest. These are most prevalent in the central region of the country among the Otomis, Nahuas, Huastecos, Huicholes and others. Christian symbols such as the cross, virgins, saints, angels and other elements were introduced by evangelists in the early colonial period.

These appear on small and large pieces such as men's shirts among the Tzotzil in Chiapas, in the fabrics of San Miguel Ameyalco, which feature churches, and the appearance of the Virgin of Guadalupe in many textiles in the Sierra Norte of Puebla. Popular sayings or phrases also appear especially in the textiles of the Purhepechas around Lake Pátzcuaro and in the state of Puebla.

Looms

Two types of looms are employed in the making are handcrafted fabrics, the pre-Hispanic backstrap loom and the introduced European foot pedal loom. Traditionally, weaving, especially on the backstrap loom, was considered to be women's work. Women still produce items such as kitchen cloths, tablecloths, carrying bags and ornamental items with traditional designs.

Although considered primitive, the backstrap loom is versatile and allows for different techniques and combinations of techniques, some of which can be very complicated. It allows for the combining of different fibres such as cotton with wool or silk. Designs are woven into the cloth on this loom by changing thread colours and/or by adding items such as shells or other matter into the finished product. The backstrap loom is most prevalent in the south of the country.

The foot pedal loom was brought to Mexico after the Conquest. Unlike pieces done on backstrap looms, pieces done on these machines have traditionally been done by men with wool being the favored fibre. This type of loom is most extensively used in the centre and north of the country. The principal advantage of this loom is that it allows for pieces of greater width than backstrap looms and has been used to create sarapes, rugs, blankets and more.

Rugs and Other Items Made in Oaxaca and Mexico State

Two states that continue to have significant handcrafted textile production are Oaxaca and Mexico State. Oaxaca is known for its variety of handcrafted textiles including rugs, rebozos, tablecloths and traditional clothing such as huipils. These are made backstrap looms or foot pedal looms. In Mexico State craft pieces are mostly produced in Jiquipilco, Tejupilco de Hidalgo, Temascaltepec de González, Temoaya, Valle de Bravo, Zacazonapan, Toluca and Tenancingo producing napkins, tablecloths, sheets, kitchen items, clothing, bathroom items, rebozos and rugs.

Both states also are significant producers of rugs. The making of knotted rugs by the Otomi in Mexico State is relatively recent. It began in 1969 when Ernesto Fernández Hurtado of the Bank of Mexico decided to promote a pilot centre in Temoaya for the study and manufacture of this type of rug using traditional Otomi designs. Today, these rugs are a distinctive feature in Mexico State crafts. The rugs are made with 100% virgin wool and have an average knot density of 140,000 m2. There are about 21 different designs offered with 250 variations in colours and size. Most are sold in upper-class neighbourhoods of Mexico City, but due to the problem of cheap imitations, some vendors only sell from their workshops.

Teotitlán del Valle in Oaxaca is known for its woven rugs. Most producers make their rugs on foot pedal looms using wool dyed with natural materials such as indigo and the cochineal bug. Rugs are also produced in Mitla, Santa Ana del Valle and Tlacolula de Matamoros along with blankets and a type of sarape. One distinguishing feature of Oaxaca rug production is the use of the cochineal insect. This insect has been used since pre-Hispanic times to dye fibre, producing colours ranging from purple to yellow, varying depending on what the ingredients, such as certain flowers or lime juice, are added. For a time, the use of natural dyes was threatened by cheaper synthetics but the use of natural dyes has made a comeback.

Value and Protection of Handcrafted Textiles

After the Mexican Revolution, references to native Mexican cultures became fashionable, including arts crafts food and regional clothing. This was expressed in the arts by those such as Diego Rivera and Dr. Atl. Since that time, there have been a number of efforts to maintain and expand the textile producing traditions, especially of the south of Mexico. The Textile Museum has a collection of 4,000 pieces and is located in the former monastery of San Pablo in the city of Oaxaca. The museum was opened in 2008 and sponsored by the Alfredo Harp Helú Foundation. The pieces include modern, colonial and pre-Hispanic textiles. Clothing items include huipils, enredos, quechquemilts, skirts, rugs and wall hangings. The collection is in three divisions Textiles of Oaxaca, Textiles of Mexico and Textiles of the World.

Sna' Jolobil, or House of the Textiles in the Tzotzil language, is a cooperative of more than 600 Tzotzil and Tzeltal women in 12 municipalities in Chiapas based in San Cristóbal de las Casas. It was founded to promote and elevate the textile crafts, especially those produced on backstrap looms, with the aim of preserving traditional techniques and designs as well as promoting the economic fortunes of women weavers.

The organization has a collection of antique huipils available for study and reproduction as well as workshops in weaving and producing vegetable dyes. The organization has been successful in attracting more young people into the craft. In 1986, it received the Premio Nacional de Ciencias y Artes (National Prize of Sciences and the Artes) and numerous members have earned individual awards for their work.

Federal agencies such as FONART and various state agencies have their own promotional efforts including annual crafts contests and the recognition of masters in various fields, including textiles. Florentina López de Jesús is an Amusgo from Xochistlahuaca, Guerrero. She learned to weave from her mother at six years of age as well as to prepare raw cotton and spin it into yarn. She continued to weave as well as to do other jobs to help out her family.

As an adult she began to make pieces specifically for sale such as tablecloths, placemats, rebozos and huipils, travelling to Ometepec to market. Her work caught the attention of FONART in between 1969 and 1971, which led to her becoming a member of the La Flor de Xochistlahuaca artisans' cooperative.

Since then, she has given workshops to people in her region as well as the Curso de Tintes Naturales sobre Algodon (Natural Dyes for Cotton Course) in 1994 and has promoted the use of brown cotton called "coyochi."

Her work has won a number of awards including 2nd place Gran Premio de Arte Popular, FONART in 1987, 1st place Gran Premio de Arte Popular, FONART in 1991 and Premio Nacional de Artesanias de SECOFI in 1993.

Juan Rayón Salinas, whose parents were craftsmen, is from Mexico State. He began working with textiles in 1970, and in 1971 the state government began work to open a Centro de Capacitación de Tapiz y de Bajo Liso to introduce European techniques for making rugs. Traditionally Rayón's hometown of Xonacatlán made wool sarapes, but he entered the centre specializing in throw rugs. He work was recognized and he began to participate in exhibitions in Mexico and abroad.

After working for a time with the Centro, he established his own independent workshop. His work can be seen in various cities in Mexico as well as in New York. Also from Xonacatlán, Reyna Rayón Salinas is known for her cloth belts and embroidery, which she has been making since she was 12. Cosme Flores is from the city of Tlaxcala, son and grandson of weavers who made wool rugs. He began weaving when he was 11 along with working in agriculture. His work has won various prizes such as first place in the Concurso Estatal de Artesanias Tlaxcaltecas in 1993 and 1994. His work is also featured in a permanent exhibition at the Museo de Artes y Tradiciones Populares de Tlaxcala.

Justina Oviedo Rangel is of the Huave ethnic group in Oaxaca. She began weaving when she was eight on her own while playing. When her mother saw her ability, she began to give her formal lessons. She specializes in napkins, placeholders and tablecloths, but also makes huipils. She also makes figures of clay. Her work has won awards such as the Concurso de Tejido de San Mateo del Mar in 1978 and various times since then until 1989.

Evaristo Borboa was born in Tenancingo, Mexico State, where the making of rebozos is a tradition. He began weaving when he was 12, making rebozos using a backstrap loom, rather than the European loom. This means that each of his rebozos are made individually rather 26-30 at a time, which is possible with larger looms. He is also known for his knotted or "ikat" technique as well as the jasper style. Interested in older styles of rebozos, he began in experiment in 1947 with these older designs.

In the 1960s, upon visiting the Virgin of Zapopan, he noticed that the image was wrapped only in a simple shawl. He offered to make the image new rebozo, something he has done every year since. Recognition has come late in Borboa's life winning awards from FONART and state agencies starting in the 1990s.

Handcrafted textiles have also been promoted as a tourist attraction in its own right. This is especially true in the state of Chiapas. Mexican handcrafted textiles have experienced a resurgence of interest due to the reassessment of them as a luxury item and the rising interest in some consumer sectors in locally crafted wares.

Many of these textiles are being incorporated into items sold by globally recognized brands. Louis Vuitton, who has manufacturing facilities in Mexico, sponsored an exhibition called "Historias de Tradición artesanal" (Stories of Artisan Tradition) at the Museo de Arte Popular in Mexico City.

However, handcrafted textiles not only compete with other types of imported textiles, but also countries like China and Guatemala are producing imitations of traditional Mexican indigenous designs. These can be found both inside and outside of Mexico.

The Asociacion de Mujeres Empresarias in Chiapas considers the imitations to be a form of pirating and puts native weavers livelihoods at risk. Organizations such as this work to have indigenous designs marked as intangible world heritage to protect it with markers for authenticity—much as is done for tequila or Talavera pottery.

Current Textile Industry

Current Importance of the Sector: Modern textile production in Mexico dates back to the era of Porfirio Díaz from the 1880s to 1910. Today, textile production plays an important role in the gross domestic product of Mexico, since it is exported and generates employment. Textile production includes the making of thread, cloth and decoration, in both natural and synthetic fibres.

It accounts for about 1.2% of the total GDP and 7.1% of the manufacturing sector. It is the fourth largest manufacturing activity in the country. From the end of the Mexican Revolution to the mid-2000s, the sector saw steady growth. Much of the growth in the last four decades was spearheaded by "maquiladoras" or manufacturing plants along the northern border, which can import raw materials duty-free to make exportable products.

Another important textile area is the state of Guanajuato, which is Mexico's third largest producer. Some of these products include clothing, thread and sewing fabric, sheets, tablecloths, decorative pillows, rugs, carpets and tarps. Clothing items include jeans, other pants, blouses, tshirts, sweaters, vests, jackets, skirts and others, for national and international brands such as Liverpool, Chipieco, Carhartt, Echojeans, Polo Ralph Lauren, JCPenney, Old Navy, Timberland and more.

However, in the mid-2000s, the sector began to decline, mostly due to foreign competition. A significant number of jobs have been lost since 2003 as well as a number of factories. Many of these operations and jobs are shifting to Asia.

Exports to the United States

The U.S. is the largest textile importer and almost all textile producing countries compete for a share of this market. Mexico ranks fourth in textile exports to the U.S. according to OTEXA. Mexico's advantages in this market is it proximity and favorable tariffs, especially since the passage of NAFTA. In 2004, all restrictions and quotas on Mexican textiles were lifted in the United States.

However, textile exports to the U.S. fell from more than 11 billion dollars in 2004 to just over 10 billion in 2005, as the U.S. imports more from other countries, who produce more cheaply.

From January through September 2004, U.S. imports of Mexican-made apparel reached \$5.069 billion, 4.3% below the total registered for the same period in 2003, according to the CNIV, Mexico's textile industry association. Meanwhile, U.S. imports of Chinese garments grew 21.7% during that period to reach \$6.69 billion Yet Mexican-made products began to lose their competitiveness in the U.S. because taxes and tariffs on imports from other countries were also dropping.

Non-U.S. Markets

While the U.S. is by far the major market for Mexican textiles, Mexico has free-trade pacts with 43 countries, one of the largest such networks in the world. Until very recently, this did not include China, which has been seen as an "enemy" rather than as a potential trading partner. There has been changes in this as Mexico seeks to expand business ties with China, especially in attracting capital.

In the Americas, Mexico is part of the Central America Tree Trade Agreement, and recently Mexico and Peru struck a deal for the import and export of clothing and other textiles. Mexico's textile exports to Canada increased fivefold by the mid-2000s, raising its market share in that country to five percent. Export growth to Canada has slowed since then but remains fairly strong.

Domestic Clothing Market

Nine major chain stores control 40% of the brick-and-mortar sales, but approximately 58% of the domestic clothing market obtains its goods through illegal channels, either through smuggling, robbery or the evasion of taxes. Much of the illegal Chinese textiles sold in Mexico enter through the United States, where labels are changed to avoid Mexico's 533% tariff on Chinese goods.

Mexico's International Competitors

In addition to those from China, Mexican textile exports face competition from India, Bangladesh, Pakistan, Indonesia, Vietnam, Hong Kong and Central America. In 2000, Mexican textiles held around 12% of the U.S. market while Indian textiles 3.84%. Other Asian countries with presence include Hong Kong (5.7%), Indonesia (5.3), Vietnam and Bangladesh (5% each) .

Much of the reason for this is that labour costs are significantly higher in Mexico than in Asia. Mexico also has regulations that inhibit investment, as well as stricter environmental laws. Mexican fabrics cost 3.45 dollars per square metre while Chinese textiles cost 2.69 dollars.

While the cost of Mexican fabric has increased 2%, those from a number of other countries in Asia and Central America have gone down. One major factor behind this is Mexico's relatively expensive labour costs. Another reason Asian products are cheaper is that utilities such electricity, gas and transport is cheaper.

China is Mexico's most important competitor. Not only are products from this country cheaper, the supply chain in China is more organized than in Mexico. For example, most threads used to sew clothing are produced in China; Mexico produces little, creating the need to import such. This can cause production delays. Mexico is also mostly limited to the making of basic items with little added value instead of more fashionable products that sell for more. In addition, Mexico also has protectionist policies designed to inhibit foreign investment and ownership of textile production facilities in the country.

One example of this is the maquiladora industries. Prior to the 2000s, maquiladoras owned by Asian concerns who imported materials from Asia to make products for the U.S. enjoyed the same tax advantages as those who used Mexican suppliers. However, this was changed during the beginning of the 21st century. This caused many

Asian maquiladoras to close and move to Asia as the tax advantages no longer compensated for higher labour costs.

Mexico has also complained to the World Trade Organization that China has been engaging in "illegal practices" such as "dumping" (selling abroad at a price lower than local markets) to the detriment of the Mexican industry. Mexico claims that the Chinese government subsidizes textiles sales abroad to gain market share.

Navajo

Navajo rugs and blankets (Navajo: diyogí) are textiles produced by Navajo people of the Four Corners area of the United States. Navajo textiles are highly regarded and have been sought after as trade items for over 150 years. Commercial production of handwoven blankets and rugs has been an important element of the Navajo economy. As one expert expresses it, "Classic Navajo serapes at their finest equal the delicacy and sophistication of any pre-mechanical loom-woven textile in the world."

Navajo textiles were originally utilitarian blankets for use as cloaks, dresses, saddle blankets, and similar purposes. Toward the end of the 19th century, weavers began to make rugs for tourism and export. Typical Navajo textiles have strong geometric patterns. They are a flat tapestry-woven textile produced in a fashion similar to kilims of Eastern Europe and Western Asia, but with some notable differences. In Navajo weaving, the slit weave technique common in kilims is not used, and the warp is one continuous length of yarn, not extending beyond the weaving as fringe. Traders from the late 19th and early 20th century encouraged adoption of some kilim motifs into Navajo designs.

Purpose

The original function of Navajo weaving was to produce clothing: "shoulder robes, rectangular panel or wrap-around-dresses, semi-tailored shirts, breechcloths, and a variety of belts, sashes, hair ties, and garters." The Navajo did not produce rugs until export markets expanded at the end of the 19th century, and their textiles served no specific religious or ceremonial function.

History

Pueblo Influence: The Navajo may have learned to weave from their Pueblo Indian neighbours when they moved into the Four Corners region during the period from 1300 to 1500. Some experts contend that the Navajo were not weavers until after the 17th century. Navajo obtained cotton through local trade routes before the arrival of the Spanish, after which time they began to use wool.

The Pueblo and Navajo were not generally on friendly terms due to frequent Navajo raids on Pueblo settlements, yet many Pueblo sought refuge with their Navajo neighbours in the late 17th century to evade the conquistadors in the aftermath of the Pueblo Revolt. This social interchange is the probable origin of the distinctive Navajo weaving tradition. Spanish records show that Navajo people began to herd sheep and weave wool blankets from that time onward.

The extent of Pueblo influence on Navajo weaving is uncertain. As Wolfgang Haberland notes, "Prehistoric Puebloan textiles were much more elaborate than historic ones, as can be seen in the few remnants recovered archaeologically and in costumed figures in pre-contact kiva murals." Haberland suggests that the absence of surviving colonial-era Pueblo textile examples make it impossible to do more than conjecture about whether the creative origins of Navajo weaving arose from Navajo culture or were borrowed from the neighbouring people.

Early Records

Written records establish the Navajo as fine weavers for at least the last 300 years, beginning with Spanish colonial descriptions of the early 18th century. By 1812, Pedro Piño called the Navajo the best weavers in the province. Few remnants of 18th-century Navajo weaving survive; the most important surviving examples of early Navajo weaving come from Massacre Cave at Canyon de Chelly, Arizona. In 1804, a group of Navajo were shot and killed there, where they were seeking refuge from Spanish soldiers.

For a hundred years the cave remained untouched due to Navajo taboos until a local trader named Sam Day entered it and retrieved the textiles. Day separated the collection and sold it to various museums. The majority of Massacre Cave blankets feature plain stripes, yet some exhibit the terraces and diamonds characteristic of later Navajo weaving.

Wider Commerce

Commerce expanded after the Santa Fe Trail opened in 1822, and greater numbers of examples survive. Until 1880, all such textiles were blankets as opposed to rugs. In 1850, these highly prized trade items sold for $50 in gold, a huge sum at that time.

Railroad service reached Navajo lands in the early 1880s and resulted in considerable expansion of the market for Navajo woven goods. According to Kathy M'Closkey of the University of Windsor in Ontario, Canada, "wool production more than doubled between 1890 and 1910, yet textile production escalated more than 800%".

Purchases of manufactured yarn compensated for the deficit in wool production. Federal government reports affirmed that this weaving, which was performed almost exclusively by women, was the most profitable Navajo industry during that era. Quality declined in some regards as the weavers attempted to keep up with demand. However in today society an average price of a rug goes for about $800.00.

Several European-American merchants influenced Navajo weaving during the next decades. The first to advertise Navajo textiles in a catalogue was C. N. Cotton in 1894. Cotton encouraged professional production and marketing among his peers and the weavers whose work they handled. Another trader named John. B. Moore, who settled in the Chuska Mountains in 1897 attempted to improve the quality of textiles he traded. He attempted to regulate the cleaning and dyeing process of artisans who did business with him, and shipped wool intended for higher grade weaving outside the region for factory cleaning.

He limited the range of dyes in textiles he traded and refused to deal fabric that had included certain commercially produced yarns. Moore's catalogues identified individual textile pieces rather than illustrating representative styles. He appears to have been instrumental in introducing new motifs to Navajo weaving. Carpets from the Caucasus region were popular among Anglo-Americans at that time. Both the Navajo and the Caucasus weavers worked under similar conditions and in similar styles, so it was relatively simple for them to incorporate Caucasus patterns such as an octagonal motif known as a *gul*.

Traders encouraged the locals to weave blankets and rugs into distinct styles. They included "Two Gray Hills" (predominantly black and white, with traditional patterns), "Teec Nos Pos" (colourful, with very extensive patterns), "Ganado" (founded by Don Lorenzo Hubbell), red dominated patterns with black and white, "Crystal" (founded by J. B. Moore), Oriental and Persian styles (almost always with natural dyes), "Wide Ruins," "Chinle," banded geometric patterns, "Klagetoh", diamond type patterns, "Red Mesa" and bold diamond patterns. Many of these patterns exhibit a fourfold symmetry, which is thought by Professor Gary Witherspoon to embody traditional ideas about harmony or Hozh.

Recent Developments

Large numbers of Navajo continue to weave commercially. Contemporary weavers are more likely to learn the craft from a community college course, as opposed to family. A Navajo woman struggles and sacrifices, but for some this is their only source of income. Contemporary Navajo textiles have suffered commercially from two sets of pressures: extensive investment in pre-1950 examples and price competition from foreign imitations. Modern Navajo rugs are indeed notable for their high prices.

Construction

Wool and Yarn: In the late 17th century, the Navajo acquired the Iberian Churra, a breed of sheep from Spanish explorers. These animals were developed into a unique breed by the Navajo, today called the Navajo-Churro.

These sheep were well-suited to the climate in Navajo lands, and that produced a useful long-staple wool. Hand-spun wool from these animals was the main source of yarn for Navajo blankets until the 1860s, when the United States government forced the Navajo people to relocate at Bosque Redondo and seized their livestock.

The 1869 peace treaty that allowed the Navajo to return to their traditional lands included a $30,000 settlement to replace their livestock. The tribe purchased 14,000 sheep and 1,000 goats.

Mid-19th century Navajo rugs often used a three-ply yarn called *Saxony*, which refers to high-quality, naturally dyed, silky yarns. Red tones in Navajo rugs of this period come either from Saxony or from a raveled cloth known in Spanish as *bayeta*, which was a woolen manufactured in England. With the arrival of the railroad in the early 1880s, another machine-produced yarn came into use in Navajo weaving: four-ply aniline dyed yarn known as *Germantown* because the yarn was manufactured in Pennsylvania.

Among the locally produced yarns for Navajo textile, indiscriminate breeding from 1870-1890 caused a steady decline in wool quality. Increasing proportions of brittle kemp can be found in well-preserved examples from the period. In 1903, federal agents attempted to address the problem by introducing Rambouillet rams into the breeding population.

The Rambouillet is a French breed that produces good meat and heavy, fine-wool fleeces. The Rambouillet stock, were well adapted to the Southwestern climate, but their wool was less suitable to hand spinning. Short-stapled Rambouillet wool has a tight crimp, which makes hand spinning difficult.

The higher lanolin content of its wool necessitated significantly more scouring with scarce water before it could be dyed effectively. From 1920 to 1940, when Rambouillet bloodlines dominated the tribe's stock, Navajo rugs have a characteristically curly wool and sometimes a knotted or lumpy appearance.

In 1935, the United States Department of the Interior created the Southwestern Range and Sheep Breeding Laboratory to address the problems Rambouillet stock had caused for the Navajo economy. Located at Fort Wingate, New Mexico, the programme's aim was to develop a new sheep bloodline that simulated the wool characteristics of the 19th-century Navajo-Churro stock and would also supply adequate meat.

The Fort Wingate researchers collected old Navajo-Churro stock from remote parts of the reservation and hired a weaver to test their experimental wool. Offspring of these experiments were distributed among the Navajo people. World War II interrupted the greater part of this effort when military work resumed at Fort Wingate.

Colouration

Prior to the mid-19th century, Navajo weaving colouration was mostly natural brown, white, and indigo. Indigo dye was obtained through trade and purchased in lumps. By the middle of the century, the palette had expanded to include red, black, green, yellow, and gray which signifies different aspects of the earth as defined by different locations of the reservation. Navajo used indigo to obtain shades from pale blue to near black and mixed it with indigenous yellow dyes such as the rabbit brush plant to obtain bright green effects. Red was the most difficult dye to obtain locally. Early Navajo textiles use cochineal, an extract from a Mesoamerican beetle, which often made a circuitous trade route through Spain and England on its way to the Navajo. Reds used in Navajo weaving tended to be raveled from imported textiles. The Navajo obtained black dye through piñon pitch and ashes.

After railroad service began in the early 1880s, aniline dyes became available in bright shades of red, orange, green, purple, and yellow. Gaudy "eyedazzler" weaves dominated the final years of the 19th century. Navajo weaving aesthetics underwent rapid change as artisans experimented with the new palette and a new clientele entered the region whose tastes differed from earlier purchasers. During the later years of the 19th century, the Navajo continued to produce earlier styles for traditional customers while they adopted new techniques for a second market.

Weaving

Traditional Navajo weaving used upright looms with no moving parts. Support poles were traditionally constructed of wood; steel pipe is more common today. The artisan sits on the floor during weaving and wraps the finished portion of fabric underneath the loom as it grows. The average weaver takes anywhere from 2 months to many years to finish a single rug. The size greatly determines the amount of time spent weaving a rug. The ratio of weft to warp threads had a fine count before the Bosque Redondo internment and declined in the following decades, then rose somewhat to a midrange ratio of five to one for the period 1920-1940. 19th-century warps were coloured handspun wool or cotton string, then switched to white handspun wool in the early decades of the 20th century.

Cultural Perspectives

Weaving plays a role in the creation myth of Navajo cosmology, which articulates social relationships and continues to play a role in Navajo culture. According to one aspect of this tradition, a spiritual being called "Spider Woman" instructed the women of the Navajo how to build the first loom from exotic materials including sky, earth, sunrays, rock crystal, and sheet lightning. Then "Spider Woman" taught the Navajo how to weave on it.

Use of traditional motifs sometimes leads to the mistaken notion that these textiles serve a purpose in Navajo religion. Actually these items have no use as prayer rugs or any other ceremonial function, and controversy has existed among the Navajo about the appropriateness of including religious symbolism in items designed for commercial sale. The financial success of purported ceremonial rugs led to their continued production.

Critical Study

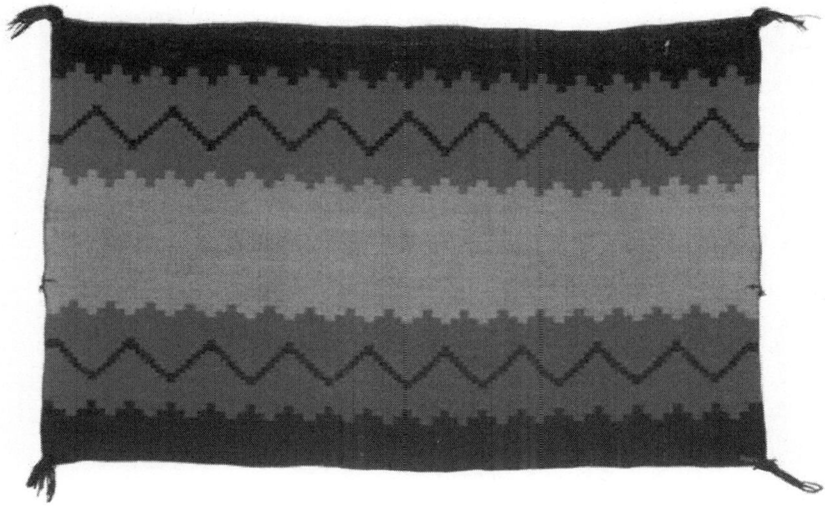

Figure: *Woman's fancy manta, circa 1865. "Navajo people believe in beauty all around and, here, this weaver is weaving her version of beauty." —Sierra Ornelas, Navajo weaver.*

Until recently, anthropologists have dominated the study of Navajo textiles. Most historic examples of these works belong to ethnological collections rather than fine art collections, which mean items have been exhibited and analyzed with an eye toward normative or average works rather than emphasizing technical or artistic excellence. These priorities have artificially inflated the market value for items of inferior craftsmanship. In general, this tendency has affected most non-European art to some degree.

Other factors that have hindered art criticism of Navajo textiles include the common distinction between fine art and applied art and the scholarly theory among some archaeologists and art historians that pure artistic expression cannot exist among non-literate peoples.

Oaxacan

The state of Oaxaca in southern Mexico has a noteworthy tradition of finely crafted textiles, particularly handmade embroidery and woven goods that frequently utilize a backstrap loom. Oaxaca is home to several different groups of indigenous peoples, each of which has a distinctive textile tradition.

Construction

Oaxacan fibres may be hand spun from cotton or locally cultivated silk. Traditional dye sources include *purpura pansa* among the Huave, Chontal, and Mixtec people. The Chontal and Mazatec also utilize cochineal to attain bright red tones.

According to Alejandro de Ávila B., founding director of the Ethnobotanical Garden in Oaxaca, the region's biological diversity yields Mexico's greatest variety of fibres and dyes, and "the technical sophistication of Oaxaca's textiles is unparalelled in the country."

Traditional clothing items among the peoples of Oaxaca include the *huipil*, a women's blouse constructed from several panels; the *ceñidor*, a type of sash among the Mazatec; and the *paño*, a Chinantec head covering. Handcrafted Oaxacan textiles employ plainweave, brocade patterns, gauze weave.

Motifs

Mexican textile expert Irmbard Weitlaner Johnson associates pre-Christian spiritual traditions with the presence of butterflies in Mazatec textile motifs. "To this day the Mazatecs identify the butterfly as the soul that leaves the body. They believe that the souls of the deceased have permission to come to this world once a year on All Saints' Day and the Day of the Dead to visit their family. This is the period when butterflies are most abundant in the area and the Mazatecs consider it a sin to kill them."

Regional motifs without specific spiritual meaning, or for which disputed interpretations exist, include a class of stepped fret known as *xicalcoliuhqui*, which means "twisted ornament for decorating gourds" in the Nahuatl language; and the double spiral *ilhuitl*, whose name translates as "fiesta day."

Pre-Colonial tradition associates colour with the four cardinal directions: yellow with east, red with north, blue and green with west, and white with south.

Another shared motif among the region's indigenous peoples is a rectangular ornament below the neckline of the *huipil*. No specific symbolism is known, but it is a frequent theme in pre-colonial codices and surviving historic textiles that remains in popular use.

Other Symbolic Uses

Traditionally, Oaxacan women wrap a red *faja* (a woven sash) around their waists as a protection from evil.

Blocking

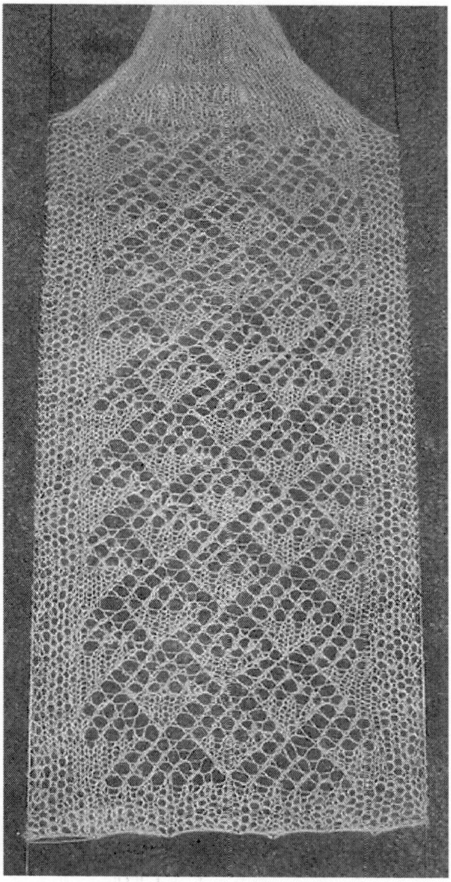

Figure: *knitted scarf during blocking*

In knitting, crochet and other textile arts, blocking is a final stage of handmade textile production that adjusts the shape of the finished piece. Not all pieces need blocking, however blocking is standard for lace work, and is not uncommon in sweaters, socks, and other solid projects. Through heat and moisture, blocking sets the stitches and standardizes the final dimensions, and may enhance the drape. Hand manufacture places natural stresses on fabrics that may result in deviations from its intended shape and size. Blocking is only effective on natural fibres, but a technique called "killing" may be used on synthetic fibres to achieve an effect similar to blocking.

The degree of malleability is determined by the type of yarn used, with wool providing the most flexibility. For projects that are produced in sections, blocking is normally done prior to final assembly.

Fibre Art

Fibre art refers to fine art whose material consists of natural or synthetic fibre and other components, such as fabric or yarn. It focuses on the materials and on the manual labour on the part of the artist as part of the works' significance, and prioritizes aesthetic value over utility.

History

The term fibre art came into use by curators and art historians to describe the work of the artist-craftsman following World War II. Those years saw a sharp increase in the design and production of "art fabric."

In the 1950s, as the contributions of craft artists became more recognized—not just in fibre but in clay and other media—an increasing numbers of weavers began binding fibres into nonfunctional forms as works of art.

The 1960s and '70s brought an international revolution in fibre art. Beyond weaving, fibre structures were created through knotting, twining, plaiting, coiling, pleating, lashing, and interlacing. Artists in the United States and Europe explored the qualities of fabric to develop works that could be hung or free standing, "two or three dimensional, flat or volumetric, many stories high or miniature, nonobjective or figurative, and representational or fantasy."

The women's movement of the same era was important in contributing to the rise of fibre art because of the traditional association of women with textiles in the domestic sphere; indeed, many of the most prominent fibre artists are women.

Since the 1980s, fibre work has become more and more conceptual, influenced by postmodernist ideas. For fibre artists, in addition to long-standing experimentation with materials and techniques, this brought "a new focus on creating work which confronted cultural issues such as: gender feminism; domesticity and the repetitive tasks related to women's work; politics; the social and behavioural sciences;

material specific concepts related to fibre's softness, permeability, drapability, and so on."

Fibre and the Context of the Textile Arts

Modern fibre art takes its context from the textile arts, which have been practiced globally for millennia. Traditionally, fibre is taken from plants or animals, for example cotton from cotton seed pods, linen from flax stems, wool from sheep hair, or silk from the spun cocoons of silkworms. In addition to these traditional materials, synthetic materials such as plastic acrylic are now used.

In order for the fibre to be made into cloth or clothing, it must be spun (or twisted) into a strand known as yarn. When the yarn is ready and dyed for use it can be made into cloth in a number of ways. Knitting and crochet are common methods of twisting and shaping the yarn into garments or fabric. The most common use of yarn to make cloth is weaving. In weaving, the yarn is wrapped on a frame called a loom and pulled taut vertically. This is known as the warp. Then another strand of yarn is worked back and forth wrapping over and under the warp. This wrapped yarn is called the weft. Most art and commercial textiles are made by this process.

For centuries weaving has been the way to produce clothes. In some cultures, weaving forms demonstrate social status. The more intricate the weaving, the higher the status. Certain symbols and colours also allowed identification of class and position. For example, in the ancient Incan civilization, black and white designs indicated a military status.

In Europe between the fourteenth and seventeenth centuries woven pieces called "tapestries" took the place of paintings on walls. The Unicorn in Captivity is part of a series consisting of seven tapestry panels known as *The Hunt of the Unicorn* by Franco Flemish from this time period. Much of the art at the time in history was used to tell common folktales that also had a religious theme. As Mark Getlein wrote, "Tapestry is a special type of weaving in which the weft yarns are manipulated freely to form a pattern or design on the front of the fabric...Often the weft yarns are of several colours and the weaver can use the different-coloured yarns almost as flexible as a painter uses pigment on canvas."

At the same time period in the Middle East, fibre artists did not make tapestry or wall hanging weavings, but instead created beautifully crafted rugs. The woven rugs did not depict scenes in a story, but instead used symbols and complex designs. An example of this type of art are the giant rugs known as the Ardabil carpets. Getlein wrote, "Like most Islamic carpets, they were created by knotting individual tufts of wool onto a woven ground."

Another fibre art technique is quilting in which layers of fabric are sewn together. Although this technique has not been around for as long as weaving, it is a popular form of art in American history. Recently, quilted fibre art wall hangings have become popular with art collectors. This non-traditional form often features bold designs.

Other fibre art techniques are knitting, rug hooking, felting, braiding or plaiting, macrame, lace making, flocking (texture) and more. There are a wide variety of dye techniques. Sometimes cyanotype and heliographic (sun printing) are used.

Fibre artists face the same dilemma of all artists; determining "what is art?" More so with fibre arts and other media associated with handicraft, because they have long been associated with domestic or utilitarian production. Typically, pieces like potholders, which just follow patterns without doing anything more, are not considered works of fibre art. Fibre art works are works of art that communicate some sort of message, emotion or meaning and go beyond just the literal meaning of the materials. Fibre arts face the challenge at times of the message or meaning of the work of art being eclipsed by the study of the materials used and their history, rather than what they contribute to the overall work of art.

Mathematics and Fibre Arts

Mathematical ideas have been used as inspiration for a number of fibre arts including quilt making, knitting, cross-stitch, crochet, embroidery and weaving. A wide range of mathematical concepts have been used as inspiration including topology, graph theory, number theory and algebra. Some techniques such as counted-thread embroidery are naturally geometrical; other kinds of textile provide a ready means for the colourful physical expression of mathematical concepts.

Quilting

The IEEE Spectrum has organized a number of competitions on quilt block design, and several books have been published on the subject. Notable quiltmakers include Diana Venters and Elaine Ellison, who have written a book on the subject *Mathematical Quilts: No Sewing Required.* Examples of mathematical ideas used in the book as the basis of a quilt include the golden rectangle, conic sections, Leonardo da Vinci's Claw, the Koch curve, the Clifford torus, San Gaku, Mascheroni's cardioid, Pythagorean triples, spidrons, and the six trigonometric functions.

Knitting and Crochet

Knitted mathematical objects include the Platonic solids, Klein bottles and Boy's surface. The Lorenz manifold and the hyperbolic plane have been crafted using crochet. Knitted and crocheted tori have also been constructed depicting toroidal embeddings of the complete graph K_7 and of the Heawood graph. The crocheting of hyperbolic planes has been popularized by the Institute For Figuring; a book by Daina Taimina on the subject, *Crocheting Adventures with Hyperbolic Planes*, won the 2009 Bookseller/Diagram Prize for Oddest Title of the Year.

Embroidery

Embroidery techniques such as counted-thread embroidery including cross-stitch and some canvas work methods such as Bargello (needlework) make use of the natural pixels of the weave, lending themselves to geometric designs.

Weaving

Ada Dietz (1882 – 1950) was an American weaver best known for her 1949 monograph *Algebraic Expressions in Handwoven Textiles*, which defines weaving patterns based on the expansion of multivariate polynomials.

J. C. P. Miller (1970) used the Rule 90 cellular automaton to design tapestries depicting both trees and abstract patterns of triangles.

Fashion Design

The Issey Miyake Fall-Winter 2010–2011 ready-to-wear collection featured designs from a collaboration between fashion designer Dai Fujiwara and mathematician William Thurston. The designs were inspired by Thurston's geometrization conjecture, the statement that every 3-manifold can be decomposed into pieces with one of eight different uniform geometries, a proof of which had been sketched in 2003 by Grigori Perelman as part of his proof of the Poincaré conjecture.

Wearable Fibre Art

Wearable art, also known as *Artwear* or "art to wear", refers to individually designed pieces of (usually) handmade clothing or jewellery created as fine or expressive art. While the making of any article of clothing or other wearable object typically involves aesthetic considerations, the term *wearable art* implies that the work is intended to be accepted as a serious and unique artistic creation or statement. Pieces may be sold and/or exhibited.

The modern idea of wearable art seems to have surfaced more than once in various forms. Marbeth Schon's book on modernist jewellery refers to a "wearable art movement" spanning roughly the years 1930 to 1960. A 2003 *New York Times* review of a book on knitting refers to "the 60s Art to Wear movement".

Most wearable art is made of fibrous materials and constitutes therefore a branch of the wider field of fibre art, which includes both wearable and non-wearable forms of art using fabric and other fibre products. Wearable art as an artistic domain can also of course include jewellery, or clothing made from non-fibre materials such as leather, plastic sheeting, metals, etc.

Artists creating wearable fibre art may use purchased finished fabrics or other materials, making them into unique garments, or may dye and/or paint virgin fabric.

Many believe that art is something that requires money in order to make it, but a lot of clothing artists are now starting local clothing companies that produce quality art work and clothing for a decent price. Wearable art is not restricted to jewellery but is also seen in graphic T-shirts and even pants.

As with any other art form, the talent and skills of artists in this field vary widely. Since the nature of the medium requires craft skills as well as artistic skills, an advanced artist can be expected to study colour theory, chemistry, sewing, clothing design, and computer software such as Photoshop and Illustrator. Classes in clothing design and marketing may be learned from such colleges as the Fashion Institute of Technology in New York City.

The New Zealand city of Nelson has gained a worldwide reputation in the field of wearable art, with its *World of WearableArt Awards*, held annually since 1987. From 2005, the show moved to Wellington. In Australia, the Shearwater Wearable Arts or W.A.V.E. (Wearable

Arts Vision In Education) has developed from a High School initiative to become a leading Wearable Arts Event.

Jewellery as Wearable art: the Mid-20th Century "Wearable Art Movement"

Some 20th-century modern artists and architects sought to elevate bodily ornamentation — that is, jewellery — to the level of fine art and original design, rather than mere decoration, craft production of traditional designs, or conventional settings for showing off expensive stones or precious metals.

In "Modernist Jewellery 1930-1960: The Wearable Art Movement" (2004), author Marbeth Schon explores unique and innovative wearable art objects created by surrealists, cubists, abstract expressionists, and other modernist artists working in the middle decades of the 20th century.

Extreme Examples of Wearable Art

Not all garments created as wearable art are made from traditional fibres or fabrics, and not all such artworks are meant for ordinary, practical use. Performance and conceptual artists have sometimes produced examples which are more provocative than useful. Trashion is another branch of extraordinary wearable art. The Portland Oregon Trashion Collective, Junk to Funk, has been using creating outrageous art garments out of trash.

A well-known example is the "Electric Dress", a ceremonial wedding kimono-like costume consisting mostly of variously coloured electrified and painted light bulbs, enmeshed in a tangle of wires, created in 1956 by the Japanese Gutai artist Atsuko Tanaka. This extreme garment was something like a stage costume. Not really wearable in an everyday, practical sense, it functioned rather as part of a daring work of performance art (though the "performance" element consisted merely of the artist's wearing the piece while mingling with spectators in a gallery setting).

In Nam June Paik's 1969 performance piece called "TV Bra for Living Sculpture," Charlotte Moorman played the cello while wearing a bra made of two small television sets.

More recently, Canadian artist Andrea Vander Kooij created a group of pieces called "Garments for Forced Intimacy" (2006). According to an essay at Concordia University's Faculty of Fine Arts gallery website, these hand-knit articles of clothing are designed to be worn by two people, and they, "as the name states, compel the wearers into uncharacteristic proximity."

Use of Polka Dots in Clothing

Polka dot is a pattern consisting of an array of filled circles. Early instances were generally equally sized and spaced relatively closely in relation to their diameters. Many modern prints include more randomly spaced, sized and coloured dots. Polka dots are most commonly seen on children's clothing, toys, and furniture, but they appear in a wide array of contexts.

The pattern rarely appears in formal contexts, however, and is generally confined to more playful attire such as bathing suits and lingerie. Occasionally, white-on-black small dots appear on more formal clothing. Polka dots became common on clothing in the late nineteenth century in the United Kingdom.

Etymology

The pattern shares its name with the dance form, making one suspect there is a connection linking the pattern to the dance. However, the name was likely settled upon merely because of the dance's popularity at the time the pattern became fashionable, just as many other products and fashions of the era also adopted the polka name.

Usage

Traditionally polka dots are used in the clothing of flamenco dancers and performers. Frédéric Bazille's Family Reunion depicts two women in blue polka dot dresses. In 1962, DC Comics introduced Polka-Dot Man with irregularly-sized and differently coloured dots. In 1965, Bob Dylan wore a large print green polka dot shirt on the EP Just like tom thumb's blues. Musician Randy Rhoads used a Flying V guitar with polka dots.

Professional wrestler Dusty Rhodes was given a black outfit covered in yellow polka dots during his time in the WWF. This seemed strange at the time but went on to become a successful and memorable gimmick. Blues guitarist Buddy Guy regularly plays a signature Fender Stratocaster painted in black with cream polka dots. Some people associate polka dots with Venezuelan fashion designer Carolina Herrera, who used polka dots on most of her dresses during the late 80s and early 90s, as well as on the boxes of perfume Carolina

Herrera, Herrera For Men, Aquaflore and Flore. In the Tour de France, the leader in the mountains competition wears a distinctive polka dot jersey (French: maillot à pois rouge). Although the King of the Mountains was first recognised in the 1933 Tour de France, the distinctive jersey was not introduced until 1975. Much of the Japanese artist's Yayoi Kusama's work features a polka dot motif.

There were many other "polka" items, some of which include "polka-hats" and "polka-jackets." Most disappeared with the fad of the actual polka dance. Only the polka dot fabric pattern remained popular, and the name has been left intact over the years.

In 2006, polka dot skirts, dresses, scarves and tops became a fad in the United Kingdom. The polka dot skirts were usually pencil skirts. This started another fashion period, after which silk replaced the polka dot. The Pipettes were instrumental in bringing about this fashion trend.

The polka dot also appears in popular music. "Itsy Bitsy Teenie Weenie Yellow Polka Dot Bikini" is a novelty song telling the story of a shy girl in a very revealing bathing suit who stays immersed in the ocean water to hide from view. It was written by Paul Vance and Lee Pockriss and first released in June 1960 by Brian Hyland. Before that however, "Polka Dots and Moonbeams" was a popular song with music by Jimmy Van Heusen and lyrics by Johnny Burke, published in 1940. It was Frank Sinatra's first hit recorded with the Tommy Dorsey Orchestra. The song is one of the top 100 most-frequently recorded jazz standards with arrangements by Gil Evans and others and notable recordings by Lester Young, Sarah Vaughn and many others.

Mountains Classification in the Tour de France

The Mountains classification in the Tour de France is a secondary classification in the Tour de France, in which cyclists receive points for reaching a mountain top first. The leader of the classification is named the "King of the Mountains", and since 1975 wears the polka dot jersey (French: *maillot à pois rouges*), a white jersey with red dots.

History

The first Tour de France crossed no mountain passes, but several lesser cols. The first was the col des Echarmeaux (712 m (2,336 ft)), on the opening stage from Paris to Lyon, on what is now the old road from Autun to Lyon. The stage from Lyon to Marseille included the col de la République (1,161 m (3,809 ft)), also known as the col du Grand Bois, at the edge of St-Etienne.

The first major climb—the Ballon d'Alsace (1,178 m (3,865 ft)) in the Vosges —was featured in the 1905 race. True mountains, however, were not included until the Pyrenees in 1910.

In that year the race rode, or more walked, first the col d'Aubisque and then the nearby Tourmalet. Desgrange once more stayed away. Both climbs were mule tracks, a demanding challenge on heavy, ungeared bikes ridden by men with spare tires around their shoulders and their food, clothing and tools in bags hung from their handlebars.

The assistant organiser, Victor Breyer, stood at the summit of the Aubisque with the colleague who had proposed including the Pyrenees, Alphonse Steinès. Desgrange was confident enough after the Pyrenees to include the Alps in 1911.

The highest climb in the race was the Cime de la Bonette-Restefond in the 1962 Tour de France, reaching 2802 m. The highest mountain finish in the Tour was at the Col du Galibier in the 2011 edition.

Since 1905, the organising newspaper *l'Auto* named one cyclist of the Tour de France the *meilleur grimpeur* (best climber). In 1933, Vicente Trueba was the winner of this classification. However, Trueba was a very poor descender, so he never gained anything from reaching the tops first.

The Tour de France director, Henri Desgrange, decided that cyclists should receive a bonus for reaching the tops first. From 1934 on, the gap between the first and the second cyclist to reach the top was given as a time bonus to the one reaching the top first. These time bonuses were later removed, but the King of the Mountain recognition remained.

Although the best climber was first recognised in 1933, the distinctive jersey was not introduced until 1975. The colours were decided by the then sponsor, *Poulain Chocolate* or Chocolat Poulain, whose chocolate bars were covered in a polka dot wrapper.

Currently the jersey is sponsored by Carrefour supermarkets, which has sponsored the jersey since 1993, initially under the Champion brand, it switched to the main Carrefour brand for the 2009 edition of the Tour.

The Tour's jersey colours have also been adopted by other cycling stage races; for example, the Tour of Britain also has a polka dot jersey.

Current Situation

At the top of each climb in the Tour, there are points for the riders who are first over the top.

The climbs are divided into categories from 1 (most difficult) to 4 (least difficult) based on their difficulty, measured as a function of their steepness and length.

A few of the toughest climbs were originally given different individual points scales, and were thus listed as "uncategorised" (*Hors catégorie*, a term that has since passed into the French language to refer to any exceptional phenomenon); however, since the 1980s in fact the *hors catégorie* climbs have been given a single points scale and effectively became, despite the name, just a top category above category 1.

In 2004, the scoring system was changed such that the first rider over a fourth category climb was awarded 3 points while the first to complete a *hors catégorie* climb would win 20 points.

Further points over a fourth category climb are only for the top three places while on a *hors catégorie* climb the top ten riders are rewarded.

Since 2004, points scored on the final climb of the day have been doubled where that climb was at least a second category climb.

Distribution of Points

The points that are gained by consecutive riders reaching a mountain top are distributed according to the following classification:

Point Distribution Grid as of 2011

	4C	3C	2C	1C	HC
1st	1	2	5	10	20
2nd		1	3	8	16
3rd			2	6	12
4th			1	4	8
5th				2	4
6th				1	2

Point Distribution Grid as of 2012

	4C	3C	2C	1C	HC
1st	1	2	5	10	25
2nd		1	3	8	20
3rd			2	6	16
4th			1	4	14
5th				2	12
6th				1	10
7th					8
8th					6
9th					4
10th					2

The points for a mountain top finish are doubled, if that mountain is an HC, 1C or 2C. The organisation of the race determines which mountains are included for the mountains classification and in which category they are.

If two riders have an equal number of points, the rider with the most first places on the *hors catégorie* cols, is declared winner. If the riders arrived first, an equal number of times, the first places on the 1st category cols are compared. Should the two riders again have an equal number of first arrivals in this category, the organization looks at mutual results in the 2nd, 3rd and 4th category, until a winner is found. If the number of first arrivals in all categories is equal for both riders, the rider with the highest position in the overall list of rankings receives the mountain jersey.

Up until 2011 the points that are gained by climbing the mountains were distributed according to the following classification:

- Hors Catégorie climbs: 20, 18, 16, 14, 12, 10, 8, 7, 6 and 5 points respectively for the 1st until the 10th rider to climb the mountain
- First category climbs: 15, 13, 11, 9, 8, 7, 6 and 5 points respectively for the 1st until the 8th rider to climb the mountain
- Second category climbs: 10, 9, 8, 7, 6 and 5 points respectively for the 1st until the 6th rider to climb the mountain
- Third category climbs and hills : 4, 3, 2 and 1 point, respectively for the 1st until the 4th rider to climb the hill

- Fourth category climbs (hills): 3, 2, and 1 point, respectively for the 1st until the 3rd rider to climb the hill.

Criticism of the System

In recent years, the system has had some criticism. Six-time winner Lucien Van Impe said that the mountain jersey has been devalued, because it goes to cyclists who have no hope to win the general classification so are allowed to escape and gather points in breakaways.

This tactic was started by cyclists such as Laurent Jalabert and Richard Virenque, but according to Van Impe, they were really able to climb. Van Impe has proposed to award time bonuses, which may heat up the battle.

4

Needlework for Textile Arts Fashion Accessories

Needlework is a broad term for the handicrafts of decorative sewing and textile arts. Anything that uses a needle for construction can be called needlework.

The definition may expand to include related textile crafts such as a crochet hook or tatting shuttles.

Similar abilities often transfer well between different varieties of needlework, such as fine motor skill and a knowledge of textile fibres. Some of the same tools may be used in several different varieties of needlework. For instance, a needle threader is useful in nearly all needlecrafts.

Types of Needlework

- Needle lace
- Quilting
- Applique
- Embroidery
- Crochet
- Knitting
- Tatting
- Lucet
- Braiding and Tassel making
- Tapestry

Europa

Bayeux Tapestry

The Bayeux Tapestry is an embroidered cloth—not an actual tapestry—nearly 70 metres (230 ft) long, which depicts the events leading up to the Norman conquest of England concerning William, Duke of Normandy, and Harold, Earl of Wessex, later King of England, and culminating in the Battle of Hastings.

According to Sylvette Lemagnen, conservator of the tapestry,t, the Bayeux tapestry is one of the supreme achievements of the Norman Romanesque, ... Its survival almost intact over nine centuries is little short of miraculous, ... Its exceptional length, the harmony and freshness of its colours, its exquisite workmanship, and the genius of its guiding spirit combine to make it endlessly fascinating.

The tapestry consists of some fifty scenes with Latin *tituli* (captions), embroidered on linen with coloured woollen yarns. It is likely that it was commissioned by Bishop Odo, William's half-brother, and made in England—not Bayeux—in the 1070s. In 1729 the hanging was rediscovered by scholars at a time when it was being displayed annually in Bayeux Cathedral. The tapestry is now exhibited at *Musée de la Tapisserie de Bayeux* in Bayeux, Normandy, France.

Origins

The earliest known written reference to the tapestry is a 1476 inventory of Bayeux Cathedral, but its origins have been the subject of much speculation and controversy.

French legend maintained the tapestry was commissioned and created by Queen Matilda, William the Conqueror's wife, and her ladies-in-waiting. Indeed, in France it is occasionally known as "La Tapisserie de la Reine Mathilde" (Tapestry of Queen Matilda). However, scholarly analysis in the 20th century concluded it was probably commissioned by William's half-brother, Bishop Odo, who, after the Conquest, became Earl of Kent and, when William was absent in Normandy, regent of England.

The reasons for the Odo commission theory include:

1) three of the bishop's followers mentioned in the *Domesday Book* appear on the tapestry;
2) it was found in Bayeux Cathedral, built by Odo; and

3) it may have been commissioned at the same time as the cathedral's construction in the 1070s, possibly completed by 1077 in time for display on the cathedral's dedication.

Assuming Odo commissioned the tapestry, it was probably designed and constructed in England by Anglo-Saxon artists (Odo's main power base being by then in Kent); the Latin text contains hints of Anglo-Saxon; other embroideries originate from England at this time; and the vegetable dyes can be found in cloth traditionally woven there.

The actual physical work of stitching was most likely undertaken by skilled seamsters. Anglo-Saxon needlework, or Opus Anglicanum, was famous across Europe.

Alternative theories exist. Carola Hicks has suggested it could possibly have been commissioned by Edith of Wessex; and Howard B. Clarke has proposed that the designer of the tapestry was Scolland, the abbot of St Augustine's Abbey, because of his previous position as head of the scriptorium at Mont Saint-Michel (famed for its illumination), his travels to Trajan's Column, and his connections to Wadard and Vital, two individuals identified in the tapestry.

Wolfgang Grape has challenged the consensus that the embroidery is Anglo-Saxon, distinguishing between Anglo-Saxon and other Northern European techniques; Medieval material authority Elizabeth Coatsworth contradicted this:

> *"The attempt to distinguish Anglo-Saxon from other Northern European embroideries before 1100 on the grounds of technique cannot be upheld on the basis of present knowledge."*

George Beech suggests the tapestry was executed at the Abbey of St. Florent in the Loire Valley, and says the detailed depiction of the Breton campaign argues for additional sources in France. Andrew Bridgeford has suggested that the tapestry was actually of English design and encoded with secret messages meant to undermine Norman rule.

Construction, Design and Technique

In common with other embroidered hangings of the early medieval period, this piece is conventionally referred to as a "tapestry", although it is not a true tapestry in which the design is woven into the cloth; it is in fact an embroidery.

The Bayeux tapestry is embroidered in wool yarn on a tabby-woven linen ground 68.38 metres long and 0.5 metres wide (224.3 × 1.6 ft) and using two methods of stitching: outline or stem stitch for lettering and the outlines of figures, and couching or laid work for filling in figures. Nine linen panels, between fourteen and three metres in length, were sewn together after each was embroidered and the joins were disguised with subsequent embroidery.

At the first join (start of scene 14) the borders do not line up properly but the technique was improved so that the later joins are practically invisible. The design involved a broad central zone with narrow decorative borders top and bottom. By inspecting the woollen threads behind the linen it is apparent all these aspects were embroidered together at a session and the awkward placing of the *tituli* is not due to them being added later.

Later generations have patched the hanging in numerous places and some of the embroidery (especially in the final scene) has been reworked. The tapestry may well have maintained much of its original appearance—it now compares closely with a careful drawing made in 1730.

The main yarn colours are terracotta or russet, blue-green, dull gold, olive green, and blue, with small amounts of dark blue or black and sage green. Later repairs are worked in light yellow, orange, and light greens. Laid yarns are couched in place with yarn of the same or contrasting colour.

The tapestry's central zone contains most of the action, which sometimes overflows into the borders either for dramatic effect or because depictions would otherwise be very cramped (for example at Edward's death scene). Events take place in a long series of scenes which are generally separated by highly stylised trees. However, the trees are not placed consistently and the greatest scene shift, between Harold's audience with Edward after his return to England and Edward's burial scene, is not marked in any way at all.

The *tituli* are normally in the central zone but occasionally use the top border. The borders are otherwise mostly purely decorative and only sometimes does the decoration complement the action in the central zone. The decoration consists of birds, beasts, fish and scenes from fables, agriculture and hunting. There are frequent oblique bands separating the vignettes. There are nude figures, some of corpses from battle, others of a ribald nature. A harrow, a newly invented implement, is depicted (scene 10) and this is the earliest known depiction. The picture of Halley's Comet, which appears in the upper border (scene 32), is the first known picture of this comet.

The end of the tapestry has been missing from time immemorial and the final *titulus* "Et fuga verterunt Angli" ("and the English left fleeing") is said to be "entirely spurious", added shortly before 1814 at a time of anti-English sentiment. Musset speculates the hanging was originally about 1.5 metres longer.

At the last section still remaining the embroidery has been almost completely restored but this seems to have been done with at least some regard to the original stitching. The stylised tree is quite unlike any other tree in the tapestry. The start of the tapestry has also been restored but to a much lesser extent

In 1724 a linen backing cloth was sewn on comparatively crudely and, in around the year 1800, large ink numerals were written on the backing which broadly enumerate each scene and which are still commonly used for reference.

Background to the Events Depicted

In a series of pictures supported by a written commentary the tapestry tells the story of the events of 1064–1066 culminating in the Battle of Hastings. The two main protagonists are Harold Godwinson, recently crowned King of England, leading the Anglo-Saxon English, and William, Duke of Normandy, leading a mainly Norman army, sometimes called the companions of William the Conqueror.

William was the illegitimate son of Robert the Magnificent, Duke of Normandy, and Herleva (or Arlette), a tanner's daughter. William became Duke of Normandy at the age of seven and was in control of Normandy by the age of nineteen. His half brother was Bishop Odo of Bayeux.

King Edward the Confessor, king of England and about sixty years old at the time the tapestry starts its narration, had no children or any clear successor. Edward's mother, Emma of Normandy, was William's great aunt.

At that time succession to the English throne was not by primogeniture but was decided jointly by the king and by an assembly of nobility, the Witenagemot.

Harold Godwinson, earl of Wessex and the most powerful noble in England, was Edward's brother-in-law. The Norman chronicler William of Poitiers recorded that Edward sent Harold to tell William that Edward had decided William should succeed him as king of England upon his (Edward's) death. However, other sources dispute this claim.

Events Depicted in the Tapestry

The tapestry begins with a panel of Edward the Confessor sending Harold to Normandy. Later Norman sources say that the mission was for Harold to pledge loyalty to William but the tapestry does not suggest any specific purpose. By mischance, Harold arrives at the wrong location in France and is taken prisoner by Guy, Count of Ponthieu.

After exchanges of messages borne by mounted messengers, Harold is released to William who then invites Harold to come on a campaign against Conan II, Duke of Brittany. On the way, just outside the monastery of Mont Saint-Michel, the army become mired in quicksand and Harold saves two Norman soldiers. William's army chases Conan from Dol de Bretagne to Rennes, and Conan finally surrenders at Dinan. William gives Harold arms and armour (possibly knighting him) and Harold takes an oath on saintly relics. Although the writing on the tapestry explicitly states an oath is taken there is no clue as to what is being promised.

Harold leaves for home and meets again with the old king Edward, who appears to be remonstrating with him. Harold is in a somewhat submissive posture and seems to be in disgrace. However, possibly deliberately, the king's intentions are not made clear. The scene then shifts by about one year to when Edward has become mortally ill and the tapestry strongly suggests that, on his deathbed, he bequeaths the crown to Harold. What is probably the coronation ceremony is attended by Stigand, whose position as Archbishop of Canterbury was controversial. Stigand is performing a liturgical function, possibly not the crowning itself. The tapestry labels the celebrant as "Stigant Archieps" (Stigand the archbishop) although by that time he had been excommunicated by the papacy who considered his appointment unlawful.

A star with a streaming tail then appears: Halley's Comet. Comets, in the beliefs of the Middle Ages, were a bad omen. At this point the lower border of the tapestry shows a fleet of ghost-like ships thus hinting at a future invasion. The news of Harold's coronation is taken to Normandy, whereupon we are told that William is ordering a fleet of ships to be built although it is Bishop Odo shown issuing the instructions.

The invaders reach England, and land unopposed. William orders his men to find food, and a meal is cooked. A house is burnt, which may indicate some ravaging of the local countryside on the part of the invaders. News is brought to William. The Normans build a motte and bailey at Hastings to defend their position. Messengers are sent between the two armies, and William makes a speech to prepare his army for battle.

The Battle of Hastings was fought on 14 October 1066 less than three weeks after the Battle of Stamford Bridge but the tapestry does not provide this context.

The English fight on foot behind a shield wall, whilst the Normans are on horses. Two fallen knights are named as Leofwine and Gyrth, Harold's brothers, but both armies are shown fighting bravely. Bishop Odo brandishes his baton or mace and rallies the Norman troops in battle. To reassure his knights that he is still alive and well, William raises his helmet to show his face.

The battle becomes very bloody with troops being slaughtered and dismembered corpses littering the ground. King Harold is killed. This scene can be interpreted in different ways, as the name "Harold" appears above a number of knights, making it difficult to identify which character is Harold. The final remaining scene shows unarmoured English troops fleeing the battlefield. The last part of the tapestry is missing but it is thought that story never continued for very much further.

Latin Text

Tituli are included on many scenes to point out names of people and places or to explain briefly the event being depicted. The text is in Latin but at times the style of words and spelling shows an English influence. A dark blue wool, almost black, is mostly used but towards the end of the tapestry other colours are used, sometimes for each word and other times for each letter. The complete text and an English translations are displayed beside images of each scene at Bayeux Tapestry tituli.

History of the Tapestry

The first reference to the tapestry is from 1476 when it was listed in an inventory of the treasures of Bayeux Cathedral. It survived the sack of Bayeux by the Huguenots in 1562; and the next certain reference is from 1724. Antoine Lancelot sent a report to the *Académie Royale des Inscriptions et Belles-Lettres* concerning a sketch he had received about a work concerning William the Conqueror. He had no idea whether the original was a sculpture or painting though he mooted it could be a tapestry.

Despite his further enquiries he discovered no more. However, the Benedictine scholar Bernard de Montfaucon made more successful investigations and found that the sketch was of a small portion of a tapestry preserved at Bayeux Cathedral.

In 1729 and 1730 he published drawings and a detailed description of the complete work in the first two volumes of his *Les Monuments de la Monarchie française*. The drawings were by Antoine Benoît, one of the ablest draughtsmen of that time.

The tapestry was first briefly noted in English in 1743 by William Stukeley, in his *Palaeographia Britannica*. The first detailed account in English was written by Smart Lethieullier, who was living in Paris in 1732–3, and was acquainted with Lancelot and de Montfaucon: it was not published, however, until 1767.

During the French Revolution, in 1792, the tapestry was confiscated as public property to be used for covering military wagons. It was rescued from a wagon by a local lawyer who stored it in his house until the troubles were over when he sent it to the city administrators for safekeeping. After the Terror the Fine Arts Commission, set up to safeguard national treasures, in 1803 required it to be removed to Paris for display at the Musée Napoléon. When Napoleon abandoned his planned invasion of Britain its propaganda value was lost and it was returned to Bayeux where the council displayed it on a winding apparatus of two cylinders. Despite scholars' concern that the tapestry was becoming damaged the council refused to return it to the Cathedral.

In 1816 the Society of Antiquaries of London commissioned its historical draughtsman, Charles Stothard, to visit Bayeux to make an accurate hand-coloured facsimile of the tapestry. His drawings were subsequently engraved by James Basire jr., and published by the Society in 1819-23. Stothard's images are still of value as a record of the tapestry as it was before 19th-century restoration.

By 1842 the tapestry was displayed in a special-purpose room in the Bibliothèque Publique. It required special storage in 1870 with the threatened invasion of Normandy in the Franco-Prussian War and again in 1939–1944 by the Ahnenerbe during the German occupation of France and the Normandy landings.

On 27 June 1944 the Gestapo took the tapestry to the Louvre and on 18 August, three days before the Wehrmacht withdrew from Paris, Himmler sent a message (intercepted by Bletchley Park) ordering it to be taken to "a place of safety", thought to be Berlin.

It was only on 22 August that the SS attempted to take possession of the tapestry by which time the Louvre was again in French hands. After the liberation of Paris, on 25 August, the tapestry was again put on public display in the Louvre and in 1945 it was returned to Bayeux where it is exhibited at *Musée de la Tapisserie de Bayeux.*

Critical Reception

The inventory listing of 1476 shows that the tapestry was being hung annually in Bayeux Cathedral for the week of the Feast of St. John the Baptist and this was still the case in 1728 although by that time the purpose was merely to air the hanging which was otherwise stored in a chest. Clearly, the work was being well cared for. In the eighteenth century the artistry was regarded as crude or even barbarous — red and yellow multi-coloured horses upset some critics. It was thought to be unfinished because the linen was not covered with embroidery.

However, its exhibition in the Louvre in 1797 caused a sensation with *Le Moniteur*, which normally dealt with foreign affairs, reporting on it on its first two pages. It inspired a popular musical *La Tapisserie de la Reine Mathilde.* It was because the tapestry was regarded as an antiquity, rather than a work of art, that in 1804 it was returned to Bayeux where in 1823 one commentator, A. L. Léchaudé d'Anisy, reported "there is a sort of purity in its primitive forms, especially considering the state of the arts in the eleventh century".

The tapestry was becoming a tourist attraction with Robert Southey complaining of the need to queue to see the work In the 1843 *Hand-book for Travellers in France* by John Murray III a visit was included on *Recommended Route 26 (Caen to Cherbourg via Bayeux)* and this guidebook led John Ruskin to go there describing it as "the most interesting thing in its way conceivable". Charles Dickens was not impressed: "It is certainly the work of amateurs; very feeble amateurs at the beginning and very heedless some of them too".

During the Second World War Heinrich Himmler coveted the work regarding it as "Important for our glorious and cultured Germanic history".

Mysteries

The tapestry contains several mysteries:

- The identity of Harold II of England in the vignette depicting his death is disputed. Some recent historians disagree with the traditional view that Harold II is the figure struck in the eye with an arrow. The view that it is Harold is supported by the fact that the words *Harold Rex* (King Harold) appear right above the figure's head. However, the arrow is a later addition following a period of repair. Evidence of this can be found in a comparison with engravings of the tapestry in 1729 by Bernard de Montfaucon, in which the arrow is absent. However, needle holes in the linen suggest that there had been something previously in this place: though possibly a lance. A figure is slain with a sword in the subsequent plate and the phrase above the figure refers to Harold's death (*Interfectus est,* "he is slain"). This would appear to be more consistent with the labelling used elsewhere in the work. It was common medieval iconography that a perjurer was to die with a weapon through the eye. Therefore, the tapestry might be said to emphasize William's rightful claim to the throne by depicting Harold as an oath breaker. Whether he actually died in this way remains a mystery and is much debated.
- There is a panel with what appears to be a clergyman touching or possibly striking a woman's face. No one knows the meaning of the caption above this scene *ubi unus clericus et Ælfgyva,* "where [or *in which/during which*] a certain cleric and Ælfgyua", a Latinised version of Ælfgifu, a popular Anglo-Saxon woman's name. The elided AE shows familiarity with English spelling. There are two naked male figures in the border below this figure; the one directly below the figure is

squatting and displaying genitalia, a scene that was frequently censored in former reproductions. Historians speculate that it may represent a well known scandal of the day that needed no explanation. However, similar naked figures appear elsewhere in the lower border where there seems to be no connection at all with the main action.

- At least two panels of the tapestry are missing, perhaps even another 6.4 m (7.0 yd) worth. This missing area would probably have included William's coronation.

Reliability

The Bayeux Tapestry was probably commissioned by the House of Normandy and essentially depicts a Norman viewpoint. However, Harold is shown as brave and his soldiers are not belittled. Throughout, William is described as "dux" (duke) whereas Harold, also called dux up to his coronation, is subsequently called "rex" (king). The fact that the narrative extensively covers Harold's activities in Normandy (in 1064) indicates that the intention was to show a strong relationship between that expedition and the Norman Conquest starting two years later. It is for this reason that the tapestry is generally seen by modern scholars as an apologia for the Norman Conquest.

The tapestry's narration seems to place stress on Harold's oath to William although its rationale is not made clear. Norman sources claimed that the English succession was being pledged to William but English sources gave varied accounts. Today it is thought the Norman sources are to be preferred. Both the tapestry and Norman sources named Stigand, the excommunicated Archbishop of Canterbury, as the man who crowned Harold, possibly to discredit Harold's kingship; English sources suggested that he was crowned by Ealdred, Archbishop of York and favoured by the papacy, making Harold's position as legitimate king more secure. Contemporary scholarship has not decided the matter although it is generally thought Ealdred performed the coronation.

While political propaganda or personal emphasis may have somewhat distorted the historical accuracy of the story, the Bayeux tapestry presents a unique visual document of medieval arms, apparel, and other objects unlike any other artifact surviving from this period. There is no attempt at continuity between scenes either for individuals' appearance or clothing. The knights carry shields, but show no system of hereditary coats of arms—the beginnings of modern heraldic structure were in place, but would not become standard until the middle of the 12th century. It has been noted that the warriors are depicted fighting with bare hands, while other sources indicate the general use of gloves in battle and hunt.

Artistic Context

Tapestry fragments have been found in Scandinavia dating from the ninth century and it is thought that Norman and Anglo-Saxon embroidery developed from this sort of work. Examples are to be found in the grave goods of the Oseberg ship and the Överhogdal tapestries.

A monastic text from Ely, the *Liber Eliensis*, mentions a woven narrative wall-hanging commemorating the deeds of Byrhtnoth, killed in 991. Wall-hangings were common by the tenth century with English and Norman texts particularly commending the skill of Anglo-Saxon seamstresses. Mural paintings imitating draperies still exist in France and Italy and there are twelfth century mentions of other wall-hangings in Normandy and France.

A poem by Baldric of Dol might even be describing the Bayeux Tapestry itself. Therefore, the Bayeux Tapestry was not unique at the time it was created—rather it is remarkable for being the sole surviving example of Middle Ages' narrative needlework.

Replicas & Continuations

There are a number of replicas of the Bayeux Tapestry in existence. Through the collaboration of William Morris with textile manufacturer Thomas Wardle, Wardle's wife Elizabeth, who was an accomplished seamstress, embarked on creating a reproduction in 1885. She organised some 37 women in her *Leek School of Art Embroidery* to collaborate working from a full-scale water-colour facsimile drawing provided by the South Kensington Museum

The full-size replica was finished in 1886 and is now exhibited in the Museum of Reading in Reading, Berkshire, England. The naked figure in the original tapestry is depicted wearing a brief garment because the drawing which was worked from was similarly bowdlerised.

Ray Dugan of University of Waterloo, Ontario, Canada, completed a stitched replica in 1996. Since its completion, it has been displayed in various museums and galleries in Canada and the United States.

Starting in 2000, the Bayeux Group, part of the Viking Group Lindholm Høje, has been making an accurate replica of the Bayeux Tapestry in Denmark, using the original sewing technique.

A hand-painted full-size replica of the Bayeux Tapestry is at the University of West Georgia, Carrollton, Georgia, United States. It is displayed in the third floor atrium of the Humanities building as part of an art gallery. Dr. E. D. Wheeler, former judge and former dean at Oglethorpe University, commissioned the work and donated it to the university in 1997.

An approximately half scale mosaic version of the Bayeux Tapestry is on display at Geraldine, New Zealand. It was created by Michael Linton over a period of twenty years from 1979. The work includes a hypothetical reconstruction of the missing final section of the Tapestry up to William The Conqueror's coronation at Westminster Abbey on Christmas Day, 1066.

Similarly, other modern artists have attempted to complete the work by creating panels depicting subsequent events up to William's coronation, though the actual content of the missing panels is unknown. In 1997, the embroidery artist Jan Messent completed a reconstruction showing William accepting the surrender of English nobles at Berkhamsted (*Beorcham*), Hertfordshire, and his coronation. In early 2013, 416 residents of Alderney in the Channel Islands finished a continuation including William's coronation and the building of the Tower of London.

In Popular Culture

The tapestry was cited by Scott McCloud in *Understanding Comics* as an example of early narrative art and Bryan Talbot, a British comic book artist, has called it "the first known British comic strip".

Because it resembles a movie storyboard, is widely recognised and, by modern standards at least, is so distinctive in its artistic style, the Bayeux Tapestry has frequently been used or reimagined in a variety of different popular culture contexts.

It has inspired many modern political and other cartoons, including the 15 July 1944 cover of the *New Yorker* magazine marking D-Day; and George Gale's pastiche chronicling the saga leading up to Britain's entry into the European Economic Community, published across six pages in *The Times*'s "Europa" supplement on 1 January 1973.

The tapestry has also inspired modern embroideries, notably the Overlord embroidery commemorating the Normandy landings invasion, now at Portsmouth; and the Prestonpans Tapestry, which chronicles the events surrounding the Battle of Prestonpans in 1745.

A number of films have used sections of the tapestry in their opening credits or closing titles, including: the Disney film *Bedknobs and Broomsticks*, Anthony Mann's *El Cid*, Zeffirelli's *Hamlet*, Frank Cassenti's *La Chanson de Roland*, *Robin Hood: Prince of Thieves*, and Richard Fleischer's *The Vikings*.

The tapestry is referenced in Tony Kushner's play *Angels in America*. The apocryphal account of Queen Matilda's creation of the tapestry is used, perhaps in order to demonstrate that Louis, one of the main characters, holds himself to mythological standards.

Floral Cording Handwork Embroidery Allover Designs

The Allover Patterns has been introduced by Our professional Designers, they are incredible and talented designers. The designers are fairly innovative and capable of developing ideal patterns for different events. This cotton cloth Allover Pattern Fashion have a mixture of floral embroidering with modern elements. The mixture of top quality materials, rich designs and lustrous floral will absolutely pleasure anybody eyes. Its ideal for design variety of casual, semi-formal, formal and wedding dresses.

Super Allover Pattern has a beautiful floral style and nice light and dark contrast colour combinations with beautiful motif and zari thread hand work design.

The pattern is in natural style and have a beautiful and nice floral designs. Its used to modify Bridal wear salwar kameez, Lehenga Suit and Anarkali dress to give latest floral style. This floral figure is very useful as a patch to design bed sheets, curtain, door ark designs.

This Allover Pattern is combination of Indian cultural embroidery work. It has glamorous floral patches with beautiful red satin patti work. Foam embroidered pattern has old-fashion but this pattern is designed after some modification so that it may follows the latest trend.

This pattern is introduce with trendy mirror outing floral with 3mm sequins stitch work looking gorgeous. It's best suits in Anarkali Suit, salwar kameez and patiala salwar style dresses.

Red and Blue Allover Pattern in beautiful floral work style this pattern has a nice stuff and designed of motifs and 3mm sequins stitches. This pattern is also called natural floral fashion. Nice and beautiful style pattern is perfect to make casual and formal salwar kameez and tops or trousers. The floral figure is also useful in jewellery designs to make earrings, anklets, bangles and bracelet.

Embroidered Linen Allover Pattern has latest and beautiful floral designs and nice welly work in arrow motifs style. This new pattern Heavy Thick Stuff of embroidery work. This pattern also decorated with 3mm sequin s stitch designs too. Its ideal to design casual wear dresses like Kurtis, Frocks or tops also in home decor stuffs like table runner, carpets and curtain designs as well.

Freehand embroidered Allover Pattern has nice multi colour design in wool thread rubber embroideries style. This types of pattern is favorite for all girls to design party wear dresses. This pattern is light in weight and glittering with mirror work which has foam embroidery and run stitch outing in blue colour. This pattern in Long Kurtis, Salwar Suit with Ladies Trouser is looking beautiful.

5

Alphabet Design Embroidery

Alphabet design embroidery is not technically a "type" of embroidery but rather a term many people currently use to describe adding letters to a piece of cloth. Victorian ladies called in "marking" linens as it made it easy for them to tell what piece of clothing or article belonged to which family member. It was also indispensable when sending items out to be cleaned to ensure their return.

The beauty of the stitching, whether white on white or using colours, was so evident, it became common place for young ladies to embroider initials on handkerchiefs and other items to be used as gifts.

Victorian ladies would have to use graph paper and/or their artistic skills to enlarge an image and then use carbon paper to copy the image onto their fabrics.

Today, luckily for us, the computer is great (and fast) for this. Even the simplest of graphics programmes can enlarge pictures with ease. Transferring the design can now be done using carbon paper as many Victorian ladies did or by using one of the many transfer methods available on the market today.

The instructions for the following alphabet design embroidery is as described in *A Treatise on Embroidery-Crochet and Knitting with Illustrations*, by M. Hemingway & Sons Silk Company, dated 1899:

Initials for Marking Household Linens

Ladies who are able to copy, will have no difficulty in following the simple characters - in drawing and enlarging them on the material to be embroidered.

By using carbon paper they can easily be transferred.

In embroidering letters make a foundation with Persian Floss, and cover the design with Spanish Floss, taking the stitches in opposite direction to those made in the filling, after the style of working Pepper berries.

The statement above "after the style of working Pepper berries" refers to the raised affect that is achieved when laying down a layer of stitches and then covering those with satin stitch in the opposite direction.

Applique Victorian Style

In this article, included under the name of Applique, or "applied" work, is every sort of embroidery which, being worked solidly on one material, is then cut out and laid down upon another, and secured by various ornamental stitches.

Figure: *Applique on Linen*

This is rather a rough-and-ready definition, and requires amplification. Suppose, for instance, that a certain material is to be ornamented by having a group of flowers repeated over the surface at regular intervals. The group of flowers, or what not, is worked on some stout ground, such as Holland or coarse linen; when finished so far, the work is cut out carefully, the scissors following round the edge of the work about a quarter of an inch or half an inch away, according to the size and nature of the work; the work is then laid upon the ground material, which is ready stretched in a frame.

When a spray of flowers is well in its place, care being taken that every leaf shall be duly laid and no curve pulled the least out of shape, the raw edges are secured by firm stitches, and the whole design is edged with a gold thread, or a twist of silk or wool, or with a gimp or braid, according to the nature of the materials which are being dealt with. This method of work is, in fact, considerably modified by the materials employed.

For a great bold Applique wall-hanging in wools on serge the same nicety of finish should not show that would be required for a delicate piece of work in fine silk and gold thread, to be laid on a choice bit of satin.

In the former, the cut edges would be covered by the broad gimp or cord surrounding the design, whereas in the finer work the edges, wherever possible, must be dexterously tucked away underneath; for the slim outline will not hide any unevenness here, and nothing looks so clumsy and ugly as a thick outline too heavy the design. This turning-in of edges and sewing down very neatly is the most troublesome part of the work, and requires deft fingers.

One has to be careful not to cut too near the work, nor too deep into the corners; but the broader the margin left, the more tiresome it is to turn in neatly, especially if the design is small or the least bit intricate. The design for such work should be of the simplest and broadest; leaves should have a simple outline, or if serrated the serrations can be shown by two or three little stitches within the outline.

There would be nothing elaborate or troublesome in this if worked in some stitches but in the form of work discussed here would be almost impossible to do neatly. It really makes no sense in trying to conquer impossibilities when there is a straight and simple way of doing what is wanted.

Now, the very fact that broad and simple forms are a sine qua non in this method, makes the work very well adapted for decoration that is intended to catch the eye at a distance; but for richer work to be admired and handled more elaboration will be wanted in finishing. Flourishes and tendrils can be added, or a whole background pattern introduced behind the solid Applique groups. This sort of "tracery" seems to give a coherence to the heavier parts of the design, and is very helpful in enriching and lightening it.

Applique is not a stitch or series of stitches, but a certain method of work, irrespective of the stitches employed therein. But certain stitches are more adapted than others for working the groups and sprays to be applied.

The more solid stitches will, of course, be used, and the various sorts of raised couching, especially gold couching, are perhaps the best for this purpose, and the stiffer worked the better. Botticelli, the Florentine artist, is said by his historian, Vasari, to have been especially fond of this work and to have made designs for it. Vasari, indeed, said that he invented it, but it is suspected this of being a flight of the historian's imagination, which was lively at times, and not likely to err on the side of understating the case.

A simple form of applied work that is far from costly so far as concerns time and material, and yet effective, consists of cutting out shapes in coloured cloth or silk, and laying them directly on the material to be ornamented, and then connecting the whole with outlines and what veining and marking of leaf and so forth the design seems to require for its completion. Even this simple work should be put into an embroidery frame; it is so much easier to manipulate the work when both hands are at liberty.

The above article, found in Decorative Needlework by May Morris, 1893, was edited for use on this site. Note that many of the pictures or diagrams are not a part of the original article but were added to show some of the many types of appliqué that exist.

Venetian Embroidery

Venetian Embroidery takes its name from Venetian lace, owing to a certain similarity in its general appearance.

This work resembles Roman Work and Strasbourg Embroidery, but is lighter than either in effect, on account of the introduction of Lace Stitches in some of the parts where the material is cut away.

Outlines are worked in high relief, and are carried out in buttonhole stitch. Connecting buttonhole bars are with or without picots, and the linen grounds are generally ornamented with filling stitches, raised dots, open holes worked in buttonhole in relief, and adorned with picots. The work is done upon strong linens, hollands, and batiste, and is used for furniture trimmings, such as mantel and table borders, banner screens, and curtain borders.

Trace the outlines of the pattern upon ecru-coloured linen, and Run these outlines with thread, both on their scalloped and plain side. Work them over with Buttonhole lines, made of silk matching the linen in colour, and while doing so connect the various parts with plain Buttonhole Bars. Be careful that the lines of Buttonhole always turn their edges, as, should they be made otherwise, they will not secure the design when the material is cut away.

Take some fine ecru silk, and fill in the parts of the design that are intended to imitate light and open flowers and leaves with Wheels, Point de Bruxelles, Herringbone, Point de Grecque, and other Point Lace Stitches. Vein the heavier leaves with lines of Rope Stitch.

After finishing all of the Embroidery, cut away the linen that is not secured by the Buttonhole lines from underneath the Buttonhole Bars and the Lace Stitches very carefully. Very sharp and small pair of scissors should be used for this.

Below is an other example of Venetian Embroidery.

Second Description of Venetian Embroidery

In this second description of Venetian Embroidery, the work is formed upon Brussels net, and is an imitation of lace.

To work: Trace a lace design of some arabesque and running pattern upon pink calico, which is backed by brown paper. Then Tack net over, and, with a needle and fine thread Run the outlines of the design on the net.

Work these over with lines of Buttonholes, made with various coloured floss silks, and work a scalloped Buttonhole edging. Cut the net away from the outside of the edging, and work in the centres of flowers or other centres to the outlines with a few long Satin Stitches.

Use more than one shade of colour on each piece of lace, but let them blend together, and only use the soft shades of yellow, pink, blue, salmon, and green, and no dark or vivid colours.

Punched Work

Victorian punched work should not be confused with today's punch work. Punch work, as most people know it, is the craft of embroidery whereby the results look similar to a latched-hooked rug. It has small loops on top of the fabric that form the design. It is quite popular and is can be very beautiful.

Victorian punched work is easiest to describe with a picture. Complete instructions are included here for those who wish to give it a try.

Victorian Punched Work Instructions

Select a rather open mesh round weave linen and a large round needle. Outline the design in coarse cotton thread. Fine linen or silk thread is then used, taking the stitches through dots in the background placed equally distant apart. It is a good plan to tie the thread to the eye of the needle to prevent it slipping out.

To Work

Draw the needle through the dot at 7, then

- Down at 1, out at 8;
- Down at 2, out at 8;
- Down at 2, out at 9;
- Down at 3, out at 9;
- Down at 3, out at 10;
- Down at 4, out at 10;
- Down at 4, out at 11;
- Down at 5, out at 11;
- Down at 5, out at 12;
- Down at 6, out at 12;
- Down at 6, out at 18;
- Down at 12, out at 18;
- Down at 12, out at 17;
- Down at 11, out at 17;
- Down at 11, out at 16;
- Down at 10, out at 16;
- Down at 10, out at 15;
- Down at 9, out at 15;
- Down at 9, out at 14;
- Down at 8, out at 14;

- Down at 8, out at 13;
- Down at 7, out at 13;
- Down at 7, etc.

The spaces to be filled do not necessarily have to be square, but more care will be needed with filling circular shapes when you come to the outer and inner edges. However, with a little practice no difficulty will be experienced.

Many beautiful examples of old Spanish drawn work have in them patches or spots or geometric figures filled in with this open work, sometimes called "Pierced work," so the work is not new except in its popular application.

Indian Floss Silk Embroidery

As described in *The Dictionary of Needlework: An Encyclopedia of Artistic, Plain, and Fancy Needlework, 1887,* By SFA Caulfeild and Blanche C. Saward. Indian Floss Silk Embroidery is work executed upon black or white net with white or coloured floss silks, and is an imitation of the Floss Silk Embroidery made by the natives of India. From the nature of the materials used, the Embroidery should not be subject to much wear and tear, but it is not difficult of execution, is extremely Oriental in appearance, and is suitable for brackets and mantelboards and evening dress trimmings.

To Work: Trace out upon pink calico an Oriental design, composed of conventional leaves and flowers, and work out the design as in ordinary Satin Stitch Embroidery. Tack down to the calico black or white net, and cover the pattern over with a series of long Satin Stitches worked in floss silk. Insert the needle in the lower part of a leaf, and carry the stitch up to the top of the leaf, here twist the needle around one mesh of the net just to hold the silk, and carry the silk back to the lower part of the leaf on the upper side of the net, so that none of the silk is wasted at the back of the work.

Work long Satin Stitches in this manner over all the pattern, slanting them outwards when forming the petals of flowers, and curving and sloping them, when by doing so the lines of the designs are more fully indicated.

Work large leaves, not from the top to the bottom, as before mentioned, but with two lines of stitches radiating from the centre vein, and stems with a number of short slanting stitches. Designs in cream white floss silk are more Oriental in appearance than those into which colours are introduced.

French Laid Embroidery or White Work

The Correct Way to Do Initialing

French Laid Work - known and appreciated the world over.

If one were asked to mention the kind of embroidery in most general use, we may say universal use, the answer would undoubtedly be "French laid work." Professional workers and amateurs in all countries and from time immemorial have seemed to thoroughly appreciate the beauty, the durability, and perfect practicability of the firmly laid Satin stitch in white embroidery. Its very nature makes it generally serviceable and appropriate to all applications of household decoration, the table and all dining-room linens, bed decoration and all toilet-table linens, clothing, both for marking and decorating it, especially infants' clothes, pillows, caps, etc.

Many people undertake French Laid embroidery without a notion that there is a proper way to do it or that upon correctness depends success. If there is any sort of embroidery which really should be learned as sewing should, for its practical value, it is this "French laid work." Household linens ought to be marked in this way. One may use the most simple letters for this marking or they can be ornate and decorative and so answer more than one purpose.

In the first place French Laid embroidery should be raised. The stitches are close and firm, so that if all the work is done with an even tension very high raising can be done even on fine fabrics. One half the success depends on the underfilling, which is indeed one half the work. The first step of this preparatory work should always be done in the direction of the length of the bar, or line, or form, whatever it may be.

The stitches should be long and the final covering stitches should be at right angles to this work. How many times a form shall be covered depends entirely upon how high one wishes to raise it, but it is necessary to cover it at least once in the direction of the length and then to bind these stitches somewhat so they will be firm and not looping. One might contend that the overwork would bind them sufficiently, but this is not the case. The overwork will never be firm if the underwork is not made hard and firm first before a single overstitch is laid. The first row of binding-in stitches should be placed at a decided slant over the long straight stitches of the first layer of the filling.

This will be sufficient for slight raising, but, for higher, another row of binding stitches should be laid at an opposite angle from the first. When the letter or device is made up of curves, the first row of under stitches must be something of the nature of overlap work in order that the line shall keep the centre of the form, instead of long straight stitches as on forms made up of straight lines.

This is all the underfilling one should place for ordinary work, and if an equal tension has been maintained and the work as carefully done as though it were to show, instead of being preparatory, the raised letter or ornament will be hard and indeed very presentable in itself. For further raising place more long stitches in the same direction as the first row, and bind these again.

The wider the form the more raising one may venture upon within a certain limit, but a difficulty arises at once in regard to keeping within the outline of any form. The more layers of filling stitches one intends to have the farther from the outline must the first of these be kept.

The outline itself is the guide to the covering layer. The reason for this care is obvious. If the underfilling approaches too near to covering the entire width of the form the result will be an increase of the original width. Often the proportions are quite spoiled in this way and a very awkward letter or device is the result. It is difficult to keep the outline perfectly in raised white work, but perfect outlines and clear cut edges are the chief beauties of this kind of embroidery.

A very simple rule embraces the method of the overwork of French Laid embroidery, but it means a great deal and must be accurately followed. The stitches must be laid at right angles to the direction of the forms, that is, straight across by the shortest distance.

As the form changes its direction the overstitches must change theirs, gradually if the deviation is slight, abruptly if they are following a curve which suddenly reverses its direction. In order to accomplish these turns it is necessary to crowd the stitches on the inside of the curve or angle and spread them a little on the outside. This must be done without being apparent and, in order that it can be, the turn or curve must be calculated on from the start.

One must see ahead, slant each stitch slightly so that none will take a decided position in contrast to the others, but all seem part of the whole unbroken series. All the stitches in this except those exactly in the centre of the curve crowd slightly on the inside and spread the least trifle on the outside.

All the stitches then are not at right angles with the upright position of the letter but *at right angles with the direction of the lines and curves which form it.* This is an unerring rule and perfectly easy to apply to all French laid work, whether letters, scrolls, leaves, or ornaments of any sort. It keeps the embroidery absolutely conventional, as it should be, and characterizes it as an especial style.

Slender lines in French Laid embroidery are embroidered over one thread, and this is placed from end to end in one stitch and drawn to the curve as the covering proceeds. It is indeed easier to keep the stitches of this narrow line even than wider ones; it looks difficult only because it is fine. The long under stitch must not be too tight nor yet too loose. The underfilling of the stems should also be a single line but laid in Split stitch, that is, the needle should cut through the stitch already laid, which should be long but not long enough to leave the outline. Each succeeding stitch should cut through the preceding.

The worker should not be discouraged if the first attempts at French Laid embroidery are failures, because this work, seemingly so simple, requires the greatest accuracy, and accuracy involves more of patient practice to obtain than any other quality. It is, however, obtainable by anyone who will work for it and this is more than can be said for many of the qualities necessary to success in embroidery.

Broderie Anglaise

English Embroidery

This embroidery is a kind of White Embroidery. It often goes by the name of Madeira Work and Irish Work. Whatever name it is called by, it is a very beautiful embroidery.

An open embroidery upon white linen or cambric, differing from Madeira work in being easier to execute, but of the same kind. True Broderie Anglaise patterns are outlines of various sized holes, arranged to make floral or geometrical devices.

To work: Run embroidery cotton round the outlines, then piece the holes with a stiletto, or cut with scissors and turn the edges under and sew over with embroidery cotton. The art in the work consists in cutting and making all the holes that should be the same size to match, and in taking the sewing over stitches closely and regularly.

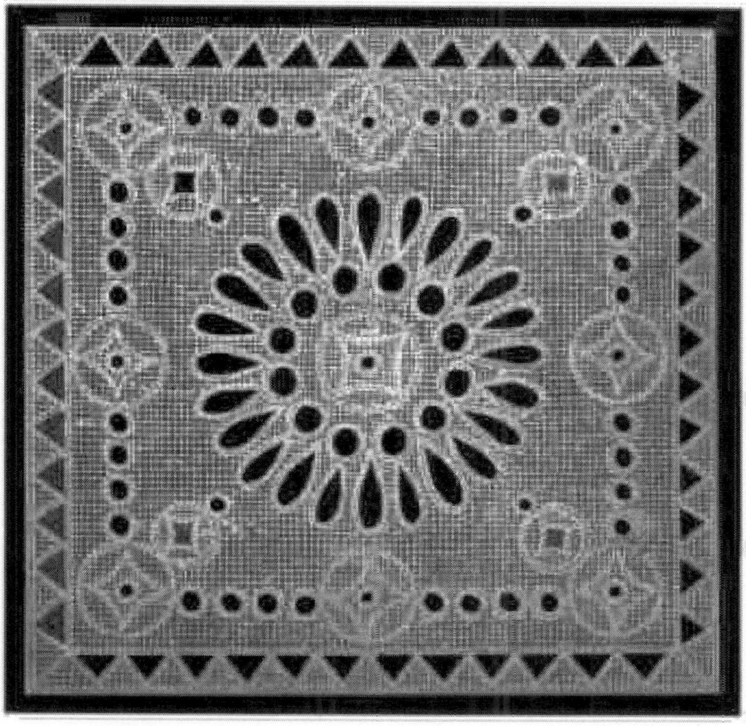

When used as an edging, a scalloped or vandyked border is worked in Buttonhole Stitch, the outer lines of the border being run in the same manner as the holes, and the centre frequently padded with strands of embroidery cotton.

Do not cut away the waste linen outside the Buttonhole until the work has been once washed, as it will then wear longer, and there is less fear of cutting the embroidery cotton in the process. When English Embroidery is used for an insertion, it requires no edging. The work is adapted for trimming washing dresses or underlinen.

The Embroiderer's Floral: Designs, Stitches and Motifs for Popular Flowers in Embroidery

Florals are the most important area of commercial textile design. In the realm of textile and fibre arts, the floral motif has always been a popular design choice; stylistically, there is a rich and varied history of its utilization. Examples are found worldwide, in cultures stretching from ancient China, Medieval India, to contemporary artists involved in grand metropolitan art circles to this day. Despite its long-standing usage, there is no shortage of innovative ways for artists to explore this imagery.

These textile artists inspired by flowers (sometimes referred to as floral textile artists) specifically highlight new and fascinating methods of bringing such a storied motif to life.

Michael Brennand-Wood

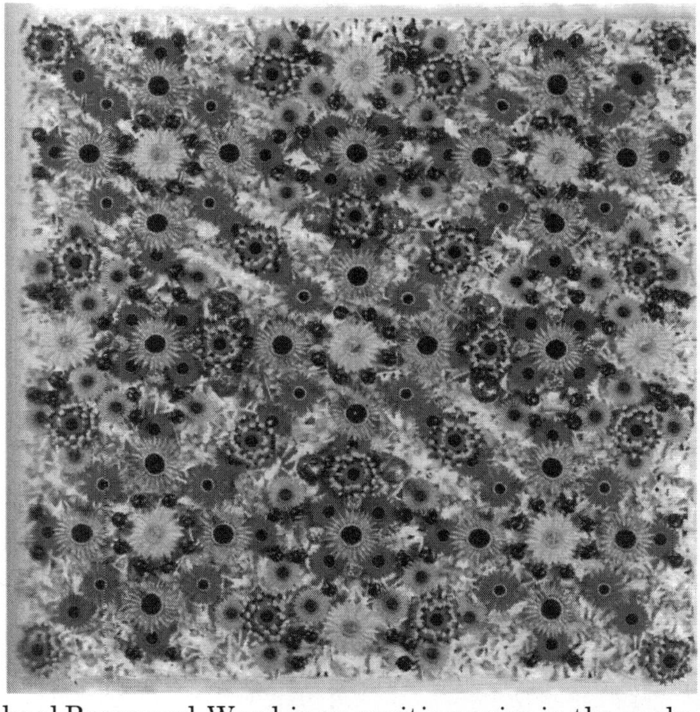

Michael Brennand-Wood is an exciting voice in the realm of floral textile art. His work is hypnotizing and radiant. For the past 40 years, Brennand-Wood has worked in textile and wood, developing an interest in the field at a very young age, inspired by his grandparents.

Brennand-Wood's grandmother worked as an industrial weaver, and he would be fascinated with the samples she brought home.

His work is generally supported by a wooden base, which was spurred by his engineer grandfather, who would tinker with wooden projects in the yard.

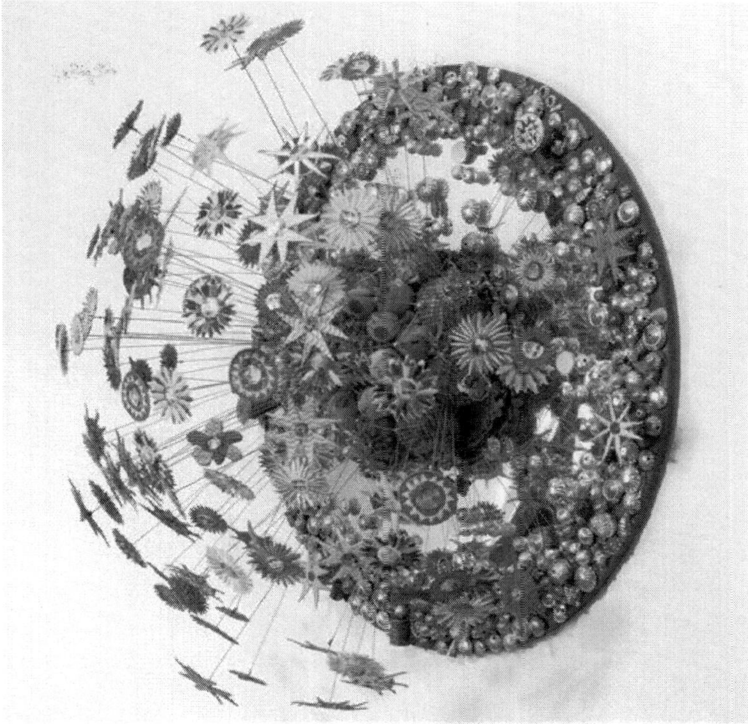

Figure: *Michael Brennand-Wood – Flower Head- Narcissistic Butterfly 60, dia x 40 cm, 2005. Collection of the artist.*

Brennand-Wood blends these two crafts, creating spectacular fine art pieces that have most recently centred around floral imagery. He has moved into computer-driven embroidery, often utilizing radiating symmetry of overlapping flowers. His floral textile designs highlight aspects of the history of ornamental weaving and embroidery in an exciting fashion, captivating viewers from all walks of artistic life. There is also a quality of depth to the work, which can sometimes be ignored in the fabric field. This plays wonderfully with the medium, as distance from the pieces can provide an entirely different perception of what they are.

Also, his work tends to play off the perception of textile as being a woman's medium, and he strives to play off these gender roles. In the 1990s, he focused on lace, and what new meaning and subcontext can be created by a material that is so loaded with a female cultural association.

6

Landscape Art

Landscape art is the depiction in art of landscapes, natural scenery such as mountains, valleys, trees, rivers, and forests, and especially art where the main subject is a wide view, with its elements arranged into a coherent composition.

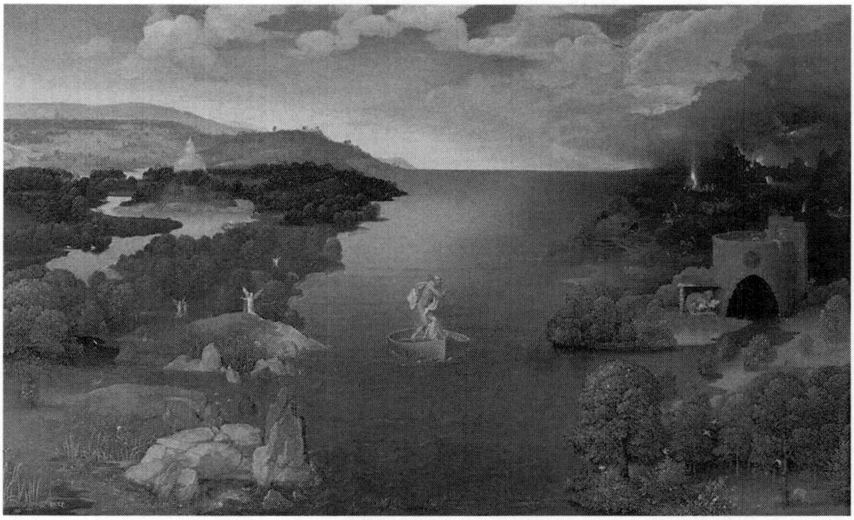

Figure: *Joachim Patinir (1480-1524),* Landscape with Charon Crossing the Styx, *1515-1524, oil on wood, Prado. He was a Flemish Northern Renaissance history and landscape painter who pioneered the "world landscape" type of view.*

In other works landscape backgrounds for figures can still form an important part of the work. Sky is almost always included in the view, and weather is often an element of the composition. Detailed landscapes as a distinct subject are not found in all artistic traditions, and develop when there is already a sophisticated tradition of representing other subjects.

The two main traditions spring from Western painting and Chinese art, going back well over a thousand years in both cases. Landscape photography has been very important since the 19th century, and is covered by its own article.

The recognition of a spiritual element in landscape art is present form its beginnings in East Asian art, drawing on Daoism and other philosophical traditions, but in the West only becomes explicit with Romanticism.

The word "landscape" entered the modern English language as *landskip* (variously spelt), an anglicization of the Dutch *landschap*, around the start of the 17th century, purely as a term for works of art, with its first use as a word for a painting in 1598. Within a few decades it was used to describe vistas in poetry, and eventually as a term for real views.

However the cognate term *landscaef* or *landskipe* for a cleared patch of land had existed in Old English, though it is not recorded from Middle English. Landscape views in art may be entirely imaginary, or copied from reality with varying degrees of accuracy. If the primary purpose of a picture is to depict an actual, specific place, especially including buildings prominently, it is called a *topographical view*.

Such views, extremely common as prints in the West, are often seen as inferior to fine art landscapes, although the distinction is not always meaningful; similar prejudices existed in Chinese art, where literati painting usually depicted imaginary views, while professional court artists painted real views, often including palaces and cities.

History

The earliest forms of art around the world depict little that could really be called landscape, although ground-lines and sometimes indications of mountains, trees or other natural features are included. The earliest "pure landscapes" with no human figures are frescos from Minoan Greece of around 1500 BCE.

Hunting scenes, especially those set in the enclosed vista of the reed beds of the Nile Delta from Ancient Egypt, can give a strong sense of place, but the emphasis is on individual plant forms and human and animal figures rather than the overall landscape setting. For a coherent depiction of a whole landscape, some rough system of perspective, or scaling for distance, is needed, and this seems from literary evidence to have first been developed in Ancient Greece in the Hellenistic period, although no large-scale examples survive.

More ancient Roman landscapes survive, from the 1st century BCE onwards, especially frescos of landscapes decorating rooms that have been preserved at archaeological sites of Pompeii, Herculaneum and elsewhere, and mosaics.

The Chinese ink painting tradition of shan shui ("mountain-water"), or "pure" landscape, in which the only sign of human life is usually a sage, or a glimpse of his hut, uses sophisticated landscape backgrounds to figure subjects, and landscape art of this period retains a classic and much-imitated status within the Chinese tradition.

Both the Roman and Chinese traditions typically show grand panoramas of imaginary landscapes, generally backed with a range of spectacular mountains – in China often with waterfalls and in Rome often including sea, lakes or rivers.

These were frequently used, as in the example illustrated, to bridge the gap between a foreground scene with figures and a distant panoramic vista, a persistent problem for landscape artists. The Chinese style generally showed only a distant view, or used dead ground or mist to avoid that difficulty.

A major contrast between landscape painting in the West and East Asia has been that while in the West until the 19th century it occupied a low position in the accepted hierarchy of genres, in East Asia the classic Chinese mountain-water ink painting was traditionally the most prestigious form of visual art.

Aesthetic theories in both regions gave the highest status to the works seen to require the most imagination from the artist. In the West this was history painting, but in East Asia it was the imaginary landscape, where famous practitioners were, at least in theory, amateur literati, including several Emperors of both China and Japan. They were often also poets whose lines and images illustrated each other.

However in the West, history painting came to require an extensive landscape background where appropriate, so the theory did not entirely work against the development of landscape painting – for several centuries landscapes were regularly promoted to the status of history painting by the addition of small figures to make a narrative scene, typically religious or mythological.

Western Tradition

In early Western medieval art interest in landscape disappears almost entirely, kept alive only in copies of Late Antique works such as the Utrecht Psalter; the last reworking of this source, in an early Gothic version, reduces the previously extensive landscapes to a few trees filling gaps in the composition, with no sense of overall space. A revival in interest in nature initially mainly manifested itself in depictions of small gardens such as the Hortus Conclusus or those in millefleur tapestries.

The frescos of figures at work or play in front of a background of dense trees in the Palace of the Popes, Avignon are probably a unique survival of what was a common subject. Several frescos of gardens have survived from Roman houses like the Villa of Livia.

During the 14th century Giotto di Bondone and his followers began to acknowledge nature in their work, increasingly introducing elements of the landscape as the background setting for the action of the figures in their paintings.

Early in the 15th century, landscape painting was established as a genre in Europe, as a setting for human activity, often expressed in a religious subject, such as the themes of the *Rest on the Flight into Egypt*, the *Journey of the Magi*, or *Saint Jerome in the Desert*. Luxury illuminated manuscripts were very important in the early development of landscape, especially series of the Labours of the Months such as those in the Très Riches Heures du Duc de Berry, which conventionally showed small genre figures in increasingly large landscape settings.

A particular advance is shown in the less well-known Turin-Milan Hours, now largely destroyed by fire, whose developments were reflected in Early Netherlandish painting for the rest of the century. The artist known as "Hand G", probably one of the Van Eyck brothers, was especially successful in reproducing effects of light and in a natural-seeming progression from the foreground to the distant view. This was something other artists were to find difficult for a century or more, often solving the problem by showing a landscape background from over the top of a parapet or window-sill, as if from a considerable height.

Landscape backgrounds for various types of painting became increasingly prominent and skilful during the century. The period around the end of the 15th century saw pure landscape drawings and watercolours from Leonardo da Vinci, Albrecht Dürer, Fra Bartolomeo and others, but pure landscape subjects in painting and printmaking, still small, were first produced by Albrecht Altdorfer and others of the German Danube School in the early 16th century.

At the same time Joachim Patinir in the Netherlands developed the "world landscape" a style of panoramic landscape with small figures and using a high aerial viewpoint, that remained influential for a century, being used and perfected by Pieter Brueghel the Elder. The Italian development of a thorough system of graphical perspective was now known all over Europe, which allowed large and complex views to be painted very effectively.

Landscapes were idealized, mostly reflecting a pastoral ideal drawn from classical poetry which was first fully expressed by Giorgione and the young Titian, and remained associated above all with hilly wooded Italian landscape, which was depicted by artists from Northern Europe who had never visited Italy, just as plain-dwelling literati in China and Japan painted vertiginous mountains.

Though often young artists were encouraged to visit Italy to experience *Italian light*, many Northern European artists could make their living selling *Italianate* landscapes without ever bothering to make the trip. Indeed, certain styles were so popular that they became formulas that could be copied again and again.

The popularity of exotic landscape scenes can be seen in the success of the painter Frans Post, who spent the rest of his life painting Brazilian landscapes after a trip there in 1636-1644. Other painters who never crossed the Alps could make money selling Rhineland landscapes, and still others for constructing fantasy scenes for a particular commission such as Cornelis de Man's view of Smeerenburg in 1639.

Compositional formulae using elements like the repoussoir were evolved which remain influential in modern photography and painting, notably by Poussin and Claude Lorrain, both French artists living in 17th century Rome and painting largely classical subject-matter, or Biblical scenes set in the same landscapes. Unlike their Dutch contemporaries, Italian and French landscape artists still most often wanted to keep their classification within the hierarchy of genres as history painting by including small figures to represent a scene from classical mythology or the Bible. Salvator Rosa gave picturesque excitement to his landscapes by showing wilder Southern Italian country, often populated by *banditi*.

The Dutch Golden Age painting of the 17th century saw the dramatic growth of landscape painting, in which many artists specialized, and the development of extremely subtle realist techniques for depicting light and weather. There are different styles and periods, and sub-genres of marine and animal painting, as well as a distinct style of Italianate landscape. Most Dutch landscapes were relatively small, but landscapes in Flemish Baroque painting, still usually peopled, were often very large, above all in the series of works that Peter Paul Rubens painted for his own houses.

The Dutch tended to make smaller paintings for smaller houses. Some Dutch landscape specialities named in period inventories include the *Batalje*, or battle-scene; the *Maneschijntje*, or moonlight scene; the *Bosjes*, or woodland scene; the *Boederijtje*, or farm scene, and the *Dorpje* or village scene.

Though not named at the time as a specific genre, the popularity of Roman ruins inspired many Dutch landscape painters of the period to paint the ruins of their own region, such as monasteries and churches ruined after the Beeldenstorm.

The popularity of landscapes in the Netherlands was in part a reflection of the virtual disappearance of religious painting in a Calvinist society, and the decline of religious painting in the 18th and 19th centuries all over Europe combined with Romanticism to give landscapes a much greater and more prestigious place in 19th-century art than they had assumed before.

In England, landscapes had initially been mostly backgrounds to portraits, typically suggesting the parks or estates of a landowner, though mostly painted in London by an artist who had never visited his sitter's rolling acres; the English tradition was founded by Anthony van Dyck and other mostly Flemish artists working in England.

In the 18th century, watercolour painting, mostly of landscapes, became an English speciality, with both a buoyant market for professional works, and a large number of amateur painters, many following the popular systems found in the books of Alexander Cozens and others. By the beginning of the 19th century the English artists with the highest modern reputations were mostly dedicated landscapists, showing the wide range of Romantic interpretations of the English landscape found in the works of John Constable, J.M.W. Turner and Samuel Palmer.

However all these had difficulty establishing themselves in the contemporary art market, which still preferred history paintings and portraits.

The German Caspar David Friedrich had a distinctive style, influenced by his Danish training, where a distinct national style, drawing on the Dutch 17th-century example, had developed. French painters were slower to develop landscape painting, but from about the 1830s Jean-Baptiste-Camille Corot and other painters in the Barbizon School established a French landscape tradition that would become the most influential in Europe for a century, with the Impressionists and Post-Impressionists for the first time making landscape painting the main source of general stylistic innovation across all types of painting.

In Europe, as John Ruskin said, and Sir Kenneth Clark confirmed, landscape painting was the "chief artistic creation of the nineteenth century", and "the dominant art", with the result that in the following period people were "apt to assume that the appreciation of natural beauty and the painting of landscape is a normal and enduring part of our spiritual activity" In Clark's analysis, underlying European ways to convert the complexity of landscape to an idea were four fundamental approaches: the acceptance of descriptive symbols, a curiosity about the facts of nature, the creation of fantasy to allay deep-rooted fears of nature, and the belief in a Golden Age of harmony and order, which might be retrieved.

The nationalism of the new United Provinces had been a factor in the popularity of Dutch 17th-century landscape painting and in the 19th century, as other nations attempted to develop distinctive national schools of painting, the attempt to express the special nature of the landscape of the homeland became a general tendency. In Russia, as in America, the gigantic size of paintings was itself a nationalist statement.

In the United States, the Hudson River School, prominent in the middle to late 19th century, is probably the best-known native development in landscape art. These painters created works of mammoth scale that attempted to capture the epic scope of the landscapes that inspired them.

The work of Thomas Cole, the school's generally acknowledged founder, has much in common with the philosophical ideals of European landscape paintings — a kind of secular faith in the spiritual benefits to be gained from the contemplation of natural beauty.

Some of the later Hudson River School artists, such as Albert Bierstadt, created less comforting works that placed a greater emphasis (with a great deal of Romantic exaggeration) on the raw, even terrifying power of nature.

The best examples of Canadian landscape art can be found in the works of the Group of Seven, prominent in the 1920s. Although certainly less dominant in the period after World War I, many significant artists still painted landscapes in the wide variety of styles exemplified by Neil Welliver, Alex Katz, Milton Avery, Peter Doig, Andrew Wyeth, David Hockney and Sidney Nolan.

East Asian Tradition

China:

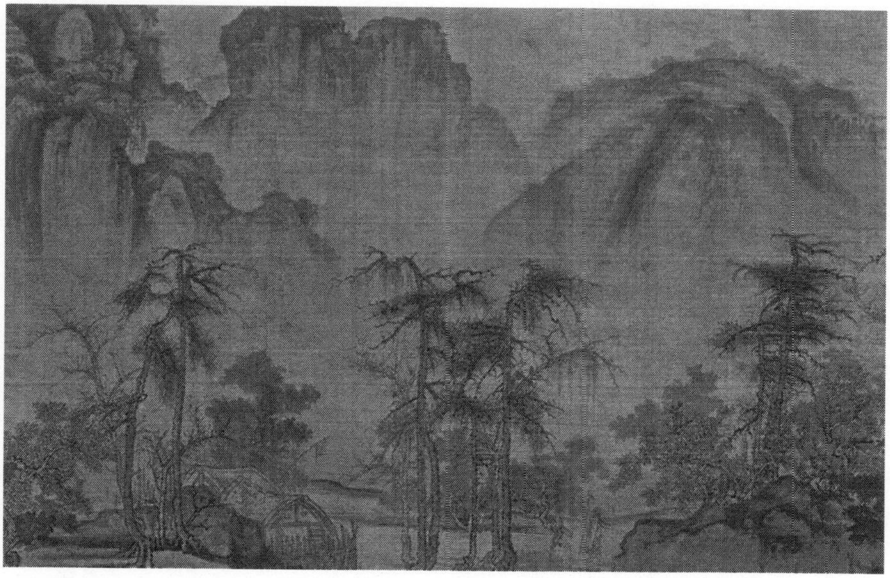

Figure: *Kuo Hsi, Clearing Autumn Skies over Mountains and Valleys, Northern Song Dynasty c. 1070, detail from a horizontal scroll*

Landscape painting has been called "China's greatest contribution to the art of the world", and owes its special character to the Taoist (Daoist) tradition in Chinese culture.

There are increasingly sophisticated landscape backgrounds to figure subjects showing hunting, farming or animals from the Han dynasty onwards, with surviving examples mostly in stone or clay reliefs from tombs, which are presumed to follow the prevailing styles in painting, no doubt without capturing the full effect of the original paintings.

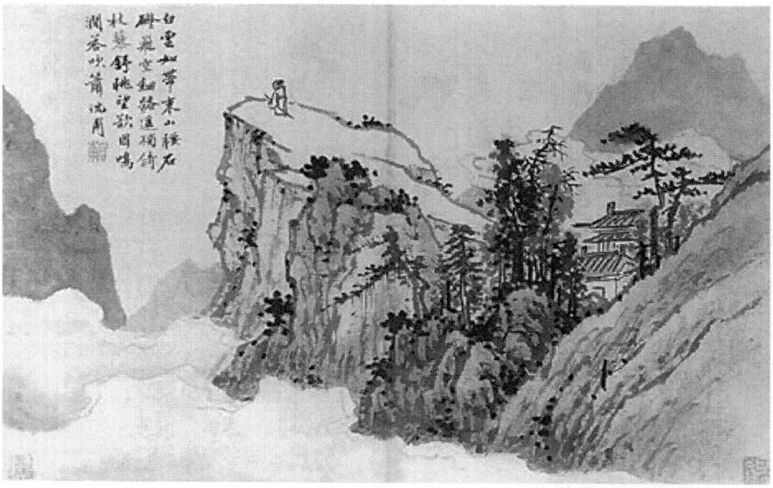

***Figure:** Shen Zhou,* Poet on a Mountain *c. 1500. Painting and poem by Shen Zhou: "White clouds encircle the mountain waist like a sash,/Stone steps mount high into the void where the narrow path leads far./Alone, leaning on my rustic staff I gaze idly into the distance./My longing for the notes of a flute is answered in the murmurings of the gorge."*

The exact status of the later copies of reputed works by famous painters (many of whom are recorded in literature) before the 10th century is unclear. One example is a famous 8th-century painting from the Imperial collection, titled *The Emperor Ming Huang travelling in Shu.*

This shows the entourage riding through vertiginous mountains of the type typical of later paintings, but is in full colour "producing an overall pattern that is almost Persian", in what was evidently a popular and fashionable court style.

The decisive shift to a monochrome landscape style, almost devoid of figures, is attributed to Wang Wei (699-759), also famous as a poet;

mostly only copies of his works survive. From the 10th century onwards an increasing number of original paintings survive, and the best works of the Song Dynasty (960-1279) Southern School remain among the most highly regarded in what has been an uninterrupted tradition to the present day.

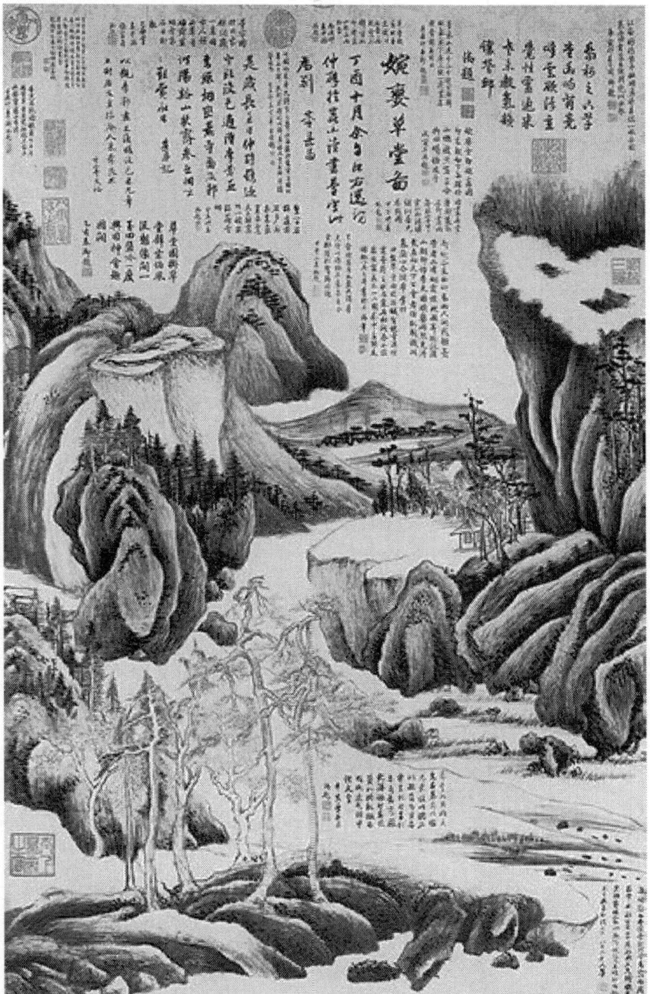

***Figure:** Dong Qichang, Landscape 1597. Dong Qichang was a high-ranking but cantankerous Ming civil servant, who valued expressiveness over delicacy, with collector's seals and poems*

Chinese convention valued the paintings of the amateur scholar-gentleman, often a poet as well, over those produced by professionals, though the situation was more complex than that. If they include any figures, they are very often such persons, or sages, contemplating the mountains. Famous works have accumulated numbers of red "appreciation seals", and often poems added by later owners - the Qianlong Emperor (1711–1799) was a prolific adder of his own poems, following earlier Emperors.

The shan shui tradition was never intended to represent actual locations, even when named after them, as in the convention of the Eight Views. A different style, produced by workshops of professional court artists, painted official views of Imperial tours and ceremonies, with the primary emphasis on highly detailed scenes of crowded cities and grand ceremonials from a high viewpoint. These were painted on scrolls of enormous length in bright colour.

Chinese sculpture also achieves the difficult feat of creating effective landscapes in three dimensions. There is a long tradition of the appreciation of "viewing stones" - naturally formed boulders, typically limestone from the banks of mountain rivers that has been eroded into fantastic shapes, were transported to the courtyards and gardens of the literati.

Probably associated with these is the tradition of carving much smaller boulders of jade or some other semi-precious stone into the shape of a mountain, including tiny figures of monks or sages. Chinese gardens also developed a highly sophisticated aesthetic much earlier than those in the West; the *karensansui* or Japanese dry garden of Zen Buddhism takes the garden even closer to being a work of sculpture, representing a highly abstracted landscape.

Japan

Japanese art initially adapted Chinese styles to reflect their interest in narrative themes in art, with scenes set in landscapes mixing with those showing palace or city scenes using the same high view point, cutting away roofs as necessary. These appeared in the very long yamato-e scrolls of scenes illustrating the *Tale of Genji* and other subjects, mostly from the 12th and 13th centuries.

The concept of the gentleman-amateur painter had little resonance in feudal Japan, where artists were generally professionals with a strong bond to their master and his school, rather than the classic artists from the distant past, from which Chinese painters tended to draw their inspiration. Painting was initially fully coloured, often brightly so, and the landscape never overwhelms the figures who are often rather over-sized.

The scene illustrated at right is from a scroll that in full measures 37.8 cm x 802.0 cm, for only one of twelve scrolls illustrating the life of a Buddhist monk; like their Western counterparts, monasteries and temples commissioned many such works, and these have had a better chance of survival than courtly equivalents. Even rarer are survivals of landscape byôbu folding screens and hanging scrolls, which seem to have common in court circles - the *Tale of Genji* has an episode where members of the court produce the best paintings from their collections for a competition. These were closer to Chinese shan shui, but still fully coloured.

Many more pure landscape subjects survive from the 15th century onwards; several key artists are Zen Buddhist clergy, and worked in a monochrome style with greater emphasis on brush strokes in the Chinese manner. Some schools adopted a less refined style, with smaller views giving greater emphasis to the foreground.

A type of image that had an enduring appeal for Japanese artists, and came to be called the "Japanese style", is in fact first found in China. This combines one or more large birds, animals or trees in the foreground, typically to one side in a horizontal composition, with a wider landscape beyond, often only covering portions of the background. Later versions of this style often dispensed with a landscape background altogether.

The ukiyo-e style that developed from the 16th century onwards, first in painting and then in coloured woodblock prints that were cheap and widely available, initially concentrated on the human figure, individually and in groups. But from the late 18th century landscape ukiyo-e developed under Hokusai and Hiroshige to become much the best known type of Japanese landscape art.

Techniques

Most early landscapes are clearly imaginary, although from very early on townscape views are clearly intended to represent actual cities, with varying degrees of accuracy. Various techniques were used to simulate the randomness of natural forms in invented compositions: the medieval advice of Cennino Cennini to copy ragged crags from small rough rocks was apparently followed by both Poussin and Thomas Gainsborough, while Degas copied cloud forms from a crumpled handkerchief held up against the light. The system of Alexander Cozens used random ink blots to give the basic shape of an invented landscape, to be elaborated by the artist.

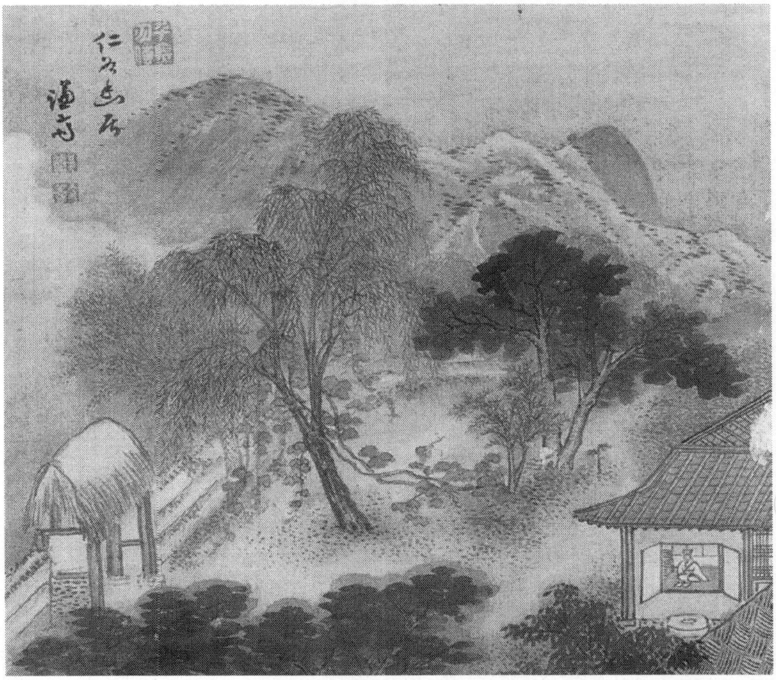

Figure: *An 18th-century Korean version of the Chinese literati style by Jeong Seon who was unusual in often painting landscapes from life.*

The distinctive background view across Lake Geneva to the Le Môle peak in *The Miraculous Draught of Fishes* by Konrad Witz (1444) is often cited as the first Western rural landscape to show a specific scene. The landscape studies by Dürer clearly represent actual scenes, which can be identified in many cases, and were at least partly made on the spot; the drawings by Fra Bartolomeo also seem clearly sketched from nature. Dürer's finished works seem generally to use invented landscapes, although the spectacular bird's-eye view in his engraving *Nemesis* shows an actual view in the Alps, with additional elements. Several landscapists are known to have made drawings and watercolour sketches from nature, but the evidence for early oil painting being done outside is limited. The Pre-Raphaelite Brotherhood made special efforts in this direction, but it was not until the introduction of ready-mixed oil paints in tubes in the 1870s, followed by the portable "box easel", that painting en plein air became widely practiced.

A curtain of mountains at the back of the landscape is standard in wide Roman views and even more so in Chinese landscapes. Relatively little space is given to the sky in early works in either tradition; the Chinese often used mist or clouds between mountains, and also sometimes show clouds in the sky far earlier than Western artists, who initially mainly use clouds as supports or covers for divine figures or heaven.

Both panel paintings and miniatures in manuscripts usually had a patterned or gold "sky" or background above the horizon until about 1400, but frescos by Giotto and other Italian artists had long shown plain blue skies. The single surviving altarpiece from Melchior Broederlam, completed for Champmol in 1399, has a gold sky populated not only by God and angels, but also a flying bird. A coastal scene in the Turin-Milan Hours has a sky overcast with carefully observed clouds. In woodcuts a large blank space can cause the paper to sag during printing, so Dürer and other artists often include clouds or squiggles representing birds to avoid this.

The monochrome Chinese tradition has used ink on silk or paper since its inception, with a great emphasis on the individual brushstroke to define the *ts'un* or "wrinkles" in mountain-sides, and the other features of the landscape. Western watercolour is a more tonal medium, even with underdrawing visible.

Related Scapes

Traditionally, landscape art depicts the surface of the earth, but there are other sorts of landscapes, such as moonscapes.

- Vedute is the Italian term for *view*, and generally used for the painted landscape, often cityscapes which were a common 18th-century painting thematic.
- Skyscapes or Cloudscapes are depictions of clouds, weatherforms, and atmospheric conditions.
- Moonscapes show the landscape of a moon.
- Seascapes depict oceans or beaches.
- Riverscapes depict rivers or creeks.
- Cityscapes or townscapes depict cities (urban landscapes).
- Hardscapes are paved over areas like streets and sidewalks, large business complexes and housing developments, and industrial areas.

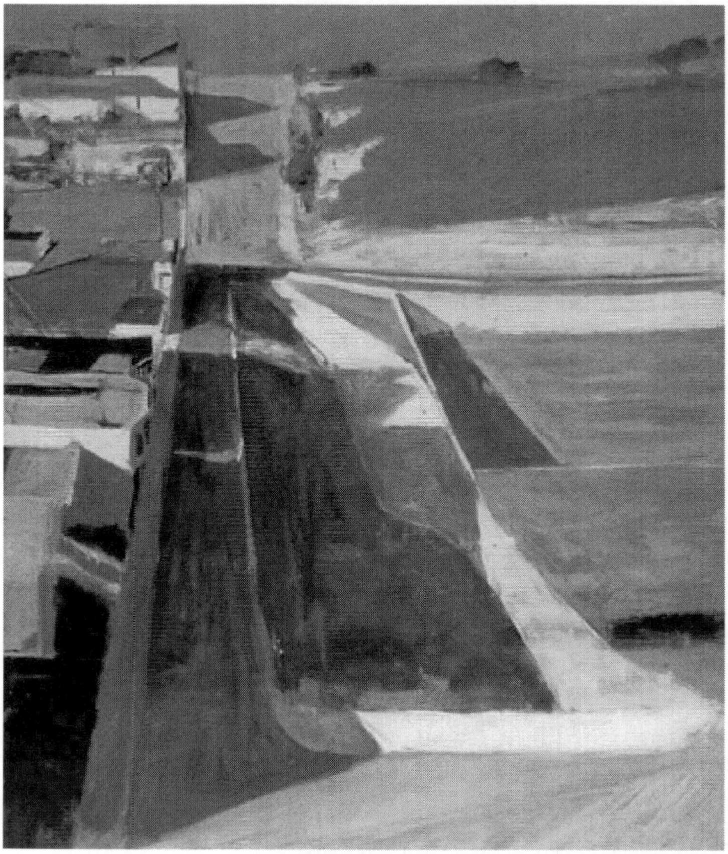

Figure: *Richard Diebenkorn,* Cityscape I (Landscape No. 1), *1963, oil on canvas, San Francisco Museum of Modern Art*

- Aerial landscapes depict a surface or ground from above, especially as seen from an airplane or spacecraft. (When the viewpoint is directly overhead, looking down, there is of course no depiction of a horizon or sky.) This genre can be combined with others, as in the aerial cloudscapes of Georgia O'Keeffe, the aerial moonscapes of Nancy Graves, or the aerial cityscapes of Yvonne Jacquette.
- Inscapes are landscape-like (usually surrealist or abstract) artworks which seek to convey the psychoanalytic view of the mind as a three-dimensional space.

Bibliography

Ambuter, Carolyn: *The Open Canvas*, Workman, New York, 1982.

Bahouth, Candace: *Flowers, Birds, and Unicorns: Medieval Needlepoint,* Harry Abrams, New York, 1993.

Barbara Snook: *English Embroidery,* Bell & Hyman, London, 1974.

Beck, Thomasina: *The Embroiderer's Flowers,* David & Charles, Devon, 1993.

Benn, Elizabeth: *Treasures from the Embroiderers' Guild Collection*, David & Charles, Devon, 1995.

Blair, Margot Carter and Cathleen Ryan: *Banners and Flags,* Harcourt Brace Jovanovich, New York, 1977.

Dawson, Barbara: *Metal Thread Embroidery*, Batsford, London, 1976.

Digby, George Winfield: *Elizabethan Embroidery*, Thomas Yoseloff, New York, 1963.

Dillmont, Thérese de: *Encyclopedia of Needlework*, Editions Th. de Dillmont, Mulhouse, France, 1968.

Eaton, Jan: *Complete Stitch Encyclopedia*, Baron's Education Series, Woodbury, N. Y., 1986.

Elizabeth Geddes and Moyra McNeill: *Blackwork Embroidery,* Dover Books, New York, 1976.

Ellis, Marianne: *Embroideries and samplers from Islamic Egypt*, Curious Works Press, Greenville, SC, 2001.

Enthoven, Jacqueline: *Stitches with Variations*, Sunset Designs, San Ramon, Calif, 1976.

Enthoven, Jacqueline: *The Stitches of Creative Embroidery*, Schiffer Publishing Ltd., West Chester, Pa., 1987.

George Wingfield Digby: *Elizabethan Embroidery,* Thomas Yoseloff, New York, 1964.

Irwin, John and Margaret Hall: *Indian Embroideries*, Calico Museum of Textiles, Ahmedabad, 1973.

Jane Ashelford: *Dress in the Age of Elizabeth I.* B.T. Batsford Ltd, London, 1988.

Janet Arnold: *Queen Elizabeth's Wardrobe Unlock'd,* W.S. Maney & Son, London, 1988.

John, Edith: *Creative Stitches,* B. T. Batsford, London, 1967.

Kim Brody Salazar: *The New Carolingian Modelbook: Counted Embroidery Patterns from Before 1600,* Outlaw Press, Albuquerque, 1995.

Lanto Synge: *The Royal School of Needlework Book of Needlework and Embroidery,* William Collins Sons and Company, London, 1986.

Lantz, Sherlee and Maggie Lane: *A Pageant of Pattern for Needlepoint Canvas,* Atheneum, New York, 1973.

Margaret Pascoe: *Blackwork Embroidery,* B.T. Batsford Ltd, London, 1986.

Marguerite Fawdry and Deborah Brown: *The Book of Samplers,* Cameron and Tayleur, London, 1980.

Mary Gostelow: *Blackwork,* Van Nostrand Reinhold, New York, 1976.

McNeill, Moyra: *Pulled Thread,* Taplinger, New York, 1972.

Morrell, Anne: *The Techniques of Indian Embroidery,* Batsford, London, 1994.

Nichols, Marion: *Encyclopedia of Embroidery Stitches Including Crewel,* Dover, New York, 1974.

Nordfors, Jill Denny: *Needle Lace and Needleweaving,* Van Nostrand Reinhold, New York, 1974.

Ohms, Margaret: *Ethnic Embroidery,* Batsford, London, 1989.

Paine, Sheila: *Chikan Embroidery: The Floral Whitework of India,* Shire Publications, Ltd., London, 1989.

Patricia Wardle: *Guide to English Embroidery, Victoria and Albert Museum,* Her Majesty's Stationery office, London, 1970.

Ramazanoglu, Gulseren: *Turkish Embroidery,* Van Nostrand Reinhold, New York, 1976.

Rosemary Drysdale: *The Art of Blackwork Embroidery,* Charles Scribner's Sons, New York, 1975.

Roy Strong: *The English Icon: Elizabethan and Jacobean Portraiture,* The Paul Meloon Foundation for British Art, Routledge and Kegan Paul, London, 1969.

Snook, Barbara: *Needlework Stitches,* Crown, New York, 1963.

Swain, Margaret: *The Needlework of Mary Queen of Scots,* Ruth Bean Publishers, Carlton, 1986.

Tashjian, Nouvart: *Armenian Lace,* Lacis Publications, Berkeley, 1982.

Thomas, Mary: *Mary Thomas's Dictionary of Embroidery Stitches,* Hodder & Stoughton, New York, 1989.

Thomasina Beck: *The Embroiderer's Flowers,* David and Charles, Newton Abbott, Devon 1992.

Wardle, Patricia: *Guide to English Embroidery,* Her Majesty's Stationery Office, London, 1981.

Index

❑❑❑